Bombs, Bliss and Baba

The Spiritual Autobiography

Behind the

Hilton Bombing Frame Up

Paul Narada Alister

Better World Books

Published by
Better World Books
PO Box 177
Maleny, 4552 Queensland
Australia
inrsong@ozemail.com.au

First Edition 1997
Second Edition 2013
Third Edition 2016

© Paul Alister 1997
paul_alister@yahoo.com.au

All rights reserved. Apart from any fair dealings for the purpose of private study, research, review and criticism as permitted under the Copyright Act, no part of this book may be reproduced by any process without written permission from the Publisher.

The National Library of Australia
Cataloging-in-Publication entry

Alister, Paul 1955
Bombs, Bliss and Baba: The spiritual autobiography behind
    the Hilton Bombing frame-up.

ISBN 9 780994402745
1. Alister, Paul Narada, 1955 -
2. Ananda Marga-
Biography. I Title.

299.1411

Cover art by Magda Wozniak (www.behance.net/mwozniak)
    with Paul Narada Alister
Book Layout & Design by Kamala Alister

Contents

1	Early Years	1
2	Ananda Marga	14
3	Going to India	30
4	The Embassy Strike	41
5	Dark Side of the Moon	51
6	Going to Jail	63
7	Jail Life	70
8	The Committal Hearing	87
9	Police Lies	99
10	The Hunger Strike	113
11	The Trials	125
12	Meditation and Service	139
13	Not a Merry Christmas	155
14	Divine Loneliness	160
15	Personalities	171
16	The Hilton Bombing Inquest	177
17	The Tide Turns	189
18	The Inquiry	199
19	Freedom	207
20	Meeting Baba	221
21	Dreams Fulfilled	230
22	Saying Good-bye	239
	Epilogue	243
	Appendix 1	248
	Appendix 2	249
	Appendix 3	251
	Glossary	254

Author's Note

The following story is my personal autobiographical account of historical events that were important to many Australians. As far as possible, I have tried to be accurate about many details and people involved. However this book is not meant to be a full legal explanation of our case. Two excellent books already exist which explain in detail the political and legal ramifications of our case. They are:

Free Alister, Dunn and Anderson:
The Ananda Marga Conspiracy Case
by my co-accused Tim Anderson
Published in Sydney, 1985 by Wild and Wooley

Spies Bombs and the Path of Bliss: Ananda Marga and the Hilton Bombing by our solicitor Tom Molomby
Published in Sydney, 1986 by Potoroo Press

Acknowledgments

Firstly I must thank my wife Kamala for the many hours of editing work, as well as to Murray Hosking, and Brian Priest of Oracle Press, who helped not only in editing but also generously gave useful advice. Finally Leslie Synge generously gave her time to help with the editing.

The man who convinced me to wrote this book, Murray Farquahar, also deserves a special mention,
as do the following:
Irena Dunn, Di Bergan, Fred Cole, Julie Sheppard Sigsworth, Sukalpa Robinson, Mukti Haigh, Kapil Arn, Gaotami Pfiefer, Mayatiita,
Dada Manavendrananda, Dada Acutananda and Dada Shubhatmananda.

Dedication

To my mother and father,
to CAADA members,
and to Baba
for all their love,
support and sacrifice.

1
Early Years

The path of spirituality is beset with numerous obstacles.
— Baba

SITTING IN THE MEDICAL ROOM OF LONG BAY'S RECEPTION PRISON, I FELT DAZED and confused as I tried to comprehend what had just happened. Blood ran down my shirt as a nurse attended to my wounds. "You're lucky you didn't lose your ear," she said, sounding half concerned and half critical. The prisoner who had attacked me had nearly ripped off my left ear.

Since I couldn't see the damage I didn't know how severe it was. All I knew was there was a throbbing pain in my ear. I felt disoriented from pain and medication and drifted in and out of waking consciousness. Dreams and memories came to me of my early life and the circumstances leading up to my recent imprisonment.

I was reminded of a similar painful experience. My father had a short temper and sometimes disciplined my twin brother Mark and I by bashing our heads together. This usually gave me a very sore ear and head.

Isolation

My father loved my mother dearly. Their marriage was very happy and idyllic until my older brother was born. Then my father discovered that he had a low tolerance for children. This brought out an awful temper that often exploded over the smallest incident. When my older sister was born a few years later, Mum and Dad decided she would be their last child. Therefore, when I came along ten years later, unplanned, and certainly for

Dad, unwanted, he was not very pleased. To make matters worse, my twin brother Mark followed ten minutes later. Twins! My father considered this a nightmare. He immediately ordered that we be fed and in bed by the time he came home from work each day.

We were born on July 15th, 1955 in Perth, Western Australia. My mother was suffering from depression and my father's intolerance of us made things worse for her. She needed to rest, so as soon as we were old enough, she left us most of the day in the backyard with our pet parrot and dog. She took care of our basic needs, but spent little extra time with us. This was how my mother dealt with the very difficult situation she found herself in.

All day we interacted with the pets and each other. We had no one else to talk to except our mother occasionally. Our older brother and sister were busy teenagers and didn't have much time to spend with us. This meant there was no one to teach us how to speak, so we didn't learn. When we wanted something, we used sign language. My mother told me later that if we wanted a drink, we panted like a dog with our tongues out and pointed to our mouths.

My twin brother Mark and I. Typically, our mother is in the background and we are paying attention to our pet galah, our regular companion.

Early Years

The doctor thought we were deaf but my mother knew we weren't because we responded to her when she spoke to us. We didn't learn to speak until we were four years old and mixed with other children at kindergarten. By that time we needed special speech lessons from child language specialists to help catch up.

Because of this very late start, I found school difficult. I was always at the bottom of the class. Being dyslexic also didn't help. I didn't care for school, although that may be because of my difficulty in learning. I remember that one time in grade six I got a sum correct. My teacher stopped the class and told me to stand up while every one applauded me for getting one right! I thought it was amusing and fortunately didn't feel insulted by such mocking sarcasm.

Meanwhile, at home my father had decided to put up with us, after making sure we'd never disobey him. If we inadvertently did, he was often physically violent. For example, one time we left out our three-wheeler bicycles in the driveway and he accidentally ran over one with his car. He was furious and chased us around the yard with a stick threatening to beat us. The fact that the stick had old rusty nails sticking out didn't seem to bother him.

Another time I banged into a glass sliding door while sleepwalking. Although I did no damage my father was very angry and said if I did that again and broke it he would send me to a home! For some time after that I went to sleep afraid that I might wake up and be told I was going to an orphanage. A sleepwalker has no conscious awareness of what is happening or any memory of what he has done.

My sweet, affectionate mother said that she would have been stricter with us but she felt she had to compensate for father's extreme authoritarianism. Nevertheless, I am grateful for learning self-discipline from Dad. He usually meant well but just could not control his temper. He only got drunk about twice a year, but when he did, he was terrifying to be around.

Despite the strict discipline and constant threat of violence, life was generally happy for me. I was very obedient and rarely did anything to get Dad upset. I never felt my life to be disadvantaged. Only later upon reflection did this occur to me.

The Search

By the time I was a teenager, I began to feel restless and dissatisfied with life. At school, I still did poorly although I was generally very good at sports. I played Australian Rules football and cricket. Later I took up surfing. However, this didn't satisfy a much deeper urge that told me there was something more to life. By the time I was 13, I was binge drinking. It was also in this year that an adult friend of mine sexually abused me. The attempt to forget this horrible experience is probably what led to the drinking.

By the time I was 15, I had discovered marijuana. This was in 1970. I left school and started a five-year apprenticeship in boiler making/welding. In those days 15 was considered very young to be taking drugs, but I felt a very strong urge to find something more in life. I was also becoming quite successful with surfing and secured sponsorship with a surfboard manufacturer. But this still didn't satisfy me.

After a year of marijuana and hash, I tried LSD. During that year, I started going to Hatha Yoga classes. I only lasted one term but it was there that the seed was sown for spirituality. Once my yoga teacher told me she had studied with a yogi who was so elevated that in his presence she felt very happy and peaceful due to the strength of his spirituality. It impressed me that a person could make you feel peaceful and happy just by his presence.

The hippy surfers that I associated with seemed superficial. While I liked them, they didn't 'feel' right. Some of them were getting interested in eastern religion and meditation and that interested me. Meanwhile, the drug taking was becoming detrimental to my mind and my happiness. My memory was starting to fail, which concerned me a great deal. Every time I had a high, it was followed by depression.

Still I wanted something more in life. Drugs were not providing an answer. It was becoming increasingly apparent they were obstructing me from finding an answer by making me more confused, cynical and depressed. Surfing was still very enjoyable but that too seemed to be lacking. I decided I wanted to give up drugs but what would I replace them with? To go back to ordinary life seemed so dry and boring. Then I remembered the yoga classes. I thought about the yogi's peaceful, happy effect on others. I decided to take up yoga again. I also wanted to learn about meditation.

I lived on John Street in Cottesloe, a beautiful beach suburb of Perth. It was not far from the port town of Fremantle where yoga classes were held. During the classes, I felt some satisfaction but still something was missing. Meditation appealed to me, so I leafed through many books. But nothing struck that inner chord. I continued searching.

On Fridays and Saturdays, my yoga teacher taught meditation. Students read from the *Bhagavad Gita*, the Bible and other spiritually inspiring scriptures. The meditation consisted of concentrating on a candle light. This didn't seem very spiritual to me but it was something—a good start on a new path.

One night at meditation class, I met Kapil and Karuna. They were members of an Indian based group called Ananda Marga, which means 'Path of Bliss'. They had joined Ananda Marga in India, but there were no other members in Perth and only a few in Australia. They made contact with one of the Ananda Marga monks who had just arrived in Australia and invited him to Perth.

I was elated when they announced that this monk, one of the spiritual teachers of Ananda Marga, would give a talk on meditation during our Friday night class. I still remember that night clearly. I waited anxiously. He was late. Suddenly, the door burst open and in walked a tall, young, handsome yogi in bright orange robes, wearing a turban and, yes, emanating a peaceful aura!

"A real yogi," I thought with excitement and a touch of awe.

The 'yogi' spoke about the search for happiness. He said the desire for happiness is infinite but we try to satisfy it through finite things. Only merging with the infinite cosmic consciousness, or God, can give infinite happiness. The method to experience this cosmic consciousness, he said, is intuitional meditation.

It all made sense to me. Although at the time I didn't realise it, he was describing what had been happening to me. I had been searching for infinite happiness through finite things like alcohol and drugs. Even with surfing and all its magic, I still felt the lack of some mystical link—a vital factor in my life.

On Saturday night, I attended the yogi's talk again. It was the same as the talk on Friday but I enjoyed just being in his presence. After the talk, he announced that there would be a meditation retreat the following weekend. However, anyone who wanted to attend had to first be initiated into his meditation. This was because there would be a lot of time spent in meditation and everyone had to know how to meditate properly.

"How wonderful," I thought. A whole weekend of meditation. In addition, the meditation instruction would be free! I later found out that all of Ananda Marga practices are taught free of charge.

Initiation

The 'yogi' was called Dada Sumitananda. 'Dada' means respected elder brother. (Nuns are called 'Didi', meaning respected elder sister) When I asked Dada about initiation he seemed reluctant. He questioned my desire to learn. Later, I realised it was because I was only 17 and he wanted to know if I really was ready. However, I persisted and so finally he agreed. A time was set, next Monday at 5 pm, at Kapil and Karuna's house where Dada lived. I was ecstatic.

In 1972, I was in the second year of my boilermaking/welding apprenticeship. I was working in Fremantle, mostly repairing ships. Work finished at 4 pm, so after work I went straight to Dada's place near Perth. After getting off a bus, I merrily walked to the street where Dada lived. I was so happy, feeling I had finally found what I had been searching for! The sun was shining, the sky seemed bright and the trees beautiful. Even the birds seemed to be singing more than usual!

I walked down the street looking for the house number written on the paper that I clutched in my hand. The number didn't exist! I walked up and down the street, but to no avail. Feeling dejected I felt my initiation must not have been meant to be. As I turned to go home, I noticed a bright orange blur in the corner of my eye. I turned and saw Dada walking out of a corner shop! I quickly called out to him and went with him to his house. I had been given the wrong number!

The yogi took me into a room in the house and we sat down on the floor. He was an 'acharya', which meant that he was specially trained to teach meditation and yoga. He was also a celibate monk and the orange robes he wore were a symbol of sacrifice and renunciation.

Dada explained that initiation involved learning a specific meditation technique using a spiritually vibrated sound called a *mantra*. Not only did I have to repeat the mantra properly but I also had to be thinking and feeling the mantra's meaning. This is called 'ideation.' Only then would I be able to experience the full spiritual effects of the meditation. Meditation without ideation can create a peaceful feeling, but ideation is needed for deeper spiritual experiences.

Dada also asked me to take three simple oaths. Not to harm others consciously, to help others, and to keep the individual meditation technique that he would teach me confidential. He explained that this was because the mantra and specific techniques are given according to individual personality and mental vibration. The proper mantra has to be given to each person to have the desired benefit, just like a doctor prescribes the right medicine to have the curative effect.

He also explained the symbol of Ananda Marga. As soon as he showed it to me, I became confused and curious. To me it looked like a mix of the Jewish Star of David, the Japanese rising sun, and the Nazi swastika!

Dada explained that there are two interwoven triangles. The downward triangle represents the inner search through spiritual practices, while the upward triangle represents service. Balancing service and meditation brings progress, represented by the rising sun in the centre of the two triangles. In the middle of the rising sun is a *swastika*, an old Sanskrit symbol which means spiritual victory or enlightenment. Dada explained that Hitler had misused this powerful symbol when he made it the symbol of conquest. Swastika is a Sanskrit word derived from 'swasti' which means welfare or wellbeing. In India it is common to see temples decorated with swastikas. It is supposed to bring good fortune and victory.

Finally, Dada taught me meditation. Afterwards we sat for

The Pratik symbolises a balance of spirituality and service. The Swastika in the centre is an ancient symbol that means "spiritual victory."

My acharya, Dada Sumitananda, around the time of my initiation. Today, 40 years later he is still dedicated in his life as a monk. At the time of this writing he is in charge of Ananda Marga organisational activities in the Middle East.

several minutes in meditation together. I was deeply at peace. I felt like a new person. This is what I'd been looking for! I was overjoyed to have found the key to my inner spiritual self!

I asked Dada many questions about spirituality and the life of an acharya. He asked if I'd like to become one. I laughed at the idea, thinking only the most elevated people could take on such a lifestyle.

Dada said that anyone practicing meditation and moral principles in their life would gradually become 'elevated.' I asked him more about the moral principles he followed. He told me that these principles were vital to success in meditation and explained them in detail.

"Meditation without morality is dangerous. According to ancient yoga texts there are ten moral principles, divided into two parts, *yama*' and *niyama*.. Yama includes non-harming, truthfulness, non-stealing, moderation and the effort to perceive God in everything. Niyama stands for purity and cleanliness, contentment, selfless service, spiritual study and faith in God."

"You said *selfless* service. Isn't all service selfless?" I inquired.

"No, what most people consider service is not real service because they expect something back in return. This is really a commercial transaction, not service. You may see a business that claims it has been 'serving the community for 20 years.' Actually, they did not serve the community at all because the community had to pay for the so-called service they provided. Even to expect praise or a thank you for service is not true service. Real service is unilateral, meaning there is no return or benefit except the satisfaction of knowing you have helped someone. Service has to be selfless and done ideally as an expression of love for God.

Dada had told me during initiation that it was important that I meditate twice a day, as regularly as possible. He also told me I must do some kind of service on a regular basis. I asked him why these things were so important.

"Twice a day for at least half an hour is the minimum time needed for the meditation to have a real spiritual effect and to strengthen your mind. Regular service purifies the ego and removes any vanity that might come from your development through meditation."

I told Dada that, inspired by the yoga and meditation classes I was taking, I had been thinking about going to India to meditate intensively.

I had even saved some money for the trip. I thought he would be enthusiastic about this idea, but his answer surprised me.

"There is no need to go anywhere to meditate. God can only be found within you, not without. Ananda Marga is different from many other spiritual groups in this regard. We say you don't have to give up your home, family and worldly life and go to the Himalayas or forests to meditate. Rather by staying in the world and fulfilling your worldly duties, while also meditating, you'll progress faster because service and duty to others helps break down the ego and induces feelings of love for others."

Dada also taught me some specific yoga exercises or *asanas* to do each day. Like my mantra, Dada specifically 'prescribed' certain asanas for me according to my health and mental tendencies. He also gave me some suggestions about foods that disturb meditation. They included all animal flesh such as red and white meat and fish. Also eggs, onions, garlic, mushrooms and all intoxicants except those given for medical reasons.

Dada also recommended fasting twice a month according to specific moon phases as a method of physical and spiritual purification. That was one of the biggest challenges for me. In fact, it was all a huge change for me and completely different from anything I had ever done. But I was feeling inspired and I understood that this was about more than just learning meditation: I was taking on a new lifestyle. I knew this was what I had been looking for, so from then on, I followed Dada's instructions carefully. I gave up alcohol, drugs and smoking from that day and felt much better for it. The high from drugs seemed quite a 'downer' compared to the high gained from meditation.

I questioned Kapil later about why eggs, onions, garlic and mushrooms were considered bad for meditation. He explained that garlic and onions create extra heat in the body, eggs have a similar effect to meat, and mushrooms have a crudifying energy.

He related an experience he had not long after his initiation. He complained to his Acharya that when he meditated he broke out into uncontrollable sweating. Dada asked him if he had been eating onions or garlic. Kapil replied that he had been eating onions. The Acharya said if he stopped eating onions, the sweating would stop. And it did.

It took me about a year before I was fully over my attachment to meat eating. After that I not only lost the desire for meat, but increasingly found it repulsive. Within a few years I found I could not even eat food if it was on the same plate as meat. The smell alone made me feel ill.

Initially, I was hassled by my friends and by my parents about my diet. In time, they came to accept my new habits and either admired me or dismissed me as being crazy! It was a good lesson in not being swayed by other's opinions. I did what I felt was right for me. I am now very thankful I ignored all the criticism and taunts and followed my convictions.

Stages of the Spiritual Path

Later, I read that the spiritual path involves four stages. In the first stage, friends, parents or colleagues put obstacles in your way. Physical obstacles like sore legs and aching backs also present themselves. Internally there are also obstacles in the form of doubts, poor concentration and impatience for results.

In the second stage, the external obstacles recede. Friends stop bothering you, your back and legs stop aching as much, but the internal mental obstacles become stronger. While there is some success in concentration and therefore bliss or *ananda* is experienced for the first time, your ego can become a major problem. It's easy to feel superior to others because of your spiritual achievements. You have to remember that everything comes from God so there is nothing for you to be proud of.

In the third stage, meditation becomes blissful and concentration becomes intense. Consequently, you may develop mental or occult powers. If these powers are not surrendered to God, it becomes easy to be tempted to misuse them for self-centred or personal interests. This can lead to your spiritual downfall.

The last stage is where complete concentration and control of your mind is achieved. You experience unshakable bliss and it becomes relatively easy to become totally self-realised.

When I was going through difficulties with my friends and parents about my new lifestyle, it was helpful to understand that this was only a phase of spiritual progress.

Correct Mantra

After my initiation, I went home. My housemate wasn't there. As soon as I walked in, I felt dizzy and sick. I collapsed on the floor. Intuitively I felt that if I drank some warm milk I would be alright.

I dragged myself along the wooden floor to our kitchen, pulled myself up and managed to warm up a cup of milk. As soon as I drank the milk the weakness, dizziness and sickness disappeared and I felt fine.

I have since learned that a test for the correctness of the mantra given at initiation is that either a pleasant or unpleasant experience should follow. This experience confirmed I had been given the correct mantra.

For the rest of the week, I went to Dada's flat after work. I could not get enough of his company or what he taught me about spirituality. At the weekend retreat, I immediately felt familiar in the new environment and lifestyle. It took a few more retreats, however, before I really began to understand the more complex concepts.

Strange Experience

Towards the end of 1973, Ananda Marga had a vegetarian food stall at a fair in a country town just out of Perth called York. The food proved very popular and several people learned meditation after joining in the collective chanting and meditation.

The following year Ananda Marga attended the York festival. At this second festival, a woman told some of us about an incredible experience. She explained how she had attended the previous year's festival and learned a simple meditation. After the festival she returned home and started practicing the meditation regularly. Her husband worked in a psychiatric hospital and the atmosphere eventually got the better of him. He started acting strangely and one night after returning home from work, locked his wife in their house. Then he went outside to get his axe saying he was going to kill her! She searched desperately for a way out but every conceivable exit was sealed.

Suddenly, she noticed a man beckoning her to escape through a door he was holding open. She was too frightened and desperate to question the man, and immediately ran out to safety. She never saw the man again until she came to this second York festival. Seeing a photo of the Ananda

Marga guru for the first time, she was completely startled. This was the man who had saved her life! I found out he is known to his disciples as 'Baba', an affectionate term that means 'beloved spiritual father'. This generated a desire in me to know more about this mysterious personality.

Margiis at one of the first retreats I attended in Perth, 1973. I am in the front row, middle, in a light shirt. Dada Dharmavedananda is clapping in the middle. Karuna is to my left. Retreats were very inspiring and helped me learn about Ananda Marga by living the spiritual lifestyle directly.

2
Ananda Marga

Errors, like straws, upon the surface flow
He who would search for pearls must dive below.
— John Dryden c.1670

MY NEW INTEREST IN SPIRITUALITY INSPIRED ME TO READ BOOKS ABOUT ANANDA Marga philosophy and other spiritual ideas. *Autobiography of a Yogi* by Yogananda, *Be Here Now* by Ram Das, *The First and Last Freedom* by Krishnamurti, were some of the more memorable books I read. Until now, I had been semi-literate and had read only one book in my life. The book I did complete was for my third year English exam, which I failed miserably! My parents were pleased to see me actually reading books rather than just looking at the pictures.

A second retreat was held a week after the first. Nearly all the followers of the Yoga school I was attending in North Fremantle had taken initiation. This upset the school's head teacher, Laxmii. Unfortunately, she never spoke well of Ananda Marga after that.

One of the school members, Lionel, became a good friend. He told me wonderful stories of the school's Guru, Swami Shivananda. This created a desire in me to visit him. Lionel had been practicing yoga and mediation for over 15 years. He liked both Ananda Marga and the school's Integral Yoga philosophy and practices. The only disagreement he had with Ananda Marga was its belief that practicing the headstand yoga posture was not good for health. Ananda Marga says the pressure from blood on the brain is harmful and can create irritability, bad temper and even brain tumours. Lionel would get quite angry when I mentioned this to him and would rebuke the allegation saying he'd been doing the headstand for over 15 years and he was as healthy as ever! After I left Perth I lost contact with him and a few years later I heard he had died suddenly of a brain tumour!

Baba Stories

Those first months of Ananda Marga in Perth were very enjoyable and carefree. The group meditations or 'dharma chakra', as they are known, were Sunday evenings at Kapil and Karuna's house. They often enchanted us with personal experiences about Baba in India. Kapila told us of one memorable time when he attended a large spiritual gathering where Baba was conducting a discourse for about 30,000 Margiis. At the end of the of his discourse Baba held his hands in a special position called a 'mudra', which created a very profound vibration. Like a wave, it swept over those attending the discourse. People young and old, professional and illiterate, suddenly went into all kinds of elevated states, some laughing, some crying, some saying nothing but feeling very moved. Kapil said he felt a jolt of bliss pass through him. Many years later, I was also to experience Baba's wonderous mudra.

Baba's devotees claim him to be fully self-realised or enlightened and therefore omniscient (all knowing), omnipotent (having all possible occult powers) and omnipresent (aware of everything and everyone, internally and externally). Being omniscient, he supposedly could speak fluently in any language—and later I heard many stories confirming this. One such story was from a man I met from the mountains of Papua New Guinea. He visited Baba and said Baba spoke to him fluently in his tribal language. He said he knew no one who spoke his language outside of his tribe.

Kapila and Karuna said Baba had many powers and could read people's minds like a book. He could even tell them what they had done or thought when they were children. He could describe in detail the geography of any remote place in the world and could speak as an expert on literally any subject. Baba has written books on many subjects including spirituality, psychology, biopsychology, medicine, agriculture, science, art, music, history, politics, economics and language.

Wherever he went he would talk in detail about the history of certain landmarks, the healing capacity of a particular flower, the evolution of a species of animal, or any subject that presented itself. The breadth and accuracy of his all-encompassing mind fascinated people. However, the greatest thing about Baba was his unconditional love for everyone and everything. Whoever visited him felt like Baba was a long lost best or intimate friend who loved them deeply. Baba also showed great affection towards birds, animals and even plants.

Sometime Baba would feign anger to correct a disciple's bad habits or thoughts, but his great love was always apparent as well. Sometimes after pointing out a disciple's specific past misdeeds, Baba would then touch a certain point on the body, and put the person into deep ecstasy. The disciple had to promise not to do it again and to serve suffering humanity wherever they could.

Baba was very modest, both in personality and dress. He rarely talked about himself, preferring to speak about the need to know and love God. He advocated teaching by example, and he was a perfect example. He practiced morality, spirituality and selfless service and taught others to do the same.

Baba slept only a few hours a night, from about 1 to 4 am. He meditated for a few hours a day, and spent the rest of the time working. He spoke with organisational workers, dictated his books, took news reports of Ananda Marga progress around the world, and met individual disciples. He ate very little—usually a few mouthfuls of food at each meal.

Baba's moods changed according to whatever was appropriate. Sometimes serious, sometimes joking, sometimes blissful, and sometimes ordinary and practical.

Needless to say, as I heard these stories, I developed a strong desire to meet Baba, although I still felt some skepticism. Some of the things Kapil said seemed a bit too fantastic to believe. However, it would not be too long before my doubts began to crumble.

I also had a strong desire to meet Swami Shivananda. He lived in the Himalayas at a place called Rishikesh. His teachings of morality, meditation and selfless service were very similar to Baba's teachings. I understood Shivananda was enlightened. However, he died before I got a chance to meet him.

Spiritual Experiences

While I found the philosophy very interesting and at times inspiring, what I wanted most was practical experience. I liked Ananda Marga because it offered a practical way to experience God in my own life. Shortly after my initiation, I had two profound experiences that confirmed I was on the right track.

I felt great energy rushing up my spine, and I heard a strange 'cricket' sound. Later I read that this experience was my spiritual energy (*kula kundalinii*) piercing the first chakra (*muladhara chakra*) or energy centre of the body. Most of the chakras produce a sound such as bells ringing, flutes playing, the sea crashing, or the Om sound. The meditator may hear these sounds as kundalinii passes through the chakra associated with a particular sound. Not all meditators experience them, however.

The second experience had a more profound effect on me. Early one morning I awoke with the most peaceful, contented feeling I had ever experienced. I felt so tranquil. For hours, I lay in bed contented just to do nothing but enjoy this wonderful feeling. Wave after wave of tranquillity rolled through me. On a deep level, I realised there was a happiness other than which could be experienced from worldly enjoyments. It was really much better.

Spiritual Becomes Political

Those first few months after initiation were very happy times, as is often the case. Then came the 'tests', which often discourage people from continuing on a spiritual path.

My test happened at an 'advanced retreat' Dada was running in February 1973. There were now about 20 people attending retreats and Sunday group meditation. All was going well until Dada said he had an announcement to make. He had just received word that Baba had been poisoned by the jail doctor under the direction of the Indian authorities! This was the first time Dada had ever mentioned that our guru was in jail! Dada explained the history of Baba's imprisonment and talked about how, throughout history, great people have been unjustly persecuted and often imprisoned for speaking the truth. Baba and Ananda Marga had been vocal against the corruption in the Indian government, the Hindu caste and dowry systems. Also, the powerful communist party felt threatened as the poor were becoming very sympathetic to Ananda Marga because of its service projects, while the intellectuals were attracted to its rational and spiritual social philosophy called 'Prout'.

Unfortunately, most of the people at the retreat chose not to hear the wisdom of Dada's explanation and left the retreat and Ananda Marga. When I heard Dada's explanation I thought it all sounded quite acceptable and remembered how Jesus and other great leaders had been mistreated and slandered. I'm certain if they lived today, they would be promptly persecuted for speaking out against injustice.

The few Margiis that remained organised an overnight vigil, protesting Baba's arrest and his poisoning. It was my first protest for Ananda Marga and something that was to be a major feature in my Margii life for many years. This was something that my parents didn't quite understand or appreciate. However, they did appreciate the general change for the better that they had seen in me since initiation. So, they did not make much fuss when they saw me on television in a tent outside Parliament House, protesting Baba's poisoning.

The Persecution of Ananda Marga

While I could accept that a guru may be imprisoned injustly, I certainly was still keen to understand the background better. Talking to Dada, Kapil and Karuna, I was able to piece together some of the history and persecution of Ananda Marga.

In the seventies, Indira Gandhi's government tried unsuccessfully to ban Margiis from holding government jobs. Gandhi's government saw the movement as a threat because Ananda Marga, with a combination of spiritual philosophy and dynamic social reform, easily appealed to Indians caught between the largely materialistic philosophies of communism and capitalism, which were vying for popularity in India. Because of Baba's relentless insistence on morality, Margiis in government jobs were exposing corruption which also rankled the government. The growing popularity of Ananda Marga especially amongst the middle classes was viewed by the government as a threat.

The Current, a newspaper of Indhira Gandhi's Congress Party reported in 1971 that:

"...it is a generally well known fact in well-informed circles that a large number of SENIOR government officials are Ananda Margiis... This is said to have been a greatly disturbing fact to the government... The Home Ministry is also believed to have come to the conclusion that the Ananda Marga has during its short history created a base in almost all the states, from Kashmir to Kerala and from Rajasthan to Assam. This was done at a striking pace and with great vigour... A more recent assessment made of the movement is said to have revealed that half the number of of police superintendents in Bihar State belong to Ananda Marga. This is said to have greatly disturbed the government of India."

Failing legal moves to stop Ananda Marga, the government turned on Baba personally. Police raided his headquarter in Patna, Bihar, twice but found nothing to incriminate him. Baba moved his headquarters to another state because of the harassment. The police raided the now empty Patna building and claimed to have found arms. Baba was arrested but later released. He was then re-arrested and charged with conspiring to murder some of his followers. Later, some of the so-called murdered Margiis turned up in court to say they had not been murdered!

Baba's case received international attention for its blatant violation of human rights. Famed American peace activist Daniel Berrigan S.J. shared my opinion:

The attempted destruction of Ananda Marga is a measure of the historical tragedy now being endured by the people of India. It is by no means wonderful that Ananda Marga and its heroic founder and guiding light Shrii Shrii Anandamurti, should be feeling the first blow of the truncheons.

Were the Mahatma [Gandhi] still among us, together with the father of the present incumbent [Nehru]—these men would most surely also be in jail, or otherwise disposed of.

Soon after his imprisonment, at the time I came into Ananda Marga, Baba said the jail doctor poisoned him. (This was confirmed in late 1974 by an inquiry commission which concluded that Baba had been deliberately administered an overdose of barbiturates by the jail doctor which amounted to poisoning.) Baba immediately went on an indefinite hunger strike demanding an inquiry into his poisoning. Margiis all around the world protested. This was during the State of Emergency in India when all government opposition groups were banned and their members imprisoned and tortured. Many Margiis and acharyas also suffered imprisonment and torture.

Years later, when Indira Gandhi lost the election and her government was thrown out of office, Baba was given a new trial and acquitted of all charges. He ended his hunger strike after an amazing five and half years! This defies medical explanantion, since Baba survived mainly on the water left over from boiled white rice. During his imprisonment, Ananda Margiis were harassed all over the world for protesting against Baba's ill treatment. Many false and malicious claims were made against Baba and Ananda Marga. For example, one was that Ananda Marga promoted violence and terrorist activites. Asked by a reporter if he supported violence to secure his release, Baba replied that he would not come out of prison other than by lawful means. He said, "I completely disavow acts of violence and even if some misguided youths who have no faith in the Marga's ideology, are involved in such acts, it will not obtain my release in this way." (Patna Jail, October 16, 1978.)

Throughout Baba's imprisonment, he remained unperturbed and continued to tell Margiis to have faith in dharma, or righteousness, and that he would be released at the appropriate time.

Indeed, following Baba's acquittal and release, Ananda Marga continued to grow rapidly.

The Path of Bliss

Baba was the founder and guru of Ananda Marga. He was born on the full moon of May in 1922. A family man and a railway accountant, he was alarmed at the corruption and poverty in India. He had been teaching Tantric spiritual meditation since He was a boy and had many private disciples. He felt the need to create a movement that would regenerate spiritual and moral life in India, and in the world generally. He also wanted to teach a practical spirituality suited to the physical and psychological nature of today's humanity. He said many of the spiritual techniques and mantras of the past were not appropriate for the complexities of modern human beings.

In 1955, he officially founded Ananda Marga. It began as a small organisation based in Jamalpur, India, a small railway town—but it was not to remain small. Ananda Marga's slogan is 'self realisation and service to all beings', which is realised by combining meditation and other spiritual practices with selfless service.

In his social writings and worldly activities, Baba used his given name, Prabhat Rainjan Sarkar. In his spiritual discourses, Baba used the name, Shrii Shrii Anandamurti, which means 'embodiment of bliss'. His disciples simply called him Baba. 'Baba' also means God in a personal sense, or one's inner spiritual self.

The type of meditation system Baba taught is called Tantra', which means, 'that which liberates one from bondage'. Tantra does not emphasise sex as is often claimed in the West. Then again, it does not deny sex or any other of our 'natural drives'. Rather, it says suppression of our lower self is worse than expression, so we should exercise moderation and restraint, while ideating on God. The spiritual feeling that gradually develops helps sublimate our natural drives to divine desire. Tantra advocates 'love of (spiritual) self and love of God' and teaches practical techniques for spiritualising worldly life and activities.

Tantra's *love* of God is in contrast to religion that generally teaches fear of God. Tantra is a spiritual path based on rationality, personal experience and fearlessness, while religion is generally based on irrational dogma, fear and blind faith. Of course, there are many spiritual people who are also religious. Tantra is a means to experience the essence of the teachings of all the great religious founders. For example, many of the Christian mystics follow practices that could be considered Tantric in spirit.

As interest in Ananda Marga grew, Baba trained some family people to be acharyas (spiritual teachers) so they could teach the spiritual practices and establish service projects. After a few years Ananda Marga became very popular in India. Soon, the family acharyas did not have time to do all the work while maintaining their family life. Therefore, Baba established an order of monks and nuns who work full-time for Ananda Marga, teaching meditation and running its vast social service projects: schools, homes, food distribution, disaster relief, medical clinics, progressive farming, cultural and artistic activities and so on.

By the mid sixties Ananda Marga had started centres overseas and by the late eighties was in over 250 countries and recognised by the United Nations as a non-governmental organisation (NGO). Ananda Marga's service work has received support and praise from many sectors.

Dreams Coming True

Soon after my protest vigil, Dada had to go back to Melbourne and Sydney. My frustration was also growing at this time with my apprenticeship and direction in life generally. At work my hearing and eyesight was diminishing due to the poor conditions. I nearly lost my life twice due to accidents at work. All this prompted me to tell my parents I wanted to leave my apprenticeship. Because of my poor education they were reluctant to support my wishes.

During this time another Dada came to Perth recruiting Margiis to attend an 'LFT Training Centre' in Sydney. He was an American named Acharya Abhiik, with a rather domineering personality and a very sharp mind. LFT stands for Local Full Time worker. This is someone who volunteers full-time to do Ananda Marga work. I jumped at the chance but my parents were not sure if volunteer work was a wise move.

"How much money can you make as an LFT?" my father asked.

"Well, none, its volunteer work, although Ananda Marga takes care of board, food and basic expenses," I replied.

My father, though he meant well, was a pure pragmatist at heart, and couldn't appreciate what I saw in being a volunteer for some strange religious sect, as he wrongly perceived it. (Not being a religion or an offshoot of a religion, Ananda Marga cannot be categorised as a 'sect.') My father tried arranging for my apprenticeship to be transferred to a bigger and safer place but I maintained my determination to leave for LFT training. Eventually my parents reluctantly agreed to my desires. Admittedly, I wondered myself if it was wise to throw away three years of a five year apprenticeship when I had no education to fall back on if the LFT thing wasn't what I thought it would be. However, I kept thinking that nothing could be better than teaching meditation and working on Ananda Marga's service projects. It seemed all my dreams could come true at once.

Astral Travel

After selling my motorbike, which I'd only just purchased and was quite attached to, I left for Sydney and LFT training. I was hitch-hiking with Kapil and Karuna. One night, in the middle of the Nullabour Plain desert, I lay down to sleep after evening meditation. Then a strange thing happened. While my eyes where shut I began to feel myself lifting up as if I was travelling in an elevator. I opened my eyes and could see clouds coming quickly towards me. I realised I was going towards the clouds! Then I thought about my body and immediately I felt myself descend back down into my physical form. "So that's what astral travel is like," I thought.

A New Name and New Understanding

We reached Adelaide in two days and met another American Dada who had come to Perth. His name was Dada Dharmapala. He was a wiry, jolly fellow with a lovable but crazy sense of humour. I had now been meditating for one year, so Dada decided to teach me the first lesson of meditation. This is the main meditation given in Ananda Marga. He taught me a new mantra and a technique for withdrawing my mind from outside disturbances, as well as from my body. Dada also gave me my Sanskrit name, Na'rada, which means, 'he who inspires devotion in others'.

Dada said that he was giving me the name after a great sage called Na'rada Muni and therefore I could use the Muni after Na'rada if I wished. Muni means 'sage' or 'intellectual,' although it also means 'one whose intellect is complete, or one who has attained God through meditation'. Sanskrit names are often given at initiation or when requested. The name acts like a mantra, creating the vibration of its meaning every time it is used. The meanings are always spiritual and positive, either representing a quality we have or need to develop.

After getting my spiritual name and new meditation (and still all free of charge!) I sought clarification of some things that were disturbing me a bit.

"Dada, how long does it take to become self-realised? I feel much better than when I started a year ago, but I don't feel I am close to enlightenment."

Dada smiled and said, "The path to enlightenment, according to yoga and Tantra, is not like taking a course where you earn a degree after so many years of study. For everyone enlightenment comes at different times. For many it does not come in this lifetime, although they will achieve many stages towards enlightenment and self-realisation. Nevertheless, to be totally enlightened or liberated is a totally different story. Only a few people become interested in spirituality and actively follow a spiritual path. Of these only a small portion follows the path for the rest of their life and attain significant elevation. Moreover, of those, only a few go all the way to reach full self-realisation.

"But don't be disheartened. Just by being on the path, each day you are making progress, which ultimately will bring you to a much deeper and fulfilling happiness. You have already admitted to feeling much better than when you started a year ago. Eventually you will attain enlightenment, be it in this life or another, as is everyone's destiny. It's just a matter of time, which is our choice. In the meantime, whatever progress you make is much better than before you started, isn't it?"

"That is true" I admitted, "but it was initially other people commenting on how much 'happier' and 'healthy' I looked, even though at the time I did not feel so different. It was only on reflection that I realised I did feel significantly better than before initiation."

"Yes spiritual progress is usually gradual, and often others notice it in us before we do. Baba always says that 'struggle is the essence of life,' and that we must constantly struggle against our weaknesses, doubts and fears. It is in this struggle that we acquire the necessary strength and conviction to reach our goal. The path of Tantra and dharma is not for the cowardly or timid."

"What is dharma?" I asked.

"It literally means 'that which is natural to us,' or the true or innate nature of something. For example, the dharma of fire is to burn and the dharma of humans is to realise their spiritual self. Dharma is what distinguishes us from animals. It is wrong to call humans 'rational animals' just as it would be to call animals 'mobile plants'.

Dharma is composed of three qualities: *vistara* or expansion and is developed through spiritual meditation. *Rasa* or flow, is about surrendering to God's plan rather than our egotistical desires. *Seva* means selfless service. These three components characterise Tantra's spiritual path and are the speciality of human dharma rather than animal dharma.

I then asked, "Why is there so much emphasis on service if people suffer because of their past bad actions? According to the law of karma they deserve to suffer, so why should we help?"

"No!" Dada replied in a firm voice, "You must not think like that—it is selfish and defective thinking. The cause of peoples' suffering is not our concern. Our only concern is if they are in genuine need of our help. You don't give a rich man your money, nor should you help people so that they become dependent on you. But also to ignore the needy saying it is their karma is pure selfishness. It will also create bad karma for your as well!"

"You mean in the future when I need help I will be ignored?"

"Something like that. We reap what we sow. The spirit of the true Tantric is the world's happiness is my happiness and the world's sorrow is my sorrow."

"Dada, you implied that true service can have no personal gain, but don't you get gain from teaching meditation? Aren't you trying to convert people to Ananda Marga?"

"My first concern is to give everyone the opportunity to experience their higher Self through spiritual meditation. I therefore teach anyone provided they are willing to follow basic morality. I know many people I teach will not become Margiis. That's fine although of course I would like to encourage them to become Margiis, but that is of secondary concern—a bonus."

Spiritual Training

In December 1973, I attended the first Australian LFT training session. There were 25 trainees, mostly from university, and Dada Abhiik was the trainer. Training lasted three months in a rented house in north Sydney. The routine was strict and austere. We woke before 5 am and then did two hours of meditation followed by yoga postures and finally breakfast. Then we had philosophy classes until noon, another hour of chanting and meditation, lunch, silence for half an hour, and class for a couple of hours. After a break, there was two more hours of meditation, more yoga postures and another class after dinner. When that finally ended around 10 pm, we had one more hour of meditation before we went to sleep.

Discipline was very strict, but the spiritual philosophy classes were fascinating. The concepts answered many questions I had about life and my own purpose. Even now I still remember and use concepts we learned in those classes.

Due to the long periods in meditation, many of us experienced physical reactions in our bodies during our practice. These occur when the mind has expanded and become more subtle than the body. These symptoms are listed in Tantric texts and include such involuntary actions as shaking, making humming and other strange noises, singing, weeping, rolling, salivating, yawning, bursting into laughter, hiccoughing, and making a long sighing sound. Some of these symptoms became quite frequent during our meditation times and sometimes I laughed to myself watching the others. Regular yoga exercises and a 'yogic diet' make the body subtle over time and these symptoms gradually disappear.

I felt very grateful to have Dada Abhiik as our trainer as he seemed so knowledgeable. Be it spiritual or social philosophy, he could always answer my queries.

"Dada, other people teach meditation mostly to relax and feel peace. But in Ananda Marga we also talk about the struggles in life. The Margiis that I have met seem to face many challenges and don't seem to always experience the calm mind other meditation groups talk about."

Dada thought for a moment and then replied, "Their meditation is different. There are many kinds of meditations, but what we do is Tantric meditation. This is concerned with raising the *kula kundalinii* (spiritual energy) until it reaches the highest chakra, the seat of consciousness. For the kundalinii to rise through all the chakras our body and mind have to be purified and perfected. This is no easy task and requires constant struggle and effort.

"The meditation or visualisation techniques many people teach for relaxation are something quite different. No major change in lifestyle is needed. But if you want real inner peace, which comes through union with Cosmic Consciousness, then effort and surrender is needed, along with a lot of God's grace."

"You don't make it sound very enticing—all this struggle and effort."

"Oh, but it is enticing, through struggle comes bliss. Just a small taste will make you mad for more. All the mystics of all the great religions talk about it, indeed live and die only for IT!"

Remembering my experience in this regard, I added:
"I have had a small taste of bliss and already I find that I am wanting more and more of it."

"You see," said Dada, "how intoxicating a taste of bliss can be?"

Another time I was present when another trainee asked Dada how to know if one is following the spiritual path correctly.

Relaxing after morning meditation around 1973. I was finding more and more pleasure in my spiritual practices.

"Generally if there is a choice to be made then pick the option which is the most difficult. The path of degeneration is nearly always easier in the beginning, while the path to enlightenment is more difficult but gets easier later on."

"Why is that?"

Dada replied, "Because spirituality is about long-term happiness—infinite bliss rather than short-lived pleasure. Say you are fasting and feel hungry. If you follow your animal urges you will break your fast and eat in order to satisfy your immediate hunger. But then you lose all the benefits of fasting, just to remove a short-term discomfort. However, if you follow your higher self and control your hunger by continuing your fast, then you will benefit from the fast."

"And have a more enjoyable breakfast," said the trainee.

"Yes," smiled Dada," and also learn self control which is indispensable on the spiritual path."

Later in life I frequently remembered this little conversation. I learned not to let short lived inconveniences or displeasures distract me from my long term goals. This gave me inner strength and resolve.

LFT Postings

It was a long three months. Everyone went through a lot and became better for it. Except for one or two, everyone agreed to work as LFTs. They would either stay at established centres or be assigned to start up new ones. Melbourne, an established centre, was my first posting and I stayed there for the year of 1974.

While I was in Melbourne it was decided to conduct a meditation intensive. Margiis would take turns in doing meditation at the centre all day and all night. My turn was early in the afternoon. After a short time of meditating, the desire to continue indefinitely became strong. So I continued for hour after hour until the intensive ended seven hours later. While I can't say I experienced anything particularly dramatic, I did feel deep peace and tranquillity, a little like what I had felt after initiation. After that I developed a strong desire to do long meditations. I know I could experience real inner peace and happiness and that was what I wanted most.

Different Gurus

One of the things I liked about being in Melbourne was the many different spiritual groups there. Sometimes I would visit them just to see how they operated and what their philosophy was. I liked philosophical discussion and debates, provided they did not become aggressive and personal. I felt Ananda Marga had the most comprehensive and balanced philosophy but was always interested to see if there was something as good or even better. Of the Eastern and Western religions, sects, and yoga paths I investigated I did not find any that convinced me to change my allegiance to Ananda Marga, even though I was quite impressed with some.

Sometimes different gurus would visit and I would go and see them. The guru of the Hare Krishnas, Shrii Acharya Prabhupada, the guru of the Divine Light Mission, Maharajaji, and Swami Muktananda were some of the more famous gurus I saw.

One guru that impressed me was Swami Muktananda. I got the opportunity to personally hand him a bouquet of flowers on behalf of Ananda Marga. It was just before he was to give a public talk. Dada Abhiik told me to walk up on stage and present the flowers to Swami Muktananda. I did this and said it was a gift from Ananda Marga. He initially looked a little surprised and then told his assistant to place the flowers under a photo of his guru—a sign of great respect. Swami Muktananda was impressed with the Margiis in Melbourne and told his disciples they should follow our example of discipline and devotion.

I also spoke with Christians but despite their best efforts, they could not convince me to leave Ananda Marga or Baba, regardless of my great admiration and respect of Jesus Christ.

Meanwhile I was developing a deep desire to became an acharya as I continued working in Melbourne as an LFT. I had no interest in getting married and I constantly thought about how to get closer to God. All I wanted to do was devote my life to self-realisation and service to humanity. The acharya lifestyle seemed to be the best way to achieve this goal.

3
Going To India

*Human beings want to emerge from the dark chasms of sleep and death
into the world of light—golden flashes of light
piercing the heart of darkness.*
—Baba

AT THE END OF 1974 I LEFT MELBOURNE AND RETURNED TO SYDNEY FOR OUR national seminar. There was five blissful days of intensive spiritual practices, philosophy classes and seminars. Dada Abhiik knew I was keen to go for acharya training and so when he asked me if I was ready to go, I immediately said yes.

"Are you sure?" Dada asked.

"Yes I'm sure," I replied.

Dada looked at me silently for several long seconds, then said, "Okay."

Dada told me to visit my parents and say goodbye to them. Back in Perth with my parents, I explained that I was going to become a celibate missionary monk, working full time for Ananda Marga.

Dad did not mount the big battle I'd expected. He just asked his usual question, "What sort of money do you get?"

"Well Dad, we don't get paid. It's like being an LFT for the rest of my life. Ananda Marga takes care of my basic needs while I run the service projects and teach meditation. I will be working overseas and you will be able to contact me at the Ananda Marga centre I'm living in."

My parents were glad to hear they could still contact me, especially my mother. I felt sad saying goodbye, thinking it would be a long time before I could see them again. I was glad when it was over and finally I was on my way to India.

India

Four of us went to acharya training. The others were women I knew from the LFT training centre. We arrived at Calcutta Airport late at night. It was my first trip to India and it was quite a memorable one. Even now I can still experience the shock I felt when driving into Calcutta that night and seeing not only such chaos and crowds on the streets even so late at night, but also of all things, cows chewing their cud in the middle of the road! Our taxi driver nonchalantly swerved around ubiquitous cows as I constantly braced myself for a collision with them.

In February 1975, Ananda Marga was under heavy persecution, especially in India. Baba was still in jail and foreigners did not display the fact that they were Margiis for fear of being deported. We were told not to go to the Global Office until after 10 pm. as it was probably being watched by police. Therefore, we didn't go there until the next night. We stayed at the Modern Lodge (I thought that was an ironic name for a very rundown place) in the New Market area of Calcutta.

Next morning we went out for a look at the area. Within seconds, I came across my first beggar—a woman with elephantitis of the neck. I felt quite an affinity for her and indeed to the whole place. I quickly developed a feeling of having been here before—perhaps having lived here in a past life? I felt more at home than in Australia. However, when I returned to India on a regular basis, this familiar feeling gradually vanished.

After 10 pm. we took a taxi to the Ananda Marga Global Office in Punditia Road. I felt quite excited about having to go at this late hour, wondering if the police were watching the office. We entered the office compound without incident and met the Office Secretary. He seemed pleased to meet us and we all were certainly happy to be in a place with so many senior monks and nuns.

While staying at the Global Office, I had time to read more Ananda Marga publications. In one magazine I found the following article by a non-Margii who had a personal meeting with Baba. This article had a major impact on me because it made me understand how Baba relates to Margiis and non-Margiis with equal love and concern:

> Baba said to me, "My boy, you are having impure thoughts."

I told him, "No I'm not," but then he held me by the ears and told me that I had had them recently. I remembered the thoughts and admitted it. Baba then told the details of the thoughts.

Then he told me that I was a good boy and that I was not really bad and I should call him Baba. He made me draw near to him and put my hands on my chest in the gesture of Namaskar [a spiritual greeting]. He told me to stand up and to gaze into his eyes. As I did so, I seemed to see balls of fire in his eyes and I could not look at him for very long. I embraced him as he had told me to do so and, at that moment, it seemed if his body entered into mine and mine into his. We became merged into one inseparable body. I felt thrilled and confidence poured into my whole system.

As we separated, he touched my left rib and told me that I was not in perfect health. He said I should avoid drinking wine with a high percentage of alcohol and that I should cut down my smoking to a minimum. I told him of a certain ailment that I had and he said that he has given me that hint for its cure. I suppose he has.

"Are you a good boy?" he asked. I said, "I am now, but before I was not so good. " He got angry and said that I have always been a good boy and that I should never again think that I have been bad because he is always with me. I nodded my head in reverent agreement.

This story increased my fascination about Baba on several levels. It showed Baba not only reading a person's mind, but also indicated his healing abilities and powers. In this case the man was not a Margii and so while Baba did not normally encourage smoking or drinking, he took a much more mild approach knowing the man would not have the same obligations as a Margii. There was also a glimpse of what it would be like in close proximity to Baba.

All of this added to the other remarkable stories I'd heard, increased markedly my fascination and desire to meet Baba.

With time I came to hear many more stories. One of my favourites was about a young student who went to see Baba, not knowing who he was or what he was capable of. The acharya who brought him saw Baba stop and talk to the student. Afterwards the student was weeping. The Dada asked the student what Baba had said to make him cry. Apparently the student had a diary that he had kept since he was very young, and which no one else had ever seen. Baba looked at the man and repeated to him a poem that the young man had written some years before, but had not yet completed. After repeating the unfinished poem Baba then added the last line to complete it!

City of Bliss

After a few days in Calcutta we were off to Ananda Nagar, an Ananda Marga model community on sacred land near West Bengal. We wanted to visit Ananda Nagar on our way to Acharya training as we had all heard what a wonderful place it was. We had heard that many Tantric yogis had been practicing meditation there for thousands of years, and some had achieved liberation. We heard that the great ancient yogi, Shiva, had visited this area of land 7,000 years ago. Because the vibration is so high, we were told one month of meditation there was like doing meditation for a year anywhere else.

I also was keen to meet some of the highly advanced Dadas who live at Ananda Nagar. I heard some had occult powers like the ability to read minds. It all sounded very exciting and so it proved to be.

Ananda Nagar means 'City of Bliss' and it is a model Ananda Marga community with both spiritual and social service projects, including preschool, primary school, college, medical clinic and various agricultural projects. It is in a very impoverished, yet ancient and culturally-rich area. Years later Baba gave a plan that turned this near-desert land into an oasis of gardens, lush agricultural projects and various self-sufficient industries.

After we arrived and were shown where to stay, one particularly vibrant Dada visited me. He said his job was to look after us. As soon as he walked into my room I felt elevated. As he spoke about Baba and meditation I could see and hear the air around him crackling and vibrating. It is something difficult to explain. Perhaps tiny explosions of blissful energy in the air best describe this wonderful experience. I felt full of peace and bliss.

There was another time when I was eating in one of the college rooms. Suddenly, another Dada walked in. He was a big, round person, and started scolding a little boy in an Indian language. The little boy looked horrified and ran outside. The Dada left also. I thought to myself, "What an arrogant, mean person!" The boy could not have been older than seven.

Later, to my total surprise, I was told that this was a very elevated Dada; some people even said he had attained liberation! I became confused at hearing this as he seemed to be so aggressive. Sometime later I met him at group meditation and he seemed quite pleasant but still not what I thought constituted an enlightened yogi.

Time passed rapidly at Ananda Nagar and soon it was time to go. My week there was truly a spiritual experience and I noticed my meditation was now deeper and better. As I was about to leave I met this same Dada again. He said:

"So you are going now?"

"Yes," I replied.

There was a long silence as neither one of us seemed to know what to say next. He was looking out into the sky in a dream-like state, but also with great intensity. Then he invited me back to his room saying he had something to give me. He pulled out a large, round, sesame sweet and said to take it for my journey. Then he pulled out two more and said to give them to the two women with me. I thanked him and left.

It was not until I was back in Australia that I understood some of his greatness. Several times, when I did meditation, he appeared in my mind. I could see him very clearly with a white radiant aura around him, and I always experienced a pleasant serene feeling with this vision. I also remembered him gazing into the sky after he asked if I was going. I felt that at this time his mind had been deeply lost in the thought of God. I realised it was not always possible to judge a person's spiritual greatness by our judgments of their external behaviour. Baba said a positive nature, simplicity, directness and love are the signs of spiritual elevation.

As for the Dada's hostile response to the little boy, who knows what the boy may have done to warrant the scolding? In later years, when I returned to India I often met this Dada and have received much valuable spiritual guidance and feelings of bliss while in his presence. Later I also read an article written by him on what it is like to be in the liberated state. The editor of the magazine noted that Dada was writing from personal experience and not philosophical theory or conjecture.

Experiencing Spiritual Liberation

On the path to complete self-realisation, a meditator passes through several stages of God consciousness, or *samadhis*.

In the first stage we experience God's presence all around. We can no longer feel God is far away— 'in the sky' or elsewhere.

In the next stage we become intimately close to God. Later we have an actual tactile experience as if we are in the lap of God. As we move further along the spiritual path, we begin to feel deeply that we are very similar to God; we no longer feel much difference. Finally, the spiritual aspirant feels, 'I am God.' It is called *savikalpa samadhi*. This is the stage Dada wrote about.

Dada explained that when we approach this state of savikalpa samadhi, we experience it for awhile and then we return to our previous condition. After repeatedly experiencing and returning, we finally become permanently established in this state.

In Sanskrit this liberated state is also called 'brahma sadbhava', which means 'perceiving everything as God Consciousness.' Here one always perceives Consciousness in a pure state, as a milky white light permeating the atoms and molecules of the manifested world. It is the state of the truly liberated person. Dada explained that whether one has the eyes open or closed one will experience a deep bliss. However, when the eyes are closed the bliss is more intense. In this state the ego is almost non existent. One feels united with God.

In this rare and highly exalted state of liberation we have transcended worldly pleasure and pain, attraction and aversion. There is only a feeling of continuous, unbroken, loving bliss. However, externally we may take on different behaviours and personalities, so as to adjust with others and the world. But internally there are no desires. We wander about the world child-like, guided by God and serving those who come in contact with us. The served people also have some of their mental impurities or bad karma absorbed into us. That explained to me why I felt so much better spiritually after being in Dada's presence. Maybe he had absorbed some of my impurities or negative karma.

There is a still greater realisation when there is no dualistic feeling at all— there is just 'IT!' In that ultimate state the ego is totally absorbed in God-Consciousness and all individuality and practical functioning ceases to exist. This is called *nirvakalpa samadhi*, or *nirvana* in Buddhism.

Training Centre

In India the taxi and rickshaw drivers are notorious for over-charging foreigners. So before going to Varanasi for Acharya training I asked what was the correct fare for getting a rickshaw from the train station to the training centre.

When I arrived at the training centre the driver asked me for a fare that was higher than I expected, so I refused to pay. I insisted I would only pay half of what he wanted, so we got into a big argument. He threw the money I gave him on the ground, spat on it and shouted even louder in Hindi at me. People gathered and also shouted at me but I was determined not to be ripped off. In the end I just walked away when some Indian Margiis from the training centre came to help out.

That night I was informed that the amount the rickshaw driver asked for was correct! I felt both ashamed and sorry for what I'd done, but also amused at the irony of an honest Westerner (albeit unintentionally) ripping off an Indian rickshaw driver! Usually it is the other way around. Fortunately, one of the trainees had given the rickshaw driver the correct fare.

The training centre for men was in a 500-year-old sandstone castle. Some papaws and a few other trees surrounded it with vultures sitting in them. Further away were fields and some sugar cane crops (which we Westerners sometimes raided secretly.)

We were about 20 trainees with two trainers. This group included four Westerners: two from Europe, and two from Australia. Since I was very keen to become an acharya and liked any challenge given to me, I accepted the job of schedule in-charge. This was despite warnings from other trainees that the last few had all left training because of the hardships this job caused. It did not take long for me to understand why it was such a difficult job. I had to run up and down almost vertical stairs informing everyone of their classes, which really wore me down. It also meant I missed much of the class myself. The extremely hot weather also did not help my work much either.

The classes covered spiritual and social philosophy, Sanskrit, Bengali, English, and conduct rules. These rules concerned many areas of health, hygiene, morality, social conduct and character building . While family Margiis follow some disciplines necessary to the yogic path, acharyas are given additional conduct rules concerning missionary life. Only after having passed exams on all these subjects does one undertake training in teaching meditation and yoga exercises. In Ananda Marga, meditation and yoga postures are 'prescribed' individually and privately by a trained acharya according to our physical and mental condition. But this special training isn't given until the trainee has reached a proper standard of conduct.

As summer began to make its very hot presence felt, food became quite an issue. It was quite scarce and mostly only white rice, potatoes and chapatis (a type of flat bread). The situation got so bad that we began to eat leaves! One day I saw a trainee dragging in a branch from a tree, while others were collecting dried leaves. I asked what the branch was for and was told its leaves were to be boiled for dinner that night. The dried leaves were to make a fire to cook our meagre meal. We were even running low on fuel. I felt really worried about the coming summer months, when, I was told, food became even more scarce and the winds got so hot that it could burn your skin if you weren't covered.

My Deadly Greed

One day I happened to notice a pile of what looked like peanuts in a storeroom. Certainly they tasted a bit like them. Making sure no one could see me I gulped down as much as I could as I was always hungry. About an hour later I started vomiting. I became very sick and continued to vomit. When I explained what I had eaten Dada informed me that I had eaten castor oil seeds! He thought it was quite funny, and now I can see why. But for months I could not even look at a castor oil seed without feeling sick. Unfortunately, the latrine was situated under a castor oil tree and often I could see seeds scattered around. This made me feel sick every time I went to the toilet.

While I recovered from the castor oil seeds, my health deteriorated quite badly from diarrhoea and malnutrition. Lying in bed, looking out at the vultures in the nearby trees, I used to say to some of the other trainees that the vultures were just waiting for us all to drop so that they could eat us!

Eventually, I was taken off any duties and the head trainer said he might need to send me to hospital. But money was a problem. Telegrams were being sent daily to Central Office in Calcutta requesting funds so we could eat but we received no reply. Everyone in Ananda Marga in India was in financial difficulty, not just us. Persecution of Ananda Marga in

India had affected many of our commerce projects which created severe financial problems.

In the end I looked forward to getting sick because it meant I got a drink of Horlicks and some fruit. But as soon as my health improved, it was back to white rice and potatoes. Fasting days were quite good because I did not have to worry about food making me sick, although, with the heat, thirst and weakness, fasting became increasingly difficult. Then again, breaking the fast became a problem. All they could give us besides some lemon water, which tasted great, was more rice and potatoes, only this time watered down!

Normally we got a treat when it was a special celebration day. At one point, when conditions were getting even more difficult we were assured we would get some sweet treat at the end of our normal rice and potato meal. We waited so anxiously for the treat! Then it came: one teaspoonful each of sweet rice! Although we Westerners laughed, we also felt hurt with disappointment.

My First Baba Dream

One interesting phenomenon I'd been looking forward to experiencing as a Margii was 'Baba dreams'. One night during training I had my first Baba dream. He seemed quite unreal. His body glowed and he seemed very blissful and loving. He came into a room and looking straight at me with penetrating and loving eyes. Baba greeting me with Namaskar by putting his palms together with his thumbs touching his forehead and then his chest. A wave of bliss engulfed me.

Baba sat down to talk to a group of acharyas.. I sat behind Baba and to his side, only a few feet away. I found it quite fascinating being so close to him and watching his movements and gestures. Every little detail seemed so controlled and perfect. Even more fascinating was to see his skin. Although he was in his fifties, I couldn't see any wrinkles on his face. His skin was soft like a baby's skin (which was how it was in real life.) I awoke feeling exhilarated and moved. "So that's a Baba dream!" I thought to myself, "I want more!"

The Great Treat!

During the two months I was in training the government was harassing Ananda Marga considerably. Baba was still in jail and things seemed to be deteriorating for Ananda Marga. We were warned about occasional raids by police and immigration officials looking for Western Margiis to deport as a means of harassment.

One day I was informed of an impending raid and told to run into the cane fields and hide until nightfall. Along with some other Westerners I ran into the sugarcane fields, then into some villages. It was all quite exciting for me and certainly a pleasant relief from the training routine. Night came and we cautiously returned. The officials had gone empty handed!

Despite all the hardship, I was keen to become an acharya. It was my goal in life. I could not think of anything else I'd rather do. But suddenly, and totally unexpectedly, I found my whole attitude completely and abruptly changed. One morning I woke up with an extreme aversion to the idea of becoming an acharya. There was no other desire to replace it and I certainly did not want to be married, but I definitely did not want to be an acharya. Was I feeling this because I was so sick, I wondered? What if I could become an acharya tomorrow? Still the answer was no. Some inexplicable part of me had changed and I didn't know what to do about it.

After giving the new feelings much thought I went to the junior trainer and told him my decision to leave the training centre. He tried to dissuade me but I would not listen and so we had an argument. I left his room and reconsidered. After about a week of soul searching I went back to him and said I still wanted to leave. Again we argued and I left to reconsider. Efforts were then made to make life better for me: cups of Horlicks each day, even if I was not sick, and a trip into Varanasi for group meditation. But it was all in vain.

For the third time I saw Dada and we argued. He started shouting, but finally said, "Okay, its fine by me but you have to get permission from the senior trainer first. He'll be back tomorrow."

He came but left again and consequently I had to wait several more long days before he returned. The morning after his return I went to see him. I waited outside for hours as he met with different people, did meditation, had lunch and saw more people. Finally he called me in.

"So I hear you want to leave?"

"Yes Dada," I said.

"And you're sure this is what you want to do?"

"Yes, I am definite."

"It is four o'clock now and there is a train for Delhi at five, you had better get ready now to go."

"Yes, Dada!" I said in surprise and relief, as I rushed out to prepare to leave. Despite my excitement, I realised I had no money for a train ticket. So, I quickly sold my watch to buy my train ticket to New Delhi where I would contact my parents for an air ticket to Perth.

As I was about to go the junior trainer called me into his room to explain the reason he had been so difficult towards me. He wanted to make sure I really wanted to leave. He understood not everyone was suited to a monk's life and hoped there were no hard feelings. I said there were not and gratefully accepted some sweets he'd purchased for me.

Back in Perth my parents were horrified to see the physical condition I was in. They said I was just skin and bones.

"Did they torture you?" my father asked sarcastically.

They made me go to the doctor for a check up. As soon as I arrived, I collapsed on the floor. The doctor said I was suffering from malnutrition and dysentery. After three weeks I regained my health and got a job from the local council digging trenches. I stayed at the job until I had paid back the money my parents had spent on my airfare.

Two months after I left the training centre, a State of Emergency was declared in India. Ananda Marga was banned and many Margiis were imprisoned. The Indian Prime Minister, Indira Gandhi, had been convicted on corruption charges and rather than go to jail she declared martial law and put all her opponents and critics in jail.

All the trainees were subsequently imprisoned for some years, including foreigners. Somehow I was spared that drama. Perhaps that's why I found an irresistible urge to suddenly leave training. Was it the hand of God that made me leave to avoid imprisonment in India—and to save me for another type of imprisonment and drama?

4
The Embassy Protest

...the greater the height reached by a person, inspired by a great ideal, the lesser shall be his or her sense of pleasure and pain.
—Baba

ONCE MY HEALTH WAS RESTORED AND THE MONEY PAID TO MY PARENTS, I RANG the acting Ananda Marga head of Australasia, Dada Abhiik, about working as an LFT again. Dada said he'd love to have me back as there was so much service work to do.

In October 1975 I was posted to manage the Ananda Marga centre in Adelaide. When I arrived Ananda Marga was in the process of taking over a large city food co-operative which had been run by the communists. Unlike India and Russia, communists in Australia had a very good opinion of Ananda Marga, probably because of our emphasis on cooperatives. My three months in Adelaide was spent managing this co-operative. During this time I developed an interest in marriage but soon, after living in the Adelaide centre with a married couple, I lost the desire. Marriage was not as idyllic or easy as I thought it would be. I was quite naive in this regard.

After the mid-year retreat in Sydney I was posted to Hobart. It was there I decided to return for acharya training because I could not see myself living any other lifestyle. When I wrote to my parents about my decision I received an angry response from my mother. I wrote back to her explaining more about of my sincere desire to work full time for the service of humanity. She sent another letter, only this time it was inspired. She wished me the best of luck and said if she were any younger she would also do the same. Mum said since she could not do what I was doing she was enclosing half her savings. She sent $500 to be used for Ananda Marga's service work.

At the end of 1975 I went to Sydney for another national conference and was told I could go for acharya training again. But then Dada changed his mind and decided at the last moment to send me to Canberra to keep the centre going there.

The Guatemala Concert

After a short time in Canberra I was informed that money had to be raised for our earthquake relief teams in Guatemala. I decided to organise a benefit concert. The local radio station agreed to broadcast free advertisements and several bands said they would play for free. Canberra University donated a hall. Having little money I hitch-hiked to Sydney where Ananda Marga had a printing press. I got posters made and hitched back the next morning. Everything was very rushed and tense. I had no one to help me and neglected my meditation and yoga postures. I put up posters, but then the bands pulled out. So I had to try to get other bands with only a few days to go. Finally, I secured a band and everything was ready. But then only a few dozen people turned up. The band played some songs and then sat with the audience and listened to recordings they made of the songs they had just played! It was embarrassing. People came but left when they saw so few people there. Eventually 50 people came and so at $1 each I raised $50. The concert finished about 11 pm. but then I had to clean up the mess left behind. Long past midnight I walked home feeling very tired, disappointed and dispirited.

For the next week I awoke every morning with a migraine headache which lasted until noon. Before I was initiated I had experienced them regularly, but this was the first time since then. The migraines were probably from too much worry and not enough meditation and yoga. Skipping yoga exercises and doing very little meditation meant I had little resistance to the stress created from all the work I was doing. I learnt from that experience the importance of keeping up my spiritual practices. Without them I risked burn-out.

As an aside, despite my small donation to the cause, Ananda Marga's relief work in Guatemala at the time of this major earthquake, was very successful. As a result of that work, Ananda Marga became became well-respected in Guatemala and still has many members and projects there.

Canberra Protest Strike

The first six months in Canberra were very frustrating. There were only one or two other margiis and it was very difficult to get people interested in meditation. Sometimes I did a six-hour meditation in the mornings, hoping to get some inspiration or direction as what to do. I also felt it was best to meditate if I could not think of any work to do.

Then, during the weekly group meditation, I got an idea to challenge the Indian High Commissioner to a public debate. The Indian High Commission was in Canberra and its Commissioner had been slandering Ananda Marga and Baba. The Indian Government was coming under attack from global human rights organisations for its treatment of Ananda Marga and Baba, so the Commission was trying to create a bad name for Ananda Marga here to support the injustice in India. They were distributing books with malicious and false allegations about Ananda Marga to members of Parliament and the media. One booklet was called *Soiling the Saffron Robe*. They made crude and extremely inaccurate accusations about Baba's character with a clear intention of influencing his case.

I told the other margiis about my plan to challenge the High Commissioner. They thought it was a good idea. A debate would give us a chance to finally tell the truth about our work and our guru.I felt quite nervous about it, wondering how an uneducated person like me would survive in a public debate with a high-ranking diplomat! But I firmly believed God had planted the idea in my head and therefore I could do it.

I went to the Sydney Ananda Marga headquarters to discuss my idea. Our public relations secretary contacted a national current affairs programme called *This Day Tonight* about holding a debate. They agreed and contacted the Commissioner who refused. The public relations secretary suggested I should do a fast until I either had the debate or the Commissioner stopped slandering Baba and Ananda Marga. I thought it was a good idea, although it hadn't been my original intention. Since the Commission would not stop attacking us and also refused to debate us to air the facts, I was interviewed on TV about my 'fast to death'! I decided to drink some Horlicks, a malted-milk drink, during the fast to prolong the hunger strike so as to keep the issue alive for as long as possible (and me, too!).

While the idea of fasting wasn't entirely appealing to me, it certainly attracted attention. After my interview, which was shown nationally, I sat for a short meditation before sleep. As I did my meditation I felt dizzy and sick. I could feel a fever and weakness coming on. Panic! The next morning I was planning to leave for Canberra to start my fast and already I was feeling too sick to do it. The publicity against Ananda Marga would be terrible if I backed down because of ill health! "Baba, you have to help me," I said in my meditation. I began to feel determined that I would not let this fever take hold. By the end of meditation the fever had gone.

In Canberra I set up a tent in a vacant block next to the Indian High Commission. During that time there was a steady trickle of media attention giving my protest coverage throughout Australia and even in India. The communist Indian paper, *Blitz*, ran a half-page article that inferred I was secretly taking solid food in my tent. Some tourist buses started to come by and a few locals visited me. They were mostly friendly, and many people tooted their car horns in support as they drove past. One motorist lent me his cassette player and some tapes. One night some not-so-friendly people threw pieces of wood at my tent. Due to my physical weakness I was in no position to defend myself. That frightened me and I asked God and Baba for protection. I was never bothered after that.

That lasted a few days until the police moved me on. A total stranger who was sympathetic to the protest and who rented the property across the road, said I could camp on his lawn. I stayed there a week with my tent and placards. Due to the media coverage, the owner of the house found out I was camping on his property. He told his tenant that I was not allowed to camp on the lawn. I wondered if the Indian security forces had pressured him to have me evicted.

A margii offered me a car to stay in. This car was parked outside the High Commission and covered with placards. No one could legally disturb me, so I stayed there until the end of the protest. A new LFT was sent to Canberra to help me. During the hunger strike he kept me in stock with Horlicks and milk. By the end of the fast he claimed he'd bought every bottle of Horlicks that existed in Canberra. We joked about me doing commercials for Horlicks.

My fast lasted 108 days. While the hunger strike was not severe because of the Horlicks and milk I was drinking, nevertheless, I did lose almost 13 kilograms. My stomach shrank so that I could only drink one cup of Horlicks before feeling completely full.

Although hunger was not an extreme issue, I had other difficulties to face. It was winter, and each morning I'd find the water frozen when I washed my face at an outdoor tap. In the cold mornings and evenings I felt the chill more keenly from lack of food.

Otherwise, I used the time as an intense spiritual retreat. I meditated eight hours a day and passed the rest of my time reading spiritual books and chatting to the occasional visitor or reporter. Every day when the High Commissioner came to work, he glared at me. If thoughts could kill I would have been dead!

Margiis kept me inspired with numerous letters and telegrams from around Australia. If nothing else, the publicity my protest received nationwide certainly made the national ' Free Baba' campaign more well known. I felt this was the real purpose of the protest strike, as well as to help me grow personally.

Baba Talking

I had one interesting experience with Baba during a newspaper interview. Due to weakness and intense meditation, I was mostly quite spaced- out and had trouble thinking coherently. However, when a reporter asked me questions my mind suddenly became clear. Prior to this interview I had just been reading the passage in Baba's book that the High Commissioner had used to justify his attack on Baba. So I was prepared when the interviewer asked me about it.

The High Commissioner had quoted Baba's article where he had written that democracy is the 'government of the fools, for the fools, by the fools.' Having read the full context of Baba's statement I was able to explain that this is really the case when the vast majority of people are illiterate as is the case in India. People voting about something they don't understand is a farce. Baba said that democracy can only be successful when a majority of people are literate, moral and fully understand the issues. He said that while democracy was not ideal, it is the best system we have now and we should make an effort to create the proper conditions for its success. The reporter appreciated my response and wrote a sympathetic article.

As soon as the interview was over, my sudden flood of confidence and clarity vanished. It became very clear to me that Baba had helped me. This experience gave me added faith in Baba's omnipotence and omniscience.

I had this experience many times later and heard of many other Margiis who experienced this sudden transformation, and then a reversal back to their normal state once the job had been done.

Video and Verbals

Towards the end of 1976, news came that Baba had lost the court appeal against his conviction. This was no surprise since Ananda Marga had now been banned in India for over a year and anyone showing support for Ananda Marga was imprisoned, including witnesses and lawyers! A total media ban had also been instituted. International observers at the trial indicated that the prosecution case would have been dismissed before trial in other common law countries. The prosecution's chief witness was said to be quite unbelievable.

The International Commission of Jurists in Geneva and the International League for Human Rights in New York had commissioned a report by Mr Claude-Armand Sheppard which was highly embarrassing to the Indian Government. Sheppard, a member of the Canadian Bar, observed the case in India and testified to the US Congress that Baba's trial was a clear political farce: "The trial is not the trial of the accused," he said. " It is the demolition of Ananda Marga."

> ...in the authoritarian climate of India today it is virtually impossible to find witnesses willing to brave the authorities by testifying on behalf of the accused. Indeed, many margiis are either in detention or in hiding. Even if they could be found... their testimony would expose them almost certainly to arrest. ...Fair trials in a dictatorial framework are difficult to conceive and probably impossible to achieve. (1976 report)

Another observer of Baba's trial was renowned British lawyer and Member of Parliament Williams Wells QC. His well-researched report also slammed the trial as an unjust witch hunt.

We planned a demonstration to protest Baba's conviction and we decided I would end my fast. Many margiis came from Sydney for the protest. As we gathered on the lawn with placards, chanting slogans. The High Commissioner lost his temper and tried to attack us. He had to be restrained by his own staff and the Commonwealth police. They dragged him back into the building. Clearly this protest was the last straw for him. The Commissioner must have demanded action from the police because the police returned after taking the Commission away, and started to arrest a few Margiis, though they had left us alone before as we were within our rights.

I was watching from outside my car while this was going on. I was still far too weak to participate. The Margiis were taken off in a police van, and were arrested on charges of resisting arrest and disobeying 'lawful direction'. Police actually claimed in court that the Margiis had assaulted police, broken through police lines, and other extreme behavior. In the end we claimed a satisfying victory because a margii had been videotaping the entire event. When it was produced in court, after the police testimony, it clearly showed that the police had simply walked up and arrested the Margiis. The case was thrown out of court. Unfortunately, these police, as is typical in all Australian states, were never charged with their own proven perjury.

Exploding Lights

During the whole year I was in Canberra, I had an unusual experience each night as I fell asleep. Regardless of the time, strange white lights appeared in my mind. They reminded me of lights exploding in clouds during a lightning storm. These lights were exploding in my mind, non-stop until I fell asleep. It was a purely visual experience; I didn't feel anything unusual. No one has yet explained to me what it was I was experiencing.

New Zealand Adventure

Dada Abhiik had said that I could go for acharya training after the January conference in 1977. Again I said goodbye to my parents and went to Sydney for the conference en route to India. But Dada changed his mind again. Some acharyas in New Zealand had been deported because a few Margiis had broken the law when trying to highlight Baba's plight. He wanted me to go to New Zealand and work as a Dada, because as an Australian citizen I could not be deported. When I pointed out the obvious, that I was not an acharya, he still insisted that I go. He felt I was capable of doing the work of a Dada, except that I could not give initiation;

I could only teach introductory meditation. Dada said I had to dress like a monk in an orange uniform and a turban. While he took responsibility organizationally for what I was doing, he could not, when I asked, say how the family and single Margiis would react to an LFT in acharya uniform. This was a big worry for me.

When I arrived in New Zealand Ananda Marga had a bad name there. This was due to false slander by the Indian High Commission, and a recent incident involving some misguided Margiis. Consequently, the public often abused me. 'Go home' was a common response to seeing me in my bright orange uniform. One time on a ferry I walked passed a woman and her daughter. The mother quickly grabbed her child in fear and held her close to her as if I was going to attack them! Most of my talks on meditation which were intended for the public were only attended by journalists and security police. At first the abuse made me nervous and self-conscious. However, in time I grew out of this and became more self-confident. The experience was very strengthening.

Fortunately, the Margiis accepted me well and helped me when ever I toured. Because I had studied martial arts for many years I gave talks on meditation at martial arts schools. These went well and usually after the talk I would train with the students. This both surprised and delighted them!

Social Service Group

After six months in New Zealand I returned to Sydney. I thought Dada Abhiik now would surely give me permission to go to acharya training. But no, other things had come up that he wanted me to do. First, he put me in the position of the Australasia President of Ananda Marga because he needed a dependable person. I lived in the Australasia headquarters in Sydney, chairing meetings of the different service departments of Ananda Marga. These included departments for disaster relief, women's welfare, education, the arts, outreach, and commerce. I learned a lot dealing with some very strong and independent-minded margiis on the board. Contrary to some misconceptions, meditation does not make people weak-minded and weak-willed. People can become very strong-willed and independent as they develop an connection with their inner spiritual self. They become increasingly unaffected by other's opinions or their external environment.

After a few months, Dada said he had to start a Social Service Group in Australia. This group was to teach margiis emergency relief skills and self defense. He asked if I would go to Manila and do some training so I could give this training here in Australia?

Reluctantly I agreed, hoping (in vain) that when I got to Manila the trainer, would give me permission to go to acharya training because he had been my senior trainer when I was in India before.

My month-long training in the mountains north of Manila with my trainer was memorable. I was mostly alone with Dada and we spent our time in study and meditation. Dada was like a wise benevolent father figure to me: strict and fearless, but also loving. He reminded me of my own father in many ways.

The Philippine margiis were very friendly, and I met many helpful and inspiring acharyas from around the world. Dada Adveshvarananda, from India, in particular comes to mind. A true devotee, everything was a play of God to him. One time he was trying to write an intellectual article but quickly got sick of that and went off to do some chanting before falling into a blissful trance. I don't think he ever finished the article.

He often experienced spiritual trances due to his constant remembrance of God. It was hard not to feel his love and everyone loved him, as did I. I was very sad when years later I heard he had passed away after a long and painful illness.

Snake Love

Patience and perseverance are just some of the vital qualities on the spiritual path and I was learning how to develop them. Back in Australia I began work organising camps and service projects around Australia.

During one camp near Sydney I had a wonderful experience with a snake. I was squatting by a river about to have a wash. Suddenly I noticed a yellow-bellied black snake about a metre away. It was looking at me with what I felt was a great feeling of kindness or friendship. I, in turn, felt a strong feeling of love for *it*. The feeling was so strong I wanted to hold the snake. However, because the snake was highly poisonous, I resisted the urge. But to this day I still think of the experience and wonder what would have happened if I had mustered enough courage to hold it. I'm sure animals sense our state of mind because we can feel theirs.

The Intimate Protest

In February 1978 an event occurred that deeply affected all Australians. I didn't hear about it immediately because I was in Adelaide holding a VSS camp. I later found out that a bomb had exploded outside the Sydney Hilton Hotel, killing three men. This was during a major meeting of Commonwealth States leaders (CHOGOM) held at the Hilton. The Indian Prime Minister, Moraji Desai, immediately blamed Ananda Marga for the bombing, claiming the bomb was meant to have killed him to create pressure for Baba's release.

Hearing this outrageous accusation I organised a protest meeting in the centre of Adelaide. A small group of margiis gathered with placards and commenced our protest. A man who seemed to be hired by police created trouble for us and tried to disrupt a Margii woman from protesting. He tried to rip one of her placards. I stood in between him and the woman, determined not to let him cause any trouble.

The man pushed his face up to mine, trying to force me to move. Being stubborn, I refused to be intimidated and stood my ground. This resulted in us standing literally nose to nose, while he yelled abuse at me. Seeing the humor of the situation I commented: "We'll have to stop meeting like this, people will talk!"

Everyone present burst out in laughter while the television crews filmed us. That night on prime time news, the first thing to appear was a shot of us standing nose to nose with this man shouting abuse at me. Another embarrassing moment in my life!

Over the following months Ananda Marga experienced several incidents of harassment by police, with allegations or speculation that Ananda Marga may have been responsible for the Hilton bombing. However, other groups were also suspects. Because of some cases where we knew the police had fabricated evidence against us, Ananda Marga made a policy of not talking to police without a lawyer present. I taught this policy in my camps and followed it personally. This all became quite important for me later on.

5
Dark Side of the Moon

No one should feel disconcerted about anything. All should know God is concerned about their welfare.. Therefore don't be afraid or perplexed under any circumstances. The force that guides the stars guides you also.
—Baba

THERE WAS AN UNPRECEDENTED REACTION BY BOTH STATE AND FEDERAL governments to the Hilton Hotel bombing. It was considered Australia's first terrorist attack, so the Prime Minister became personally involved. He asked for daily reports, changed the venue for the Commonwealth Heads of State (CHOGOM) meeting and called on the army to protect the delegates.

Special Branch, the state intelligence police, put out a public request appealing for assistance to find the bombers. Richard John Seary, who was to play a leading role, presented himself to the New South Wales Special Branch investigation team. He said he had just seen the movie *Star Wars* and felt inspired to fight for a cause. Seary said he had information the investigators could use. Special Branch either did not have or did not follow a policy of checking the past history of its informants, because if they had done so, they would have found Seary far too unstable to be credible. He had been addicted to a variety of drugs since he was 12 years old: marijuana, LSD, cocaine and heroin. He was later diagnosed as psychotic with schizoid traits. His penchant for writing science fiction might have hinted at the fantasy world he lived in.

Seary initially said he thought that members of Hare Krishna may have done the bombing and that he was once a member of their organisation. He offered to spy on the Hare Krishnas for Special Branch, but they asked him to secretly investigate Ananda Marga instead. The Indian Prime

Minister, Moraji Desai, who thought the bomb was aimed at him, publicly accused Ananda Marga. So Seary was assigned to join Ananda Marga as an undercover informant and to report every week on any information linking us to terrorism, specifically the Hilton Bombing. Special Branch assigned Detective John Krawsczyk to oversee Seary's spy mission.

No one asked us, but from our point of view, Ananda Marga would have been a very unlikely suspect in the bombing. At the opening of the CHOGOM meeting we had taken the opportunity to present Desai with a letter reminding him of his pre-election promise to release Baba. He had only recently been elected and had promised to re-examine Baba's case, so we had felt quite hopeful that he might help our cause. We would have had nothing to gain and everything to lose by threatening to kill him.

Other CHOGOM delegates also said they thought the bomb was for them. Many of the delegates seemed to be using the incident for a bit of grandstanding and finger-pointing.

The Stage is Set

By April 1978, a couple of months after the Hilton bombing, I had moved to the Sydney suburb of Burwood where I'd set up Volunteer Social Service headquarters. Sunday night group meditation was held at the Ananda Marga headquarters on Queen Street in Newtown in the inner city. I attended it regularly and it was during one of these meetings that I was introduced to a newly initiated member named Virat. He was Richard Seary.

Seary did not make a very strong impression on me. He was thin and a little unhealthy looking, but quite amiable. He also seemed nervous but I thought that was because he was new to Ananda Marga. I was asked to explain group meditation to him. When I had finished he asked me what I did. When I explained he seemed quite interested so I asked him if he would like to get involved. He smiled and agreed. One of my projects was weekly soup distribution for homeless people. Every Friday night a group of volunteers would come with me to bring soup to homeless people in the inner city area. Seary said he'd done a similar service project while working for the Wayside Chapel, a Christian service project in Sydney's notorious Kings Cross. He agreed to come with me the following Friday.

During the soup run Seary told me that when he was doing this kind of work for the Wayside Chapel, he'd often seen police beating derelicts they found sleeping in deserted buildings. This outraged me and I said in future we should take a camera and recorder just in case we came across any such police brutality.

Richard Seary's outward personality was usually easygoing. However, at times he seemed agitated and restless and I would encourage him to do more meditation and yoga exercises.

He often had many strange stories to tell. For example, he told me he was dying from lung disease because he had burnt one lung out with chemicals at a factory job, and had cancer in the other lung. Another time he told me he had been involved with the Hare Krishnas and had used guns and explosives to try to blow up an abattoir. He also told me, in secret, that he had a police record and had killed someone, but added that it was in self-defense.

I was very suspicious about much of what he said and felt he was trying to impress me because he actually believed the propaganda about Ananda Marga being a terrorist group. So I just ignored him and kept on emphasising the spiritual practices and service. I told him we were not into illegal activities. Once, he told me in confidence that if I ever wanted to do anything illegal for the mission then he was willing to help. Seary seemed to ignore my rebuff of this offer.

Indeed, most of what he said was false and calculated to bait me into talking about or joining him in terrorist activities. Later in court all of his stories were proven false.

Probably the most bizarre incident that happened with Seary was in May when I met him by accident in the middle of Sydney.

Seary said, "Can I show you the birthday present I have planned for you?"

Quite surprised I replied, "But my birthday isn't until July."

He replied, "It doesn't matter, I'd like to show you anyway."

"OK, let's see what you have in mind." I didn't want to dampen his enthusiasm and desire to please me. He had become very friendly towards me.

He took me into a gun shop and showed me a rather large hunting knife. It was a real shock for me but not wishing to seem ungrateful I told him that I didn't really have any use for it. Unperturbed Seary insisted, "Surely you can think of something to use it for."

All I could say was, "Not really."

"What about this rifle?"

"No, I'm not really into rifles, and anyway I don't have a gun license."

"It doesn't matter," Seary said, "You can get one for a few dollars."

Then Seary gave me a lecture on rifles, bullets and the type of damage they can cause to people. He could see I was not that interested in such things. I asked him, "What about that fencing set on the wall there?" Seary didn't seem very impressed with my suggestion but said he'd see about it.

Looking back I can easily see Seary was trying to incite or induce me into some kind of violence. I guess he needed something for his weekly reports. Each week he reported that there was no indication that Margiis were involved with the Hilton Bombing or any other acts of violence. It seems he'd targeted me as the head of this Service Group I'd started in Australia, because it had been wrongly termed a 'paramilitary wing of Ananda Marga.' The closest thing it got to paramilitary activities were my self-defense classes, and we didn't use weapons.

By about the third month of spying on us, Seary was coming under more pressure to find something to implicate Ananda Marga in the Hilton bombing. There was a lot of political pressure to find a scapegoat and the obscure, little known Ananda Marga seemed ideal.

At the same time, a Neo-Nazi group called the National Alliance had covered Sydney with racist posters in a 'Keep Australia White' campaign. Many margiis were talking about these horrible posters. Tim Anderson (known in Ananda Marga as Govinda) was the public relations secretary for Ananda Marga and a Margii I had known since LFT training. He was a tall, well built man with a serious, intense personality. He could also be quite friendly. He was planning to do an article on the National Alliance for *Dharma*, an Ananda Marga magazine. He wanted to interview the leader but couldn't locate his telephone number as it was unlisted. I was also thinking about what could be done to combat the racism they were spreading.

The Conspiracy to 'Wall Write'

On June 15th, I was at the Ananda Marga headquarters in Newtown with Ross Dunn, a small-framed man with a friendly, sweet personality. Ross (whose Ananda Marga name was Vishvamitra) was an LFT who was particularly interested in social issues, so we started talking about the number of new Neo-Nazi posters that had been put up around town. I told him I was thinking of getting a small poster printed up with 'Fight Racism-Support Universalism' to post over the racist ones.

Seary came in and asked what we were talking about. I told him of our plan, which he thought was a good one. Then I asked if he could give any money towards the posters. He said he thought he could afford something. We found out later he was planning to ask the police for the money.

Tim joined us and we all discussed the National Alliance. Seary asked what were we going to do about it.

"I'm writing an article for *Dharma* on racist groups," Tim said. It turned out that Seary had the address for Robert Cameron, the leader of the Neo-Nazi group, which would help Tim with the article. He wrote it out on a piece of paper and gave it to him.

Later, Seary suggested to me that we go to Cameron's home and check it out for some possible anti-racist wall writing. I thought that was a good idea but agreed we should survey the place first as I had read that Cameron had a guard dog. Seary added that he was seeing a friend that night. He was sure he could borrow his car since none of us had one.

"I'll bring some paint just in case," he added. I said okay and invited Ross to come along.

"Why can't we go tomorrow night?" he asked.

"No, I've got the soup patrol to do then and besides Virat [Seary] can get a car tonight," I replied.

Ross agreed and Seary said he couldn't get the car until about 11 pm. We arranged to meet him at the front gate of Sydney University. We believed the Ananda Marga headquarters was being watched and the phone tapped by the Commonwealth police, and so we didn't want to be seen leaving the building.

I took a bath and did about an hour and a half of meditation then some yoga exercises. Tim had his office at Queen Street and I usually stayed with him when I spent the night there. He asked me why I was staying that particular night and I told him.

It was about 10.30 pm when I got my parka and went to the back shed to get some old clothes for wall writing. I was thinking that if it seemed safe to do the wall writing we should do it that night and not have to come back later. The old clothes would also act as a disguise in case we were seen.

As I was leaving, I saw Tim and we talked about my soup patrol. Since it was Thursday, and I wanted him to help me with it the next day, I invited Tim to come along on my walk towards Seary's car, so we could talk about it some more.

It was a dark, cold winter night and the ground was soaked from an earlier shower. As I crossed the road to the University, I had an ominous feeling that we were being watched. The scene was just like in the movies with stormy weather and the wind blowing. It was very eerie but I quickly dismissed the thought and reasoned that the police would not be watching us at this hour. Later, we found out that the observation squad were watching us. Perhaps I was having a premonition of things to come!

The Journey to Hell

I saw Seary flashing his car lights nearby. Tim went to speak to him while I got into the front seat of the car next to Seary.

"Did you get any paint?" I asked.

"Yeah, everything is set to go."

Noticing Ross' absence I asked Seary if he had seen him. Just as Seary answered that he hadn't, Ross came out of the University gate and I waved to him. He got into the back seat where Tim was now sitting.

Seary asked if Tim was coming with us. He wasn't so we dropped Tim off at a corner near the Ananda Marga office.

We were now ready to go to Cameron's house, but Seary said first we needed some petrol.

"I hope this car doesn't have a lockable cap, because my friend only gave me one key," he said.

He pulled over and asked Ross to have a look. He confirmed that it was a lockable cap. Seary said we would have to bust it open.

"Won't your mate mind?" asked Ross.

Seary dismissed Ross' concern and said caps were cheap to get at car wreckers. But he added, "We will have to do it in a quiet street to avoid suspicion. I know of a lane we can do it in. When I was in the Hare Krishna's I used to go in this area."

After about 15 minutes Seary managed to break open the petrol cap and used an old rag to replace it. As I got back into the car I looked in the back seat and noticed there was no paint. I asked Seary where it was and he told me it was in the boot. This was in fact a lie. There was no paint anywhere in the car.

Later when we stopped for petrol, Seary became agitated when Ross took a long time in the toilet.

"What's your mate doing in there?" he asked.

I told him to calm down. By now I was getting suspicious of him. It did cross my mind that he may not be telling the truth about this car being lent by his friend, but what could I do? Soon he calmed down and I turned on some Pink Floyd music. Ironically the song was 'The Dark Side of the Moon.'

We continued out to the Sydney suburb of Yagoona. As we drove I started joking around by pulling up my polo neck sweater to cover my lower face. I put on some dark glasses I found in my pocket and pulled down my beanie to my eye brows. I asked Seary how he liked my disguise. He muttered something unintelligible but didn't seem to find it funny. Later, in court, Seary claimed this was how I dressed at the time of the Hilton Hotel bombing. It's surprising he got away with such a story at all, given that I was dressed for winter while the bombing occurred in the middle of summer.

It was a long drive, so after awhile I decided to do some meditation but soon fell asleep. I only slept about ten minutes before Ross woke me with a hand on my shoulder.

"Narada, Virat thinks we should blow up Cameron's car. He says we should give Cameron a real scare."

"What?"

"He's got explosives in the back of the car."

I was shocked and scared. "Are we safe?"

Seary said, "Sure, the detonator's not attached."

"What exactly are you suggesting?" I asked.

"Let's blow up his car. It will be much better publicity than graffiti. I know how to wire it up. All you need to do is put it under Cameron's car."

By now I was feeling annoyed and frustrated.

"Why didn't you tell me about your plan before?" I demanded.

Ross jumped in and said: "Christ, Virat, this is a pretty dangerous game playing with this stuff!"

I told Seary I thought it would be very dangerous for Ananda Marga if we were caught with explosives, not to speak of the fact that we could all be killed. Seary argued about our tactics and said we weren't 'revolutionary enough'.

I scoffed at him and said, "What do you think we are Virat?" and asked him to take us back. Ross said he would not have come if he'd known about 'this stuff' Seary had with him.

"You don't have to use the gear, but let's at least have a look at the place," Seary said.

I thought about his proposal for a moment since we were nearly there. But I felt too frightened by the explosives. Before I could tell him I wanted out, Seary was saying we were almost at Cameron's house.

Still in a quandary as to what we should do, I told him to drive down the next street, then after a short pause added that I thought we should go back. Nervously Ross said he wanted to go back as well.

Suddenly I heard shouting and turned to see a car alongside ours. The men inside had guns that were pointed at us. They were in plainclothes but I knew it was the police.

"Pull fucking over," one of them shouted at us. Seary pulled the car over onto the side of the road. I got out and put my hands up. My mantra was going a hundred miles an hour as I tried to stay calm and assess the situation.

One of the men came up to me and ordered, "Lie down on the ground!"

I quickly obeyed and my hands were cuffed behind my back. As I lay on my stomach I was searched. From where I was, I could see Ross lying against a pile of bricks. A man was growling at him angrily. Ross looked shaken and very frightened and later I found out he had been punched in the face several times.

Perhaps it was because of my mantra, or simply God's grace, but I quickly felt calm and composed. There was no fear, just curiosity. I was told to turn over and was searched again and then told to get up. A very big detective asked, "What's your name?" I didn't reply as this was Ananda Marga's policy.

"What's your name?" he repeated angrily.

"I'm not answering any questions."

"What's in the bag?"

I didn't answer. They kept harassing me about the explosives but I wasn't going to answer any questions without a lawyer. For a short moment my composure and detachment was nearly lost as I felt the distinct possibility of this big police officer beating me. Fortunately, it didn't come to that.

We were moved over to a fence and told to sit on the ground. I told them both, "Whatever happens, don't say anything until you get a lawyer." Seary seemed very scared so I said, "Don't worry, everything will be alright."

They told us not to talk. They searched me again and ordered me to take my shoes off while another detective held a gun at my head. Surprisingly, I wasn't afraid and noted the humour of the situation. They seemed so threatened by me, even with my hands handcuffed behind my back.

"What do you think I am going to do?" I asked.

"We can't take any chances," said one detective.

We were separated and I was put into the back of a police van. Many police had now gathered. Several were surrounding Ross and Seary. The police were afraid the explosives would go off and had called in the army bomb disposal unit. Ross offered to go with the army specialists to get the bag to prove it was safe. He had seen that the detonator wasn't attached to the gelignite sticks. Nevertheless, they still evacuated the neighbourhood. It was an impressive drama with the police and the army running around, shouting orders and leading bewildered people from their homes. It was about midnight and most of the people were in dressing gowns or pajamas.

Meanwhile, I sat in the van and decided to try to sleep. But this was difficult with my hands cuffed. With a bit of wriggling (and some yoga flexibility) I was able to get my hands in front of me. Then I pulled off the extra pair of trousers I had put on for wall writing and used them as a pillow.

For the second time that night I tried to get some rest, but it wasn't to be.

The detectives took me out of the van and showed me some objects on the ground that I didn't recognise, except for what I thought looked like a few sticks of gelignite. Back at the van, I asked,

"What was that all about?"

"You'll soon find out," a detective said.

He was smiling and he asked again, "What is your name?"

I didn't reply.

"I've got to call you something."

"Okay," I said, "Call me Bill."

"Bill is your name then?"

"You can call me that."

I was put into the front of a police van and later into a car with three detectives. In the van I heard a police officer say into his walkie-talkie, "Anderson has been arrested." I could hear that they were cynical as they discussed that he was the public relations secretary of Ananda Marga.

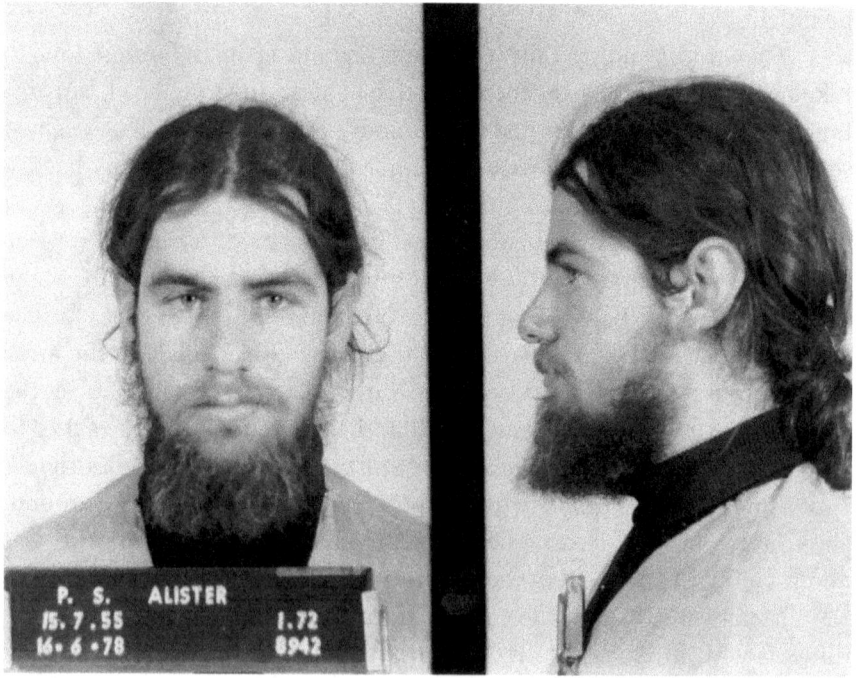

My mug shot. I wasn't looking my best after a full night of interrogation and rough treatment by police.

They knew Tim because he had been publicly critical of the police. He complained about the way they had been harassing and framing margiis in order to appease the Indian government who wished to stop our 'Free Baba campaign'.

I sat in the police car and wondered what was going to happen next. I felt bewildered and confused at why the police would have followed us when we had only planned to do some graffiti. I could only think they must be really desperate to harass Ananda Marga. The gelignite that had turned up in the car really complicated the situation. Seary had always wanted to impress me but this time he had really gone too far!

It was well after midnight before we finally drove off. The officer sitting next to me asked me how I got my hands to the front. I told him that I did yoga and that made it easy for me.

Silent Night

They took me to the Central Investigation Bureau (CIB) where I was taken into a room with two detectives who played the nice guy/nasty guy roles. This is a standard police modus operandi aimed at convincing the suspect to tell all to the nice guy in order to avoid the mean one.

They searched me for the fourth time that night and handcuffed one of my wrists to the leg of the table. They told me I was being charged with conspiracy to murder Robert Cameron. I was shocked to hear this but remained expressionless. By God's grace I felt detached and confident that everything would turn out alright in the end.

They began to interrogate me, but I remained silent.

"You are going to make it worse if you don't answer," they said.

There was still no response from me. For some hours they tried different psychological methods to get me to talk. Sometimes they acted in a nice way, sometimes in a nasty way. They sat in silence staring at me, and when I just closed my eyes and tried to sleep, they kept talking at me.

"I would say you're in your twenties. So that would make you around 35 or 40 when you get out. Such a waste of the best part of your life—gone down the drain. It could be a lot less if you cooperate," they threatened.

Finally, they stopped talking to me and let me sleep for an hour or so. Then they handcuffed me behind my back again and drove me to the Central Police Station to be charged. On the way, we turned down a narrow street and one of the detectives turned to me and said:

"I think we'll let you out here so that we can finish you for good." The car slowed down considerably and he said:

"Why don't you make a run for it so we can finish you off?"

Fear gripped me as I realised what they where trying to do. I thought if they were going to murder me they would have to do it in their car. I was not going to move an inch! A few long, tense seconds passed before the car sped up again. Later in jail I heard many stories claiming that detectives of this branch had killed suspects.

At Central Police Station, I saw Ross and Tim. After fingerprints and mug shots we were locked up. What a strange night. I went out to do a little graffiti against racism and ended up charged for murder!

6
Going to Jail

> However dense the cimmerian darkness may be,
> the crimson dawn must follow. The fiends of hell may burst out in loud
> laughter, but all must fade in the void with the sunrise.
> —Baba

WE WERE BOOKED AT THE POLICE STATION AND THEN PUT INTO INDIVIDUAL BARE cells. It was now 6 am and I found it hard to sleep. A lot was going through my mind so I just lay down on a mattress on the floor, shut my eyes and meditated. I had a strong feeling of divine presence but I still felt vaguely uneasy. I just didn't know what to expect, even though I felt God's hand in it all. Eventually I dozed off.

Tim and Ross were equally uncomfortable in the other cells. Later Tim told me he couldn't sleep because there was too much going on in his mind and he felt isolated and frustrated in the emptiness of the cell. Tim found out later that during the night his mother woke up from fright after a nightmare at the same time as his arrest. Ross said he felt devastated. He couldn't believe this was happening to him. Soon things got even worse.

We were brought before chief magistrate Murray Farquahar at about 10 am. We had been held incommunicado for 12 hours with no opportunity to contact a lawyer or anyone else. We stood before the magistrate for a few minutes while the charges were quickly read to us. We were shocked to hear that not only were we being charged with conspiracy to murder Neo-Nazi leader, Robert Cameron, but also that Ross and I were facing additional charges of conspiring to murder all four arresting officers. They alleged we had planned to blow them up in a suicide attempt during the arrest. We were also charged with possession of gelignite, though this was later dropped. Because of the severity of the charges, there was to be no bail allowed.

I thought the whole thing was absurd. What would any of the charges matter if the facts came out at a committal hearing? We certainly wouldn't be convicted, I reasoned. It must all be a big cosmic game. I guessed the police were just taking another opportunity to try to damage Ananda Marga's reputation because of our attempts to free Baba.

It was ironic that we should appear before Murray Farquahar. Nearly seven years later he was convicted of corruption and ended up in a cell next to me. It was Murray Farqauhar who encouraged me to write this book about my unusual experiences.

After this surprising news, we were taken off to the cells again for an hour of lonely waiting. There we talked about what had happened and wondered where Seary was, why he was not with us, and speculated what the police might be doing to him.

We were handcuffed and put into a huge police van with other prisoners destined for Long Bay jail. We quickly understood why it was called a 'meat wagon'. Twelve or so men were crammed onto two hard wooden benches that faced a stark, steel partition that ran down the centre. There was no light, fresh air, windows or vents. Most of the other prisoners were smoking, so the hour long trip became a shocking ordeal. We were non-smokers and we were particularly sensitive to such a foul concentration of smoke. We felt quite sick for some time afterwards. The meat wagon was later to be our normal mode of transport for court appearances.

The events finally began to catch up with me. I had been charged for conspiracy to murder and attempted murder. "It can't be true," I tried to tell myself.

A cold feeling suddenly swept through me. I tried to think positively and reminded myself that we would certainly be released once all the facts became known. Baba would not let me go to prison for something I didn't do. Then I remembered the many margiis who have suffered innocently. I thought of Baba and numerous spiritual leaders throughout history who have suffered social injustice. To take my mind off my thoughts, I tried speaking with other prisoners but this only made me more aware of the tough company that I was in and of my frightening destination.

To make matters worse, the other prisoners already knew about our case. It had been all over the news. It was on the front page of the *Sydney Morning Herald*, the *Daily Telegraph* and on many television news shows. Many believed that we were guilty terrorist and thought we had done the Hilotn bombing!

Entering Jail

Going into jail for the first time was a humiliating experience. After we were let out of the meat wagon, we were herded into a cage to await processing. It was like an animal cage, complete with cold steel bars.

Processing began with a strip search. We were made to walk one at a time into a room and undress. A guard searched through our clothing and inspected our naked body to make sure we weren't concealing anything. Officers and anyone else who happened to be in the area just stared at us.

After we had been stripped of both our clothes and our dignity, we were given jail clothes: gray trousers, a green T-shirt, jacket and shoes. The fact that most of the clothes were ill-fitting didn't seem to concern the sneering officers. Some of them seemed to get enjoyment out of seeing us look so foolish.

While I was waiting for the others (more eternal waiting!), I heard a prison officer say, "Those are the Ananda Marga terrorists."

"They don't look so tough to me," another replied.

"We'll see how tough they are after a few years," said another.

Then they grunted in agreement. I wondered exactly what they meant by that last statement and I felt an uneasy emotion in my stomach. I wasn't going to let the future bother me and so I redirected my mind to the present moment. I focused on God and was rewarded with a wave of optimism.

While other prisoners were marched off to one of the jails, we were taken to the segregation area. Tim and I were put into a 2.4 x 3.6 metre cell, and Ross was put into another. Our cell had a double bunk, small sink, toilet, chair, table and a steel cabinet.

It was a strange feeling being locked into such a small area. It was worse knowing that we would be here for 16 hours a day for an indefinite period. The prisoner in charge of cleaning our wing and giving out meals came over to our cell and introduced himself. He said he had heard about our case on the radio and in the newspapers. Later that day we saw the front page headlines about our arrest.

Again, I was frustrated and repulsed as I read our portrayal as mad, murderous religious fanatics while the police were praised as heroes. I was all the more disgusted because the newspaper insinuated that we were guilty when we hadn't even gone to trial. After all, they claimed, we had been caught in the act.

The Cage

According to the cleaner, the prison authorities wanted to keep us in segregation. They were afraid we might bring 'terrorism' into the jail, so for the first few days, that is where we remained.

At night we were confined to our cell and during the day we were put into the 'cages'. These were normally set aside for punishing prisoners or protecting them if other inmates endangered them. It was a jail within a jail and reminded me of the old style zoo cages for big cats and other wild animals. They were large rooms with a concrete floor and three brick walls with bars in front and across the top. Some had a toilet and wash basin. Today, zoos have become more humane and give the animals bigger and more natural environments to live in. That is not the case with prisons. Most maximum security jails in New South Wales still have cages.

After a few days, the authorities must have changed their minds because we were taken out of segregation and put into the normal routine with other prisoners. Tim and I were put into one cell and Ross shared a cell with another prisoner. Ross had trouble with his cell mate because he smoked, causing Ross considerable annoyance, and at times illness.

Tim and I got on quite well, despite the expected argument or two from living so closely together. Ironically, Tim was one of only a few Margiis I had difficulty in liking. We had been through LFT training together and had known each other for five years, but I found him too critical and overly intellectual. It was one of God's ironic games that of all the margiis, I not only had to learn to live with him closely for several months, but that I eventually came to feel quite close to him. I had only known Ross for a few months but we also grew closer during our time in jail. A shared adversity usually brings people together.

Not long after our arrest we were allowed a visit from some Margiis. The Margiis were concerned about us, but were pleased to see I was quite happy and positive about the future. By then we had all realised that Richard Seary was a spy.

Explaining to my Parents

Not long after the arrest I had the opportunity to write to my parents. What could I say to them? They would certainly be grief stricken. Perhaps they would not recognise me from the media reports because at the time of my arrest I was using the assumed name of Alister rather than my family name, O'Callaghan. This was a tactic some margiis used to avoid harassment by Indian custom authorities. When I was arrested I was planning to head back to India for acharya training, so I had just changed my name legally.

I finally decided to write the letter to my father and ask him to tactfully tell my mother, Eve, the bad news:

> 18 June 1978
>
> Dear Father,
>
> How are you, how is your health? I hope it is fine. During the last few days some rather bizarre events have taken place which have left me in a most undesirable position, and so I am letting you know of the facts first so that you can tell mother in a tactful way so she is not too upset.
>
> As you know, by what I've been telling you in the past, Ananda Marga has been persecuted quite a bit in this country and several margiis have been falsely charged, but released later when the facts were proven.
>
> But as you may have guessed (by what has been in the papers lately about AM), two other margiis and I have become the victims of a police attempt to discredit AM. Yes, I was one of the three charged in Sydney for conspiracy to murder a man, his wife and policemen. All I can say at this stage (not allowed to say much) is that if truth prevails in court then I'll be out in several months time. (It will take that long for the case to end).
>
> This is certainly serious and I want you both to know that I am very optimistic about the near future and that I am very well and happy here in the Remand Centre. I'm with the other two Margiis and have plenty of time to myself, which, consid-

ering some of the things I do with my time (like meditation) it is to my liking and advantage.

Please stress to mother that there is nothing to worry about as far as my happiness is concerned. I am sincerely not bothered by being here.

Of course you realise that papers are blowing it up out of all proportion, so don't take much notice of what they say. I have no guilty feelings about having done something wrong because I haven't and tell that to anyone else who questions you. I realise it will put a lot of strain on you from both our relatives and friends, but that's something you'll have to be strong about and stand up against.

I get plenty of visits when it's allowed(three times a week).

Your loving son, Paul

Before this letter arrived in Perth, my father had already left to come visit me. He said he had to find out from me directly if I was guilty or not. He said he wondered if maybe I'd done one of those crazy things young men do. He didn't think I would try to kill a person but he thought I might have wanted to threaten Cameron with the gelignite.

After listening intently to my story, he understood that I was innocent and had been framed. As my father left the prison I felt his hidden grief. I wished he could have shared the confidence I had but I would have felt the same grief had I been in his shoes.

After this meeting, my father took up my cause with great fervour. Over the years he worked tirelessly on our case. I know my arrest devastated my parents but over time their strength and love pulled them through. This gave me a lot of comfort as well.

Generally speaking, after the first shock of jail, I was in very good spirits. I was sure it would all be over when we went to court to explain our side. God graced me with a carefree optimistic mind. Sometimes I even felt excited that I was part of some event that had great significance but I was not sure how it would end.

Ross's Parents

Ross also got a visit from his parents. Understandably, they were shocked. By the time of their visit the bruising had become visible from the punching he'd received during the arrest. This upset and enraged his parents even more. In court Ross's parents gave evidence of the bruises because the police had denied the assault. The police lawyers tried to say he didn't have bruises or that he had received them in prison. This was alleged despite the fact that he was in segregation. Their comments insinuated that Ross's parents were lying.

Years later Ross's mother, Mrs E. Dunn, wrote me a letter about how she reacted to Ross's arrest and imprisonment:

> Dear Paul,
>
> I remember vividly, the day we learned of Ross's arrest—on a charge of conspiracy to murder. I had gone with my husband to get a trailer load of flooring and while he was waiting for the trailer to be loaded, I went for a walk. It was a freezing cold morning, so I decided to buy a paper and go back to the car. I came out of the shop, leaned against a lamp post and opened the paper. I saw the headlines and read that our son Ross was in serious trouble.
>
> I was so shocked, that it took me some time to get myself together and get back to my husband at the car. When Alf saw me, I must have looked awful, because he said:
>
> "What is the matter? Have you got pains in your chest?"
>
> I said: "The bottom has just dropped out of our world!"
>
> Never again were we able to greet the day with a happy heart, or to have any peace of mind.
>
> We flew to Sydney to see Ross and to hear his story about what had taken place. You only got a half an hour visit in those days. Alf and I stood at the gate of Long Bay Jail and cried! We were numb! The thought of Ross being locked up was torturous. The worst part of visiting was when I had to turn my back and leave.

Ross told us his story and then he said: "Don't worry mum, everything will come right when we get into court. Ultimately justice lies with God!"

At that time I believed in British justice. Not because I knew anything about it, but because I had been brought up to believe in it. I was soon to learn what a naive little lady I was. I was about to embark on what I call a 'Journey into Shame!' For what I was about to learn in the next few years would not only take all the sunshine out of my life, but would leave me completely devoid of any faith in our system of justice. It would make me realise what a very fragile position one is in when one gets caught up with the law...

7
Jail Life:
Boredom, violence & more boredom

If anybody, whether a judge or a citizen, takes some sort of requital against someone else, it should be corrective, not penal. Then the offender will have no cause for accusing anyone. Regardless of the flaws in the judgement, it will not harm him or her in any way. —Baba

LIKE MOST PRISONS, THE REMAND CENTRE OF LONG BAY JAIL WAS A VERY BORING place. After being awakened at 6:45 am and eating breakfast we were sent into the yards. We had to stay there in all weather until lunchtime at about 11:30 am. We were given lunch on our way into the building and at 1:30 pm we were sent back into the yard until 3:30 pm. Our dinner was given to us after the muster as we went inside and up to our landing. We ate our dinner there in the dining room at about 4:30. This monotonous repetition went on for 14 months.

The Remand Centre was nearly all concrete and steel bars, making it very harsh and sterile except for a tiny patch of grass. There were four yards. Each one was about 30 by 15 metres and had to hold up to 60 prisoners. When I first went into the yard, I thought it was strange to see prisoners walking up and down all day. I soon found myself walking much of the time as well. It was a good form of exercise and better than sitting down all the time. Two yards had a television set that most of the prisoners watched. A radio often blared out from a PA system, adding to the confusion. Prisoners sat on benches and stared into space, read, played cards, talked, slept or walked up and down. The yards without television had a game called 'wall tennis.' It's a bit like squash, only we used a wooden bat the size of a tennis racquet, and a tennis ball that we hit against one wall. The three of us often played wall tennis and became very good at it.

In the evenings we spent a lot of time in the communal room watching television. There was nothing much else to do. Before jail I didn't watch TV much but I soon developed the habit. It was a relief, at least, from the boredom. The communal room was very stuffy with cigarette smoke. The rough, tense feeling of the inmates was palpable. An occasional fight broke the monotony. The fights were over petty things but then our whole existence there was based on petty restrictions and privileges. Jail was not a magnanimous place.

What I hated most about the evenings was the constant noise. I tried shutting my cell door but often an officer would insist it remain open.

"Why?" I asked.

"Just because," the officer replied stubbornly.

"Because why?"

"Because it just is, it's the rules," the officer said, getting more annoyed at my persistent questioning. Other times they would just say "Because I said so," and throw the door open.

I found many of the prison officers quite insecure and unhappy. They vented many of their hang ups on the powerless prisoners. To be fair though, some of the prisoners would push the officers to their limit. It became quite a power game of who could frustrate or upset the other the most. The prisoners called the prison officers 'screws', and called themselves 'crims'.

We were surprised to find ourselves rather popular among prisoners when we first arrived. In segregation we heard a group of prisoners calling "Ananda, Ananda" and "Long live Ananda." They thought we were heroes because they believed we were really trying to blow up the police.

When we were moved to the normal section, some of the 'heavy' prisoners would come up to us in the yard and say, "Good on yer, glad somebody's got the guts to have a go at the pigs!" We tried to tell them that we were not really terrorists in the way the police and media described us. But they never believed us.

"Yes we know, sure," nudge, nudge, wink, wink.

They really didn't believe we were innocent. But as time passed and they got to know us they realised we could not be as dangerous as the media was portraying us. At this time our case was all over the news and we were branded as fanatic religious terrorists.

Meals and Mail

The meals were poor and for a vegetarian they were atrocious. Everything was cooked in the morning and kept warm until we ate it in the late afternoon. We were only able to eat mashed potatoes and overcooked cabbage for dinner, cold cereal for breakfast and sandwiches for lunch.

Once a week there was the weekly canteen where prisoners could order food with their own money. The prison retained this and the amount we spent was deducted from it. No fresh food was available and everything was either tinned or refined. We bought cheese and peanut butter and sometimes powdered milk and a few treats.

We ate poorly and our health suffered because of it. Tim and I wrote letters and communicated with the authorities about getting a proper vegetarian diet. After about a year it was granted. They said we couldn't be given a special diet unless all other prisoners had the same opportunity. So as a result a special diet was offered to all vegetarian prisoners in New South Wales.

While this diet was certainly an improvement, it still remained far from satisfactory. Because of the disturbing effect onions, garlic and mushrooms have on a meditator's mind, Margiis do not eat them. Unfortunately for us, most of the vegetarian food had onions in it and consequently we could not eat it, so our diet still remained inadequate. It was not until a few years later, in other jails, that we were able to get fresh fruit and vegetables in small amounts, which greatly improved our health. Our diet still lacked protein and whole grains and was never very well balanced or palatable.

Mail was censored and I remember Ross once getting called down to the main officer. He was handed back a letter he'd written with black pen lines through most of it. The officer had censored his letter! Ross was outraged by this action but had no choice but to accept it. A few years later mail censorship was officially banned. Prison officers, however, still read prisoners' letters, particularly incoming mail. The officers expressed great delight in reading personal mail and often used what they read to taunt prisoners about their personal lives. This was particularly unfair in a remand centre when most inmates had not yet been convicted of any offence.

The entire routine created enormous frustration, humiliation and powerlessness for prisoners who often vented their feelings violently on other prisoners or, occasionally, towards prison officers. Later, after release, the frustration was often vented upon society.

A Violent Meditation

One fine sunny morning I was practicing my regular routine of 45 minutes meditation before lunch. I sat on a nice grassy patch of the yard and was enjoying the thought of God's infinite love and bliss all round me. I was distracted from my peaceful state by a nearby voice and realised it was a prisoner I knew quite well, saying something to me. I knew him because, like me, he was familiar with martial arts so we often sparred with each other in the yards. I opened my eyes to see him standing in front of me looking quite menacing.

"I want to fight you!"

"What on earth for?" I asked, realising he was serious and did not just want to play round.

"Because you think you are a better fighter than me."

Feeling surprised, I replied, "Don't be stupid, I've never thought that."

But he was unrelenting, "Come on, fight me."

"Well, I have no desire to fight you," I said, feeling rather annoyed that he'd disturbed my enjoyable meditation with such crazy talk. "Let me finish my meditation."

But then he changed his tune and started to show his mentally disturbed side. "You're trying to psyche me out when you meditate, aren't you?"

"Don't be ridiculous," I snapped, not believing what was happening.

"I've been watching you meditating and you're trying to send me insane!"

"You're mad," I replied, "You don't know what you are talking about. Just leave me alone." I was thinking I didn't have to do anything to make him crazy because he already was!

"I am going to fight you," he said with more determination than before. I stood up when I realised that he was not going to leave without a fight. If I did not stand up I would have been in danger of being kicked in the face.

He was 15 cm taller than I was and a reasonable fighter. He stood there waiting for me to attack him. By now I was feeling impatient with him and wanted to resolve the issue one way or another. He was obviously not interested in talking. So I decided to oblige him and threw a punch to his face. My punch did not have much impact since I only just reached him. He grabbed me and we scuffled for a short while. Then we stood face to face again. I thought how silly this all was but didn't know how to escape peacefully. As we eyed each other off I became aware of all the prisoners surrounding us and cheering us on.

Because he was taller than I was, he seemed to think he did not have to guard his face. I thought how easy it would be to kick him in the head, as I was very flexible and quite fast with my kicks. Then I thought of the damage a good kick to his head would cause. By now I was feeling more pity for him, realising he was not quite responsible for his actions. He seemed mentally unbalanced. After about five minutes of this stand off, he suddenly walked off. I was relieved it ended that way.

That night a prisoner said to me, "I heard you had some trouble in the yard this morning with the crazy one?"

"Yes" I replied, "He's off his head. He thought I was trying to psyche him out during my meditation!"

The prisoner replied, "When I was eating in the dining room, I saw him turn around and stare at me. I told him 'fuck off, what are looking at,' but he kept on staring. When I threatened to smash his teeth in, he turned away."

Later, I heard he was put in to the section of the jail for mentally disturbed prisoners. Apparently he had kicked a prisoner in the stomach for no apparent reason. I hoped he would be okay.

A Full-Blooded Friend

While there was confrontation with certain officers and prisoners, generally I had no trouble. I went out of my way to avoid it if I could. I was quite happy doing plenty of meditation and feeling optimistic about our future.

The committal hearing had come and gone in the first six weeks. Our lawyer told us we couldn't present our case at this first hearing. It was only to find out what the police had on us. The magistrate decided there was enough evidence for a trial and set a trial date for six months later. I waited optimistically for the occasion when I was sure the truth would be finally heard. In the meantime, I tried to use my time constructively and viewed it as a special learning experience sent to me by God. I also made some good friends.

One in particular was Jabananda, a full-blood Aboriginal from central Australia. When he came to Sydney he began to drink, which led to fighting and to his imprisonment. He was a good boxer and he had a humble temperament, except when under the influence of alcohol. He told me what it was like living in the outback and how he worked with cattle for a living. He showed me a big scar on his belly that was the result of the manhood initiation he went through when he was a young teenager. I was impressed.

Jabananda had decided to go back to the bush when he got out of prison because he didn't like city life. One day he said, "You know what I have noticed about you that is different from all the others in here?"

"No," I replied, feeling surprised and curious.

"You don't swear."

"That's right," I said. "Since I've been in Ananda Marga I stopped swearing. I don't like it."

His mother always told him off for swearing which he had had picked up from his friends.

"When I came to jail," I said to him, "I decided I wouldn't let jail change me. In particular I would not do things like swearing because if I did it would mean I'd come under the influence of jail's negativity. I felt my mind was stronger than that."

Jabananda expressed interest in meditation so I taught him. He was grateful and practiced meditation regularly.

Jail Tyranny

While the prison rules were clear, their enforcement was not as straight forward. It was often quite arbitrary. Often it depended on the individual officer and his mood at the time. This included the Superintendent as well.

At one time, at the Remand Centre, a senior officer told me to wait in a cage with my court clothes until it was time to go to court. Then a

Long Bay Jail complex, our home for some four years and a place full of boredom and violence.

junior officer told me to wait in the yard. I pointed out that I'd just been instructed to stay in the cage by a senior officer. The junior officer, however, insisted I wait in the yard. I refused thinking I'd better follow the order of the senior officer. I was then charged with disobeying an order. When I explained to the Superintendent that I could not follow both orders and therefore chose to follow the orders of the most senior officer, he said he'd let me off with a warning. I asked what I was being warned for. Was it for disobeying the orders of a junior officer over the one given by a senior officer? He would not answer and ordered me out of his office.

At least I was able to argue the situation with some clarity and logic. Many prisoners did not possess such skills and would get charged thereby increasing their frustration and anger towards an inherently unjust system. Upon release they felt justified in their anti-social actions as a payback for the injustices experienced in jail.

One evening while I was sitting in the eating/TV room, a loud explosion came from the Wing next door. Everyone jumped up and shouted while looking out of the window. "What was that?" someone shouted.

"Don't know," replied another, "probably the Ananda Marga."

We were often blamed for anything to do with explosions, particularly since the Hilton bombing. Some things were said in jest, other times not. However, for us, it became a constant source of irritation and stress, knowing we would never support such activities.

Ray Denning

Tim and Ross were sharing a cell together directly above that of an infamous prisoner (or famous depending on how you looked at him) called Raymond John Denning. Ray was known as a jail radical and had spent most of his prison life in segregation, including the 'program section' of the Remand Centre. We had been put in the 'programs' for the weekend while the authorities decided if it was 'safe' to let the 'religious terrorists', as they saw us, mingle with the normal jail population.

In the program section, a system had been devised by prisoners for talking with an inmate directly above or below oneself. By emptying out the water in one's toilet bowl, one could 'talk' with the other prisoner providing his toilet was empty of water too. Each night Tim and Ross would call out to Ray to get ready for a 'talk' and then engage in long conversation with their heads down the toilet! Through these conversations Ray became interested in Ananda Marga, particularly because it fused spirituality with social activism.

Tim taught him basic meditation and Ray grew to appreciate its value in coping with jail life. After practicing this meditation for some time Ray applied to register his religion. The Governor at first was happy to see this, thinking Ray had become a bit more passive. However, when he said he wanted to register his religion as Ananda Marga, the Governor's jaw dropped in horror thinking he had gone from troublemaker to terrorist.

Meanwhile, I had been elected as one of the prisoners' delegates for their Grievance Committee. Soon after my election a major dispute occurred which had far reaching repercussions for myself and the other margiis.

One evening a prisoner became too sick to collect his medication. He asked if it could be brought to his cell. The duty nurse was a belligerent person and refused to either bring him his medication or agree to allow anyone else to bring it to him. The other prisoners became concerned because the medication was for the man's heart condition. It was decided that no prisoner would go to his cell until the sick man received his medication. Despite various threats from the officers the prisoners remained outside their cells until the nurse finally gave the prisoner his medication.

During this dispute I spoke with the nurse and a senior officer on behalf of the prisoners. I tried to explain the seriousness of the prisoner's condition. They both responded to my pleas with abuse and contempt. The next morning I saw the Governor regarding the incident and complained about the conduct of the senior officer and nurse concerned. He was not interested even though the prisoner concerned could have lost his life. Instead, he warned me that demonstrations would not be tolerated again.

Not Cricket!

While making this complaint I also used the opportunity to formally complain about the mistreatment of Ray Denning and two other prisoners in segregation. According to Ray they were refused the right to bring assault charges against certain officers. They were also denied water and toilet facilities. There was nothing being done about the broken glass in Ray's cell window that allowed rain to enter and flood his cell. Governor

Bowden got angry with me and said I was not allowed to make complaints on behalf of individuals, only general complaints. This was ridiculous because delegates were elected specifically to represent individual and collective complaints or grievances.

After this unfruitful meeting I spoke with Ross and Tim. I decided to see the Governor again and to be more firm about Ray's complaints. Ray was clearly in the right, according to prison rules. When speaking to the Governor the next morning I deliberately remained calm and rational so as not to do anything that would upset him or give him reason to dismiss my complaint. I said what was being done to Ray and the other two was inhumane and illegal. I asked that he look into the matter immediately and have it stopped. He quickly exploded into threats of "How dare you!" The Principal Prison Officer, Mr Wilson, standing next to me, told me that 'troublemakers' would have to be put on protection(segregation). This was because of the prisoners' reaction when jail privileges were removed due to the disruptive activities of 'troublemakers'.

I took this as a direct threat to have me locked away for 'my own protection'. The Governor also warned me that he could have me 'taken out of circulation'. This could have several meanings, none of which are pleasant. I realised then that I was playing with fire but felt strongly not to let Ray's inhumane and illegal treatment go unchallenged. Ross and Tim felt the same.

That afternoon I was playing wall tennis. I remember leaning over to hit the ball when suddenly I was on the ground. My ear was sore and I was in a daze. I looked up and saw a prisoner with a cricket stump in his hand. He was going to hit me with it again. Instinctively I covered my head. My mind was racing as I wondered whether to cover up and lie down or try to get up, despite the repeated blows to my head. I decided to get up. This all happened in a few seconds. When I did stand up, I realised my attacker had stopped assaulting me. I quickly moved away and turned to see another aggressor coming at me with a cricket bat! I quickly moved back as he came towards me with a menacing look. My mind raced as I tried to regain a bit of calm and decide how to deal with this man. In a daze I kept on walking backwards, trying to gain time to recover from my disorientation. Suddenly a prison officer shouted out, "Put down the bat!" The prisoner turned away and left me alone.

Prior to this confrontation with me the same person had attacked Tim. He was watching me playing wall tennis when this prisoner attacked him from behind, hitting him on the temple with his bat. Blood gushed out of his head as Tim turned to try and rush his attacker. Tim tried in vain to grab the attacker's bat but it slipped out of his grip. He backed under a toilet shed to shelter himself from the attacker's swinging bat. Applying finger pressure to his head, Tim also tried to stop the flow of blood.

"What are you on about?" asked Tim. The attacker didn't reply and then turned onto me.

When I was first attacked Ross was sitting down away from me. To his amazement he saw the madman standing over me and bashing me with a cricket stump. After the initial shock, Ross jumped up and ran to my aid. My attacker turned and attacked him, stabbing him just under the eye with the stump he'd broken over my head. With a nasty gash under his eye, Ross pursued my attacker.

Meanwhile, I had gotten to my feet to see Ross now exchanging punches with my attacker. Tim's attacker had left the yard we were in. I tried to help Ross, considering he was a small 162 centimetres and the attacker about 20 centimetres taller. But in the confusion Ross kept getting between the attacker and me. Eventually, Ross backed off when he realised the damage to his eye. Both he and Tim went to the clinic to get treatment. Meanwhile I chased our assailant asking, "Why did you attack me? What's going on?"

I did not understand why he attacked me when we had gotten on reasonably well before, but he just snarled back, "Look fuck off, the screws are watching, piss off or I'll have to give it to ya again!"

I kept on asking what it was all about until I realised blood was dripping onto my shoulder. I went to the clinic for treatment where I met Tim and Ross. Tim was shocked at how much blood was pouring onto the floor. He was taken to Long Bay Jail hospital for X-rays and stayed the weekend. Ross received stitches under his left eye and my ear, which had been nearly ripped off, was stitched up. I was lucky not to have lost it. Fate can be strange and unjust, I thought.

Officer Wilson arrived and offered Tim and I protection but we ignored him, feeling quite contemptuous towards his offer. While Tim was being taken to hospital, Ross and I went to reception to get a change of clothes. The blood had spoiled the ones we were wearing. When we arrived the prison officers could hardly hide their delight in seeing what had happened. One serious looking officer came up to me and said, "Do you know what that was all about?"

By now I had put two and two together but wanted to see what information I could get from this officer. "Not really," I said innocently.

"I hear that the attack was because one of you Ananda Margiis were going to cause trouble and some prisoners didn't want to lose their contact visits because of it." Contact visits were being introduced in a few weeks. I acknowledged what he said, but made no comment. I considered he'd made up a story to scare us.

I later asked some friends to see what they could find out about the cause of the attack. They all came back with the same story. Certain authorities told a 'heavy' crim to shut us up or there would not be any contact visits. Apparently the crim then told some of his lackeys lies to induce them to attack us.

My original attacker was told that we were going to murder him that afternoon. He was a paranoid man at the best of times and, given our reputation from the media and police as mad religious killers, it did not take much to convince this guy to attack us. He got another prisoner to help him.

After the attack the remand prison was very tense. Both prisoners and prison officers waited to see if and how we were going to retaliate. Given our 'terrorist' reputation they may well have wondered if we would have bombs smuggled in and used to blow up those involved in our attack! We had no intention of planning any retaliation.

Later, I did speak to the two men involved to make sure they didn't have any similar plans. I found my assailant alone in his cell shortly after the attack. He panicked when I entered, thinking I was going to assault him. I calmed him down and asked him to explain his story. He told how he thought we were going to murder him. He did not believe this now and realised he had been used. I also assured him we had no intention of murdering him! But I also cautioned him never to do such a thing again. He assured me he would not. Ananda Marga does not promote violence but it does not promote pacifism either. It promotes doing no harm intentionally to others but believes people have the right to act in self defense if necessary. Ideally, defence should be performed out of a sense of self preservation without any hatred or malevolence.

In the meantime, Ray Denning visited the Governor and accused him of being behind the attack. Ray made threats saying there would be a few wooden boxes taken out of the jail if anything like that happened again. Ray was furious and the Governor was said to have looked a little pale after Ray's threats. As it happened, Ray's condition improved after this incident and the contact visits took place, despite the 'trouble'.

What a delight it was to have contact visits. Previously, visits were conducted behind a clear perspex and wire grill. Contact visits involved sitting around a table with limited contact. Touching hands or a hug were only allowed at the beginning and end of visits. To have this sort of contact made a big difference to the visits by making them much more humane.

"To be able to touch your misses or girlfriend is so wonderful," exclaimed one prisoner after a contact visit. "To not have to shout to be heard with that bloody partition between you and your visitor and being able to cuddle and hug each other. It's wonderful."

Ray the Folk Hero

Not long after the attack, Ray Denning registered Ananda Marga as his religion. At that time he was taken out of the segregation units and transferred next door to the Metropolitan Reception Prison (MRP), a maximum security jail. Ray gradually gave up meditation due to his limited access to us, although he did remain a supporter of Ananda Marga.

Some weeks after his transfer he escaped from the MRP and began a campaign to clear his name and fight police verbal abuse. Ray spoke of an 'unseen but felt' entity guiding him and telling him what to do and where to hide while on the run. We presumed it was Baba as he often helped those in need if they had accepted him as their guru. We believed this was the case for Ray.

Ray was outside for about 18 months before he was recaptured. During that time he haunted and frustrated the police with his 'anti-verbal' graffiti and media stunts. He became something of a folk hero and was compared with Ned Kelly, the bush ranger. Unfortunately, he also developed a heroin habit. After his recapture the police used this fact, along with the promise of an early release, to bribe Ray into falsely making a statement implicating Tim in the Hilton bombing. The officer who fabricated Tim's confession (called 'verballing' in prison culture) was Roger Rogerson. He was eventually convicted and imprisoned on corruption charges—but not until after our case had been finished.

Psychic Violence

On reflection, the experience I had when being attacked by the prisoner was quite frightening. At the time things happened too quickly for such feelings to sink in. There was very little pain initially as the blows had more of a numbing effect than a painful one. The pain came the next day. However, the experience that occurred some weeks later was much more frightening.

One day I was taken to the MRP jail next door, for a dental checkup. The MRP had dental facilities that catered for all the inmates at the Long Bay Complex. The dentist was notorious for his poor work: fillings often fell out, wrong teeth were pulled, and so on. There was no alternative.

According to the system, those of us wanting to see the dentist were taken through to the MRP. We were put into a small yard and waited for our name to be called out to see the dentist. I paced up and down the brick and concrete yard. There were two of us walking when I noticed a few 'heavies' looking in my direction. After the bashing I'd become, understandably, very sensitive to any potential threat of violence. As I walked up and down, I wondered if they were intending to attack me. I could not think of any reason why they might want to but often violence in prison didn't wait for a good reason. Jealousy towards my 'notoriety' as one of the Ananda Marga terrorists could be reason enough. Beating me would, in turn, give them a reputation. Maybe someone had been spreading false rumours about Ananda Marga or me that may have angered them. I had no idea. The main thing was that they seemed very displeased to see me!

As these thoughts were going through my mind and I was becoming increasingly nervous, two of the heavies began pacing up and down the yard—coming from the opposite direction!

My adrenaline started to pump as I quickly tried to think how to deal with them. Out of the corner of my eye I also noticed the other heavies looking towards me with a glance that seemed to say, "You're going to get what you deserve!" The only thing between a fight and me was the other prisoner I mentioned who was walking up and down the yard. He walked in front of the two heavies, while I was walking towards them.

Then I saw the expression on the two thug's faces turn dark as they sped up their pace towards me. First, they had to pass the prisoner in front of them. They moved to each side of him and walked directly towards me. I prepared for the fight of my life!

Suddenly one of the heavies turned to the prisoner they were passing and punched him to the ground. The second one, on the other side, also started punching him as he fell. I heard a thud as the victim's head crashed on the concrete. His head bounced a little and I noticed his eyes had taken on a stunned look. He was either badly dazed or knocked out. One of the attackers grabbed his legs and dragged his limp body to a wall, presumably out of view of prison guards. There, they kicked him several times before leaving to join a welcoming reception from the other heavies looking on.

All this happened in a matter of seconds, although at the time it seemed much longer. I experienced conflicting feelings. I was certainly relieved that I was not the intended victim, but I was also shocked and appalled at the treatment of the man they had beaten. By the time I had recovered from the initial shock and confusion, it was all over. Seeing the victim lying there disorientated I wondered if I should go over and help him. I recalled the repeated advice given in jail to stay out of other people's trouble. I hesitated, fearing they might attack me. I also wondered if the victim had, in fact, done something terrible to another prisoner and this was a revenge attack. Maybe he was a 'dog', and had told on a prisoner to the authorities? Nevertheless, my heart said to help him.

In the meantime, the prisoner got to his feet and seemed to be recovering fairly well, all things considered. One of the attackers came over to him again and said some very stern words. He had obviously done something to upset them. Later, I heard a rumour that the victim had turned another prisoner in to the authorities, which is definitely not tolerated in jail culture. He was lucky he was not stabbed or bashed with an iron bar!

I felt sick and a bit shaken after this incident and realised even more the potential for violence in jail. Thereafter, I became a lot more cautious around prisoners and found it difficult to go deep into meditation when sitting out in the yards. Always in the back of my mind was the fear of attack.

Unusual Diet and Unconventional Travel

Despite a long wait, I didn't end up getting to see the dentist that day, so I had to return the next week. While I was waiting in the yards again, Ray Denning came over and we enjoyed each other's company as I waited for my name to be called out to go back to the Wing.

"How is it to be out of solitary confinement Ray?" I asked.

"Great, and I am especially glad to get out of that Remand Centre, it's such a hole," Ray said angrily.

"How's your meditation going?"

"OK," replied Ray, looking a bit uncomfortable, "I don't do it as much here— there are a lot more distractions."

"Yes there are, but try and do it twice a day, even if it is only for ten minutes, otherwise the effect will not be so deep. How are you going with your vegetarian diet? Still able to keep it up?"

Ray looked down a bit and with a kind of dissatisfied tone replied, "It's hard being vegetarian in here, especially when your mates aren't. They give me a hard time and I can never remember all the reasons you guys gave for not eating meat. Just that it was more healthy and better for meditation. Is that right?"

"There are political, social and moral reasons as well," I added. "The amount of land needed for raising beef cattle is much more than the amount of land needed to grow the same amount of vegetable protein. So by eating less meat we can grow more food to help reduce the food shortages in the world."

"Morally there just is no reason to kill animals for food. It's really out of greed that we do it. If you were starving or had some special health reason for eating meat it would be okay. But generally we don't need it. It's a habit, but it's not very healthy or natural."

Ray nodded and then changed the subject, "Hey you once told me you had done astral travel. How come you don't astral travel out of jail?"

"I like it here too much," I said jokingly. Ray laughed.

"But seriously, have you ever gone out of jail astral traveling?"

"No" I said, "I'm not interested in all those occult things. When I first started meditation I was, but I have come to realise the energy put into developing such skills is much better spent on just going deeper in my meditation. Ultimately, that's where real happiness and freedom is found. And besides, dabbling in the occult can be quite dangerous psychologically. Unless you are very advanced it can get you into a lot of trouble. Ananda Marga discourages using occult powers, even if it comes naturally with the advancement of meditation. Generally, it's considered interfering with God's natural laws."

We talked a little longer before I was called to go back to the Wing. That was the last time I ever spoke to Ray. He was later found dead from an overdose of heroin. It was a sad and pathetic end to someone who had shown so much promise. We suspect the police may have had something to do with his death because Ray knew a lot about police corruption. The constant allegations of police corruption eventually brought about a State inquiry that implicated many police officers.

8
The Committal Hearing

A truly benevolent society will never come into being under the leadership of those who are solely concerned with profit and loss... The basic ingredient for building a healthy society is simply genuine love.
—Baba

THE COMMITTAL HEARING IN LATE JULY GAVE ME HOPE FOR OUR RELEASE. I FELT sure this would be our chance to prove our innocence. Surely once the facts of our case were revealed, we would be freed and all the media and police hysteria calling us religious terrorists would end. I thought, naively, that truth must soon be victorious.

Truth didn't even get a say. I soon learned that we wouldn't be giving our side of the story. During more than seven weeks of trial, we'd only be attempting to discredit the falsified evidence of the police prosecution. Our lawyers could only vigorously cross-examine Crown witnesses. We would not present our defense until the actual trial itself began because it was considered to be more prudent to use this committal hearing to simply hear the prosecution's case.

Our Barristers were Michael Adams and Peter Bowdor. Ross and I were allocated Michael through legal aid. Tim's parents hired Peter. We were quite happy with Michael's cross-examination although Tim had some disagreements with Peter. Peter has a quiet style, while in contrast Michael can be quite dramatic.

When we first entered the courtroom, the atmosphere was very tense. It was packed with reporters, Margiis and members of the public. The police were there too, adding to our terrorist image. The atmosphere was very tense with police and sharp shooters on the roof of the court looking down on people coming in and out.

Slippery Seary

We sat behind our lawyers feeling like prize exhibits. The spectators were sitting behind us. A combination of tension and excitement gripped me. I was keen to hear what evidence the police had against us. In particular I was curious as to what Richard Seary would say.

Seary was a wild card because while he was definitely working with the police, he also seemed to have his own agenda. He said later that he originally was not going to give evidence. However, after seeing a poster around town about him, he decided he would attend. The poster was put up by Ananda Marga saying, 'This man is an agent provocateur.' He had thought he could slip away from our case unnoticed.

When Seary appeared there was murmuring and a sense of intrigue from the public and lawyers alike. He had been depicted as a mysterious character by the media. When he appeared he looked washed out and was wearing a suit too small for him. I really didn't know what to expect from him, so I listened keenly.

First Seary explained that he was working for the police to spy on Ananda Marga. He claimed that on the afternoon of the arrest, the four of us met in the back shed behind the Ananda Marga headquarters. We told him there was going to be a 'hit' tonight against Cameron and that we were going to blow up his house because of his racist beliefs. He said we told him to steal a car and that Tim had given him a car ignition barrel to aid in the theft.

He claimed that after the meeting he called Special Branch Detective, Les Krawsczyk, (pronounced Kraw-zak) to pick him up. He was the agent that Seary had reported to each week about Ananda Marga. He had tape-recorded Seary's story about the so-called 'conspiracy'. Krawsczyk made several tape recordings with Seary about Ananda Marga activities, which were later sought by our counsel for the trials but were denied on the grounds of national security.

Bulging Socks

Krawsczyk took Seary to CIB headquarters where he was further interrogated by the Special Branch boss, Chief Inspector Perrin. Seary repeated his 'conspiracy' story and said he had to get a car and pick us up by 11 pm outside Sydney University. Perrin asked if he could get a car

Richard Seary in 1985. "One of the least credible, least plausible witnesses ever to step into a witness box in this country," according to former Federal Attorney General, Senator Gareth Evans.

and Seary assured him he could get one from a friend named Les. Seary didn't tell Krawsczk or anyone else about Tim supposedly giving him car break-in tools and an ignition barrel, which he said he had put down his socks! Seary maintained the tools and barrel stayed in his socks during the whole interview.

Why didn't the detectives notice this during several hours of interviews? The barrel would be at least 15 cm to 20 cm long and about two centimetres in diameter. It seemed to us that this was proof that some detectives were involved with stealing the car.

Seary said that at about 9 pm he left police headquarters and tried to phone his friend for the use of his car but was unsuccessful. He said he stole a car instead and went to the University where he met us. The prosecution could not offer any explanation why:

• Seary had not told police that same day about his possession of car break-in tools, or of Tim allegedly giving them to him. This would have been, after all, incriminating evidence against Tim.

• Seary had stolen a car in the middle of a police operation without telling them.

Our defense argued that Seary owned the tools himself. (They were found in the car at the time of arrest.)

Confusing Confessions

Seary's testimony was full of inconsistencies. During his CIB interview, Seary said he told them that he thought we would detonate the bomb if anyone tried to stop us. It seems extremely unlikely that Seary would drive a car if he had heard us say we were going to blow ourselves up if stopped- when he knew for sure that we *were* going to be stopped by the police. We also found out in court that Cameron hadn't lived at the house in Yagoona for one and a half years. If in theory we were going to murder someone by blowing up his house, it would seem logical that we'd first make sure he was living there.

Seary did admit in court that when we were arrested I told him not to say anything without a lawyer. This was important because police alleged that Ross and I made admissions to them.

During his testimony Seary also admitted that he often did typing for me on our office typewriter and that he had stolen stationery and other items from our office. He had spent ten minutes in our typing room around the time of the big event. This was important because after our arrest, the police raided the Ananda Marga headquarters and arrested Tim. They alleged that they found press releases in his coat pocket claiming responsibility for the attack on Cameron. They were signed by the 'One World Revolutionary Army'. It seemed clear to us that Seary could easily have planted these press releases. We knew Tim hadn't written them.

The Dog
Seary looked strange when he was giving his evidence, perhaps even doped, as one national newspaper speculated. As he got down from the witness box, I looked at him wondering why he said these things. I heard either Tim or Ross mumble, "The dog."

A 'dog' is jail language we'd picked up meaning someone who tells on another person. It's the lowest thing someone could call you in jail. Dogs often have to be put on protection because of the violence usually meted out to them. I once asked a prisoner why dogs were used to describe 'give ups' or 'dobbers'. "Well," said the prisoner, "have you ever tried to hide from someone when a dog was nearby? They immediately start barking and give you away. That's why informers are called dogs."

'Dogs', of course, don't always tell the truth. As a rule, they are police informants and tend to say what the police want them to say, irrespective of what actually happened. In Seary's case there seems to be a mixture of motives for what he said. Evidence came out, particularly in his journal, that he didn't like the police. Some of his old friends gave that impression too. His girlfriend indicated that he was being pressured by the police to find incriminating evidence against us. We speculated that perhaps he was being blackmailed into informing because of his former heroin habit. He had also been with a friend at their time of death of a drug overdose. By law he could have been charged, but may have been spared this by the police in exchange for informing on others.

His motives for our frame-up could also possibly have been the Hilton bombing reward money. At the time $100,000 was being offered. He once told a friend, who testified at our inquiry about it, that if he spied on Ananda Marga he could solve the Hilton case and collect the $100,000 reward.

The Great Surprise

A few days into the trial, Seary pulled out his trump card:

"Alister said that he, Vishvamitra, Govinda and another Margii did the Hilton bombing."

I nearly fell off my seat. "He's mad," I thought. I couldn't believe my ears. Ross was flabbergasted! Tim was disgusted. He said that during the car ride to Yagoona we had a conversation with him about the Hilton Hotel and that we had confessed to the bombing. This malicious lie was the most dramatic moment of the committal hearing.

Clearly there had been no such conversation. But it matched the constant allegations in the press that Ananda Marga was responsible for the bombing.

After Seary made this damning allegation, there was a sudden dramatic rush of reporters as they fought to get out through the court door. The next day there were front page headlines plastered all over the Australian newspapers:

> SECT LINK WITH HILTON BOMBING - *The Australian*
> COURT TOLD SECT MEN ADMITTED HOTEL BOMBING!
> - *Sydney Morning Herald*
> HILTON BOMB, SECT BLAMED: WITNESS NAMES ANANDA
> - *The Daily Telegraph*

Interrogation

I quickly got over the initial shock and reaction to Seary's vicious lies. I thought, "Oh well, it's just another lie we are going to have to expose at the trial."

I knew I could prove I was in Adelaide at the time of the bombing, so I didn't really care what was said now. However we all felt concerned at how our parents would feel with this news in the press.

That afternoon we were taken away for interrogation relating to the Hilton bombing. I was put in a large cell that reminded me of a lion's den—all concrete and bars. There was no natural light and I was with several other people. One by one we were taken to different rooms in the courthouse for the interview. Plainclothes detectives took us up an elevator while I was wondering what was going to happen next. Would I get a bashing like Tim and Ross at the time of our arrest? I always felt the threat of violence when I was around police.

Nothing to Say

I was brought into a small office with a table and three chairs. Two detectives from the homicide squad proceeded to ask me questions about the Hilton.

"I've got nothing to say," was my firm reply.

"Now all we want to know is where you were during the Hilton bombing. This has nothing to do with your present case. We are only concerned about finding out who did the Hilton bombing and we have reason to believe you may know something about it. We don't want to cause any trouble for you. Just tell us where you were then. That's all."

"You can do what you like to me," I said, feeling some anxiety that they may use force. "I'm not going to say anything until I have my lawyer with me."

"Oh, we aren't going to beat you or any thing like that. I know some officers do use those kind of methods but we don't believe in them. We just want to help clear your name if you are innocent. Just tell us where you were during the Hilton bombing?"

"I told you, if you want me to answer your questions let me contact my lawyer and I'll answer all the questions you like."

"That could take all day before he's contacted and gets here—we can't wait around all day. We have other things to do." The detective was now starting to show signs of irritation at my refusal to talk.

"Well", I said feeling afraid that my answer was going to anger the two detectives but knowing I had to stay firm, "I'm sorry but I'm not talking about it until I have access to my lawyer."

There was some silence for some time. They said that Ananda Marga had a terrorist wing and that I was a member.

"That's not true. Ananda Marga does not support terrorism and I'm not a terrorist, nor do I support terrorism!" I responded, feeling annoyed and defensive about the old terrorist allegation being made towards Ananda Marga again.

"Come on," said one detective, "We caught you red-handed near Cameron's house. You're a terrorist all right."

"I tell you I am not a terrorist. We were framed and you know it!"

"Why would we want to frame you?" said one detective trying to look surprised and innocent.

"Because we were speaking out against police corruption—both State and Commonwealth."

There was a short silence before one of the detectives asked me:
"Did you do the Hilton?"
I said nothing
"You did it didn't you? We have witnesses who claim that someone who matches your description was seen just before the bomb went off."

I laughed a little knowing what he'd said to be untrue.

"Why don't you cooperate with us? If you're innocent what have your got to fear from telling us where you were that day? If you say nothing it sounds very suspicious that you are guilty."

This comment got me more annoyed and I responded, "Not letting me speak to my lawyer before speaking to you is what sounds suspicious! Why won't you let me make a phone call? Then I'll answer all your questions—after the lawyer comes. You know, I'm only doing what the Council of Civil Liberties advise everyone to do during an interrogation."

"We are not interrogating you, we just want to ask you where you were during the Hilton bombing. I don't know what harm there is in doing that."

"You might twist what I say," I replied.

"You don't think we might do that do you?"

"Why not, you guys have lied enough about Ananda Marga before. Why should I trust you now?"

"I admit some police are corrupt, but you shouldn't judge all police just because a few are corrupt."

"A few! You mean a few are not. Corruption is rampant in the police force."

"Now what have you got to prove that? That's not true at all."

"It's common knowledge and besides we have own experience with the police force."

"Like what?" one of the detective asked, looking indignant.

"Like the time three of our members were arrested on false charges of assault in Canberra. They were acquitted in court when a video tape showed what really happened."

"I mean State police."

"Not so long ago one of our members was arrested in Perth on possession of marijuana. He was acquitted when it was found that the shirt pocket the officers said he had the marijuana in, actually didn't exist on the shirt. It had false pocket flaps. After the arrest he was interrogated for two hours, but not for drugs, but a stabbing in Melbourne, by Victorian police who were present during the arrest. They used the drug charge to detain him so they could pin a stabbing charge on him to discredit Ananda Marga."

"Yes, but you can't tell of anything that we have done here in New South Wales."

"What about how you guys smashed down our front door in Sydney after our arrest and looted our valuables, like money and a cassette player?"

"Yes, it was a pity that the door got broken. It was a lovely door but I was not in that raid and had nothing to do with it."

"I suppose you would have stopped them if you were?"

"Yes of course."

I laughed in disbelief. Then there was some silence for some time.

"I know many police are corrupt but many aren't. It's natural in such a big organisation to find some corruption," one of the dectectives said.

"Are you trying to justify corruption?"

"No I'm not, but you must realise we want to help you. Why don't you trust us? What have we done for you not to trust us?"

"Because I think you are corrupt and a hypocrite."

He was taken back a bit when I said that but then composed himself and said with indignation, "That's not true, how can you say that?"

"I can tell by your vibration."

"My vibration?" He looked a bit shocked and didn't seem to know what to say.

"Yes, I can tell what kind of mind you have."

The second detective then asked me, "And what kind of vibration do you get from me?"

"The same as him," I said, looking at the first detective.

Some food was brought in and offered to me but I declined. After more silence and small talk they began again. "We know you did the Hilton."

"I heard that another Margii has been arrested for it." I replied, testing out a rumour I had heard.

This took them by surprise and they said, "Yes, where?"

"In Queensland I believe."

"How did you hear of this?" Both were getting restless and a little confused.

"I have contacts."

"Are they reliable?"

"Yes."

"What can you tell us about it?" They seemed to get more excited and frustrated.

"Nothing much. Ask my contacts if you want to know more."

"Where are they?"

"At our Sydney headquarters."

"They never tell us anything."

"Well ask the Commonwealth police. They made the arrest."

"They won't tell us anything either."

"Oh well, I guess you'll read about it in the papers."

More silence...

"You know we are your only friends. Ananda Marga will not help you. Maybe they'll help Anderson, he's got a chance, but you and Dunn are on your own. We want to help you and if you help us find the Hilton bomber then we have the power to help you in your case. What do you say?"

"I don't know anything about the Hilton except what I've read in the papers."

"Come on, think about it. Twenty years in prison. It's a long time. Most people crack up before they get out. Just tell us who did it."

"We are not terrorists."

"If you give us names we can get you off your charges. We have the power to do it if you cooperate fully. Think about it."

One of them went out and the other asked me again why I wouldn't talk about the Hilton.

"I might if you just let me make a phone call."

"Well, I don't mind."

"Okay, let me make the call."

"You will have to wait until my partner comes in and see what he says."

The other detective returned.

"Can I make a phone call?"

"No."

"Why not?"

"No need to. We have nothing more we want to say to you, unless you help us."

I was taken down the elevator and back to the cell. On the way one detective said to me, "Well, what do you think? We have the power to help you. No one else does."

After some silence I replied emphatically, "No!"

After the interrogation I met with Ross and Tim. They had both been interrogated as well. Both were asked where they were during the Hilton bombing and both refused to offer information without a lawyer. On reflection I realised I should not have spoken at all— I had broken my own policy, which I had taught other Margiis at my service camps. To protect myself, at least, I wrote down everything I remembered from the interrogation as soon as I got back to my cell that night. I was learning something from the trial already.

We were put into the van and taken back to the Remand Centre. As usual, when something about our case was sensationally published, many prisoners came up to us and said they had heard we were now confirmed as the Hilton bombers.

"Did you know you were on television about the Hilton bombing?" someone asked.

"Couldn't miss it if I wanted to," I replied, "It's another verbal."

"The cops must really be dirty on you guys hey? Well don't let them get on top of you. Keep fighting the maggots."

"Don't worry, we are going to fight it all the way."

The prisoners that did take the time to speak with us about the case were always positive and supportive and I can safely say that this was also the experience of Ross and Tim. Prison officers were not usually supportive however. One officer said to me in a spiteful and cynical tone during the committal, "So you have been accused of the Hilton bombing. You Ananda Margiis were supposed to be peace loving people!"

Taking care not to lose my balance of mind I controlled my reaction to his attitude and said, "First, you are supposed to be innocent until proven guilty and no one has proven we did the Hilton. Besides, I can prove definitely that I didn't do any bombing. Furthermore, we do love peace but have never said we wouldn't defend ourselves if we had to."

The officer looked a bit lost for words although he tried to cover it with a skeptical remark, "They all say they are innocent in here."

"And some of them are," I quickly remarked, "like us!"

He didn't seem to want to comment any further and turned away.

Most officers didn't say anything but they looked at us like we were convicted killers.

9
Police Lies

Those who deprive others of justice are themselves usually deprived of justice in the end.
—Baba

AFTER THE HILTON BOMBING ALLEGATIONS, THE COMMITTAL HEARING DRAGGED ON, BUT it was only a well planned anti-climax. The police and media thought they had the terrorists they wanted. They had carefully staged the most explosive and damaging testimony at the opening of the trial when media were there. In the two weeks of trial the police gave their evidence against us. As with Seary's story, the police stories were filled with discrepancies and outright lies.

Their publicity stunt was a success for the time being, but now that I had begun to see the extent of the injustice that could occur in court, all police attempts to shame us only added to my contempt for the charges.

Bagged

It was revealed in court that a police observation squad had been watching us get into Seary's car at Sydney University on the night of our arrest. Their so-called observations that night were important evidence in the case, though they were rife with discrepancies. The observing officers falsely claimed that Ross walked with Tim and I from the Ananda Marga Headquarters. They actually met him at Seary's car. They claimed he was carrying a blue bag similar to the one found in the car with the gelignite and detonator. We knew very well that Ross came from the opposite direction through the university and did not carry any bag, let alone explosives.

On face value it came down to our word against the observation squad, including Krawsczyk. He was the only officer who kept notes of what he saw that night. His notebook, which our lawyers subpoenaed, was for several reasons one of the most revealing pieces of evidence in the whole case.

Krawsczyk had recorded all details of the clothing we had on yet there was no mention of the blue bag Ross was supposed to have carried. Krawsczyk's notebook also confirmed several demonstrable mistakes of observation, which may not have been so significant had not a number of detectives made the same mistake. This indicated their collective fabrication of evidence.

The detectives also claimed that Ross was wearing white sand shoes. Photos taken later at Yagoona proved that he was wearing dark brown boots. Earlier in the day Ross had been wearing white sand shoes. This fact suggests that he was probably under observation much earlier than police admitted in court, before he was even supposed to have been a suspect.

Surprisingly, no detective reported anything even vaguely resembling a blue parka that I carried to the car and that was tendered in evidence by the prosecution. They gave *identical* descriptions of something that was not even there: a 'gray safari jacket' with buttons and belt that they said I was wearing. It was proven, by photographs and their own reports, that I was wearing a gray and black skivvy with no buttons or belt.

The same detectives described Tim's corduroy pants as denim jeans, at a distance of only three metres. Several detectives described a khaki shirt Tim was wearing but said nothing about the bright red windcheater that was covering his shirt.

Every detective made the mistake of saying that Tim and I had walked 'straight across' to the car. This was in stark contrast with what Seary, Tim and myself had reported. We all said the car was parked some distance down the hill from where we came from.

Later on after conferring with our lawyers, we were able to put all these small discrepancies together to reveal that the police had all made up their testimony *after* our arrest. Their mistakes weren't related to memory lapses. That number of common mistakes could not possibly occur if each detective was giving their own independent recollection of the events, as they claimed.

When Krawsczyk was asked how his notebook came to include the colour of my socks and the clothing I was wearing underneath the skivvy, he changed his story to say that he had written the notes later in the evening at CIB headquarters. He had taken down the details of my clothing after our arrest so that he could say that was what he saw at the University. In exactly the same way, they said they found the blue bag in the car at the time of our arrest and then concocted a story to show how they thought we must have carried it in. What really happened, of course, was that Seary had the bag in the car before we got in.

An Explosive Situation

More conflicting evidence came up in the varied stories of our arrest. The police charged us with attempted murder of the arresting police. This was based first on Seary's strange testimony that we had planned to blow ourselves up if we were arrested. Again we asked, why was he in the car with us if he thought that we were going to blow it up? Oddly, he said he had told the police that *before* we left that evening, but later in court he said we didn't tell him that until we were in the car. Either Seary was a clairvoyant or he was blatantly lying.

To build up the story of our attempted murder of the police, one detective said he saw Ross sitting in the back seat with the bag on his lap and his hands in the bag. He said he grabbed Ross by the throat and pulled him out of the car. But two other detectives swore in their testimony that they grabbed the bag out of the car, saw that it contained explosives and then dropped it and ran. Then the whole area was evacuated once gelignite was discovered.

A key point is whether the bomb was ready to go off, as police claimed. One detective said the detonator had been twisted onto another wire. However, evidence from the independent army explosives expert, after their 'render safe' operation was complete, was that the detonator was wrapped up and in it's 'pristine' condition. It was as if it had just come from a factory. It had never been connected to anything. This was a remarkable contradiction of the police evidence.

Detectives say that we started to 'confess' from the time of our arrest. But Seary supported our evidence that I told everyone, soon after our arrest, not to say a word until our lawyers were present. It was significant that the two army officers supported our story of what happened at the arrest scene and directly contradicted the detectives evidence in doing so.

Planted

When detectives arrested Tim at the Ananda Marga headquarters later that night, Detective Krawsczyk was there. He claimed that within a few seconds of entering Tim's room he found press releases claiming responsibility for an attack on Cameron in Tim's coat pocket that was sitting on a chair.

Krawsczyk and Seary both said that Seary told Krawsczyk about the releases. Seary said that he did not know to whom these releases would be addressed. However, recorded in Krawsczyk notebook four hours before the raid, were details of how many press releases there were and to whom they were addressed. There is simply no other explanation for this evidence other than the fact that Krawsczyk knew a lot more about the releases than the case allows. He either had them in his possession at that stage, having typed them himself, or he knew where to find them because Seary told him where he'd planted them.

Armed Hold-Up Squad detectives alleged that Tim started to confess as soon as he was arrested. Other Margiis at the office support Tim's evidence that he made no statements other than to continually ask why he was being arrested.

Bashed

The police description of what happened at the CIB headquarters that night also had major discrepancies. Our lawyers questioned the police about Ross's bashing during the arrest and Tim getting beaten up at police headquarters.

Ross Dunn's parents later both gave evidence of seeing their son the next day with two black eyes and a swollen face. Detectives produced a photograph taken two weeks after the arrest that had been backdated to the day of the arrest. (Ross was not photographed the day of the arrest as Tim and I were) The black eyes had disappeared by the time this photo was taken and police therefore claimed that Mr and Mrs Dunn were lying.

Tim's evidence of a split and swollen lip was supported by a police photograph taken that day, as well as by the evidence of his father and a family friend. Police denied it.

Police Verbals

After the Hilton Hotel bombing allegation, the next most astonishing thing was to hear the police lie about us confessing to the charges. We sat in amazement as one detective stood in front of the court and *under oath* conjured up the most obscene, implausible and nonsensical admissions we could imagine. We speculated that because they wanted us to be seen as religious fanatics, they concocted verbals that you'd expect from fanatical Christian or Muslim zealots. However, everyone who knew us couldn't believe that we'd said any of the things they attributed to us.

The main evidence the police had against us is that all three of us independently confessed to the alleged conspiracy to kill Cameron and the police officers, but that we claimed our right to silence when a record of the confession was proposed. This was against our policy of not talking without a lawyer present of course. Seary and army officers agreed with us that we never confessed.

It's important to note that at this time police refused to record confessions on tape recorders although they were freely available. All confessions were typed or handwritten by police. This, of course, could easily lead to fabrications. There was already a campaign to change this practice at the time of our arrest as many people claimed it had been used against them.

One detective from the Armed Holdup Squad read this supposed conversation with mild-mannered Ross from his notebook: "You were going to blow up the Cameron house weren't you?"

Ross supposedly replied: "He is a racist pig. He doesn't deserve to live in our world. We are humanitarians doing a service to humanity...We will never be stopped. Ananda Marga will cleanse this earth...We are committed, you people deserve to die for stopping us...we have been persecuted by your kind all over the world and it was decided that should our mission fail in this way, we would sacrifice ourselves to destroy the persecutors of our people."

My confession was supposed to have been like this:

They said, "I have received information that you intended to place a bomb...where a man named Robert John Cameron lives. Do you have anything to say about that?"

To which I allegedly replied: "Nazi racists do not belong here. You have prevented us from doing this but others will follow...Cameron is a Nazi racist and he and his type will infect others. You think you have done well by preventing us from doing this, but you haven't. I do not wish to say anything more about this matter."

For Tim, they concocted this question and answer: "Is there anything you wish to say about these two letters...which were found in the pocket of your coat?"

Tim: "Our views must be made known to the people."

Officer: "I am going to ask you some questions. I want you to understand that you are not obliged to say anything unless you wish, as anything you say will be recorded by Detective Howard and may later be used in evidence, do you understand that?

Tim: "Yes, I do not intend to say a lot. I will say this. It will not stop here. What was going to happen tonight is the only justice that Cameron and his kind deserve. You will suffer the consequences for this."

"Are you prepared to tell us the connection between the Ananda Marga movement and the One World Revolutionary Army?" (This is the group that supposedly signed the press releases.)

"One is part of the other. Until tonight the outside world did not know this."

When Seary made his Hilton Hotel allegations our lawyers turned around to us to check if there was any truth in what he had said. We were completely shocked and we shook our heads in vehement disagreement. Again, after the police verbals, our barristers turned to us for assurance, "You didn't say any of that did you?"

Ross still looking a bit stunned: "No, nothing like that...it's rubbish." Tim and I responded in a similar way. I certainly remembered how I had refused to answer the police at all when they had questioned me that night when, after a few hours, they gave up and let me go to sleep.

This was our first-hand experience of the notorious police verbals. Some of our detectives were infamous in jails and legal circles alike for this malicious practice.

Naturally, the police wanted to be able to say they had found the Hilton bombers. But it was obvious to us that there were other political motivations behind our frame-up. Well known journalist, David Marr, reported the Committal Hearing in the *National Times* (August, 1979), and revealed some of the political implications in our case:

This may emerge as the first round of the NSW Special Branch case concerning the Hilton Bombing...convictions in this case would appear to have certain, almost inevitable consequences. If the jury convicts Alister, Dunn and Anderson for the Yagoona business, it would vindicate the methods and style of the Special Branch. The Hilton trial proper would almost certainly follow. And should conviction be obtained in THAT matter, the current paranoia about terrorist activity would appear well-based, and draconian new laws proposed to protect us from terrorists and to increase police powers would appear concomitantly justified. At the moment, for instance, the Federal Government is considering setting up yet another security force in Australia, described as a 'crack' outfit of spies, police and army, to protect VIPs from terrorists. In that context, the Yagoona hearing could turn into the most important security case in Australia since the Petrov affair of 1954 – 55."

Accused

On the 14th September, 1978, Magistrate Kevin Waller found a *prima facie* case against us on the conspiracy charge. Also a case was found against Ross and I for attempted murder of police officers.

At the closing session we were given our first chance to address the court. We had planned what we would say so Tim got up and addressed Mr. Waller. He sounded nervous at first but soon became more relaxed as he read on from his prepared speech. Tim declared our innocence and explained:

> ...This case and the charges we are now facing are a direct result of a politically motivated campaign. Immediately before our arrest came the assertion to the press by certain police that Ananda Marga was responsible for the Hilton bombing, although there was no evidence. It's now very clear that the circumstances of our arrest were carefully planned in an attempt to give credibility to that idea.
>
> Your Worship, this court has heard numerous police lies and collaboration of lies under oath. These people are purporting

to be officers of the law. Your Worship, this court has been used for political purposes to help propagate the myth that Ananda Marga is a violent terrorist organisation. The charges against Mr Dunn, Mr Alister and myself are part of a programme that has included the deportation of innocent people, confiscation of passports, numerous false arrests and other types of harassment. In fact, there are very few areas the Federal Government of this country hasn't gone into in the process of suppressing Ananda Marga. A security hysteria has been developed for crude political ends. This hysteria built up around Ananda Marga apparently with the help of many sections of the media. It has already begun to make inroads not only into the personal liberties of Ananda Marga members but into the entire civil liberty situation in Australia.

In respect of our case and despite the prejudicial effect of such propaganda, all three of us are confident that none of these charges will stand in the final trial. We are certain that we will be found not guilty of all charges, but what we are not certain of is whether real justice will be served in that the authors of this elaborate and very expensive set-up, the situation which we find ourselves in now, whether these people will be prosecuted themselves. And so Your Worship, I plead not guilty and reserve my defense for the trial.

After Tim sat down, I got up and began nervously to read from my speech. Towards the end I felt more relaxed but I was glad it was over. I commented on how the charges were contrary to our ideology:

Our ideology is universalist and anti-exploitation. Exploitation and injustice are fought by either humanitarian appeal or pressure of circumstances—the latter basically means exposing injustice to the public. Our ideology clearly states that we should never think even for a moment for the destruction of any person no matter how bad they may be. Murder is immoral and we do not support it. We are neither extremists nor murderers and there is no lawful proof to suggest this, despite what the police may say. I'm totally innocent of all charges and I resent the bogus image and fabricated evidence that the prosecution has presented to the court in order to have us convicted.

By the time Ross stood up Tim and I had covered most of what we wanted to say. So Ross just added his support and said: "I'm innocent. I have, under no circumstances, made any admissions, and I reserve my defense."

Our barrister then addressed the magistrate as to why we should go to trial. The magistrate was unmoved and though he did commit us to trial, his final address did show that he saw the serious flaws in the case against us:

> Of course the Hilton bombing, which was mentioned in the case, has attracted the most press as one might expect. The Hilton bombing is not on trial here. I myself was surprised by the introduction of the evidence that I certainly didn't know was coming. And I think defense counsel must also have been surprised because they made no objection to it. The evidence is in and I suppose the damage has been done... its prejudicial effect outweighs its probative value.
> However, that's not something I will have to finally decide, but it's going to be a terrific question for both prosecution and defense at any trial, because I suppose one of the best sticks which the defense can beat Mr Seary over the head with is that he did not, at his first opportunity, inform the police of the alleged conversations in the car to Yagoona in relation to the Hilton bombing. And I think that is the weakest link on which Mr Seary has to stand.
> ...Mr Seary's evidence has been attacked, as indeed it must be because if Mr Seary stands the defendants fall. It is not my function to decide whether his evidence is credible or not. What I believe I have to do is decide whether his evidence is capable of belief...Certainly, he is a cross-examiner's dream

in that he has not only given evidence in the witness box, he has also prepared a journal of his own, and he reminds me of a saying I heard years ago, 'Oh that mine enemy should write a book because the more that one sets down in writing, the more one can be attacked later on.'

...The police say Mr Dunn had possession of explosives. Not being denied by any evidence, if it is true, what on earth is he doing with explosives and what were Mr Dunn and Mr Alister doing at Yagoona? That has not been explained in any shape or form.

The police say Mr Anderson had possession of certain incriminating documents. This has been denied in effect from the floor of the court. There is no evidence about it and if that evidence is accepted, what on earth was Mr. Anderson doing with those letters in his pocket...Of course the defense were under no obligation to put the defense and they are entitled to say as they are saying today that the evidence is just not strong enough...but again it's a matter in my view (which) has to be put before a jury...Mr. Adams says the events of this night and the evidence given is extraordinary and I agree with him one hundred percent. However, I'm pleased to be able to pass the matter on. I think this should go before a jury for determination and I will commit for trial and, as I say, gladly pass the matter to that tribunal.

Bail was refused because of 'the serious nature of the charge'. We were bundled off to the court cells and awaited a police van to take us back to Long Bay Prison.

Seven Difficult Weeks

Overall, the Committal Hearing was dramatic and at times draining. We sat in court for hours at a time for over six hours each day. We weren't accustomed to this. Of course there were also moments when time had no meaning because of the adrenaline rush we felt during some of the more shocking moments.

It was also hard to adjust to the abnormal 'anti-terrorist' security in and out of the courtroom, as well as the formality and alien nature of the court system. During court Tim once turned to me and said, "You really can get buried by the formality and coercion of this atmosphere."

"Yes," I replied. "The way things are going on."

"You wouldn't think it was to do with us—everything seems to be moving independently," Tim remarked.

"The way the cops are verballing us it seems just a matter of routine to them."

"They do it in such a matter-of-fact way."

"A crim once told me its called 'institutionalised perjury'."

"It's criminal the way they can get away with it...It's tense in here isn't it?"

"Yes," I said, looking around at the many police surrounding the room.

It was bad enough to hear all those slanderous lies about us, but it also hurt to read about them the next day in the newspapers as if they were established facts. The worse thing about court was the ordeal we had to go through every day to get there and back.

We were woken up at about 6 am and had to have breakfast and be showered by 7. For most people that would be enough time, but we wanted to do our meditation and yoga before breakfast as well. So we usually had to wake up much earlier, or miss out on breakfast.

But the worst was yet to come. Prisoners going to court were gathered together and shunted into one of the cages we encountered when we first came to jail. They were open at the top and sides and were often cold and let in the rain as it was winter. The open cells often had only one toilet, which frequently didn't work. It was usually clogged up and stinking. Most other prisoners in the cage with us smoked, which made matters worse for us.

For some unknown reason, we were kept in these cages for about an hour before getting marched to yet another cage, this time next to the reception area. Again we were crowded into a small cage and made to wait in boredom.

After about half an hour to an hour, the Police meat wagon arrived. We were handcuffed (usually to someone else), searched and then packed into the wagon. No pens were allowed because someone might be stabbed with them. If you were lucky, the officer who took the pen would remember to give it back. We were always asking our lawyers for pens.

The hour-long drive to court was nauseating and claustrophobic. Even in winter the wagon became hot and stuffy and choked with cigarette smoke. Despite a shower each morning, by the time we arrived at court, we looked and felt like wrecks!

Then we had to sit through the boredom and drama of court. We were put through much of the same ordeal to get back to jail. When we arrived we were searched and made to change into our jail clothes and taken back to our wing by around 6 pm. They kept a meal for us but it was cooked early in the afternoon. It was given out at 3:30 pm, so it was not very appetizing when we received it. Usually, it had meat all over it anyway and being vegetarians we wouldn't bother even looking at it.

Once in our cell, we usually felt exhausted. We would meditate and go to sleep immediately. Then we were up again early the next morning for the same routine. We spent the weekend recovering. This was especially true for our trials that continued non-stop for three weeks. During the Committal Hearing there were days of adjournments and breaks.

Only A Meal on Paper

Despite all the hardships life had its lighter moments, even if only on reflection.

One time, while we were on a protest fast, a Margii slipped me a note about something. Police didn't allow notes to be passed to us by the public and so I was a bit nervous when suddenly one dropped in my lap. I quickly covered it, knowing police were constantly watching us. As I sat wondering what to do next, I noticed an officer staring at me:

"He's seen me get the note!" I thought.

Not wanting him to get the note I decided I had to somehow destroy it. The conclusion I reached was to eat it! It wasn't a big note.

I planned how I would have to get the note from my hand to my mouth without being noticed. I thought if I just stuffed it into my mouth, the officers would jump onto me and try to force it out. They had such a violent, reactionary air about them.

I tried different positions of sitting but most looked too awkward and suspicious. Finally, I decided to nonchalantly put my elbow on my knee and put my palm with the note clasped in it on my chin. Then when I thought no one was looking, I slipped it into my mouth.

Slowly I began to chew it, trying not to draw attention to myself. I don't think eating was allowed in court. Besides, we'd begun a hunger strike to get contact visits with our acharya and I didn't think it would look good for us if I were seen chewing.

I tried to break it up into as many small pieces as I could but found it too difficult without becoming obvious. The detective that was staring at me before was watching again and I was feeling uncomfortable. I then decided to swallow and swallow I did. However, it only went down half way and got stuck.

I didn't know what to do. I didn't want to draw attention to myself by saying I had a piece of paper stuck in my throat, but didn't know how long I could take it without getting help from someone. Finally, the paper went down after repeated and frantic gulps. I thought amusingly, "Fancy eating paper for the first time in about a week of fasting. I had better not say anything or I'll be accused of breaking my fast!"

After court ended that day, as we were being escorted back to our cells to await a van back to jail, the detective who was staring at me said, "I know you have that note one of your mates gave you."

"I don't have any note on me," I replied.

Getting angry the detective said, "Look, don't get smart with me. I saw your mate give you a note. Now hand it over or I can have you strip searched."

When I decided to eat the note it occurred to me that I might be searched and so now I was feeling relieved that I ate it.

"You can strip search me if you like, but you won't find any note *on* me."

He was silent as we kept walking. I felt the tension from his anger and frustration in deciding if he really wanted to search me. Our lawyers had already complained to a magistrate about the way these police had interrogated us about the Hilton Hotel without prior notification. Perhaps he thought our lawyers would complain about him harassing me, especially if he didn't find anything. Whatever he was thinking he didn't search me. I never did find out what was in the note either.

A Taste of Freedom

After the last day of the Committal Hearing, I reflected on my future as the van drove us back to Long Bay Prison. If anything I was feeling more defiant and determined than ever to fight and beat this frame-up. I had learned a lot about the injustices of the legal system. Little did I realise what a long, hard road lay ahead.

One prisoner in our van was a safe breaker. He spoke to us about our case and then talked about his profession. He said how easy it was to break into safes and get out of the handcuffs.

"Would you like me to take them off for you?" he offered. We felt some skepticism and wondered if he was joking. He took out a key he'd made and unlocked his cuffs. Then he unlocked ours. He locked them back on before we reached the jail. It was a strange and pleasant feeling to be in our van and not be shackled. However, since we seldom met, it was the closest taste of 'freedom' we would have for several years.

10
The Hunger Strike

One can develop the capacity to bear sufferings at the time of hardship by the grace of the Supreme Consciousness. It is indeed a great blessing from God. —Baba

NOT LONG AFTER OUR COMMITTAL HEARING, A MOST DRAMATIC EVENT OCCURRED involving us doing a five month hunger strike in early October, 1978. This was provoked by the Prison Officers Union refusal to allow us religious contact visits. Every other prisoner was allowed them, but not us. The prison officers said they believed the acharyas might incite us to violence if they were allowed to visit us.

Originally Governor Bowden agreed to the contact visits but reneged when the officer's union threatened to go on strike if they were granted to us. Then he denied ever agreeing to the visits. Dada Abhiik suggested we go on a hunger strike to protest against this discrimination.

While I thought this was a good idea, Ross and Tim did not agree, and an argument ensued. However, they agreed to go on a hunger strike too after I said I would do it alone if necessary. Tim later said they decided to cooperate only to give me support. I'm glad they did.

I had decided to announce my fast at the end of our Committal Hearing so I could capitalise on the media's presence. Tim and Ross didn't want to make the announcement at this stage. The committal was nearly finished and on the way back from court Ross snapped, "What are you trying to do? Jeopardise the whole case? You're bloody mad—it's just what the police want, to confirm that we are crazy fanatics going on indefinite fasts over visits."

Feeling defensive I told Ross that there was a principle at stake and the police will call us mad fanatics no matter what we do. Unconvinced, Ross angrily continued his disapproval. He said, "They'll think we are all sheep, fasting till death just because our leader can't see us for visits."

I was getting angry with Ross by now and pointed out that I wasn't a sheep and I was going to do it regardless of what others thought. He mumbled something derogatory and gave up trying to talk me out of it.

Tim said nothing all this time but basically agreed with Ross because he felt making an announcement like that at the end of the Committal Hearing, especially after the police had tried to make us out as fanatical terrorists, was unwise. Tim thought it would detract from the real issue of our innocence and the frame-up.

I reasoned it wouldn't matter what the police or media said about my statement because all would be forgotten when our trial came, even if it was used against us. I felt confident that a convincing argument could be given to counter any prejudicial effect it might have on a jury.

When we went to court I told Michael Adams, our barrister, of my proposed speech to the magistrate regarding the hunger strike and he took the same view as Ross and Tim. He said that it would be used against us at the trial to support the Crown's case that we were religious fanatics. Adams spoke to me while we were in a police cell and asked me to seriously reconsider my decision. He spoke with genuine concern but I was unmoved. He then told me I was quixotic and I said that I thought it was a fair description of me.

Court Statement

It was a tense time for me because of the court atmosphere. Also because I knew that Tim, Ross and our lawyers were all strongly against me making the announcement, although Ross and Tim had decided to fast as well. I thought that at least no one can say we all thought the same and acted like programmed sheep.

As it turned out, my judgment and intuition proved correct. Neither the police nor the Crown said anything at our trials about my statement. Nothing I said was used against the others or me. This confirmed my convictions that what I was doing was not unreasonable. It also taught me the value of following my convictions.

The Fast Begins

After the prison authorities learnt of our hunger strike, the first thing they did was to try and force us to eat. They demanded that we pick up our meals and take them into the eating area, saying that what we did with them afterwards was up to us. We refused, knowing they would then say to the media that we were eating. They soon got tired of trying to make us take meals and left us alone in that regard.

As with all fasts, the first few days were the worst. Hunger and headaches were the biggest problems. Since we normally fasted for a day from two to four times a month anyway, we were somewhat accustomed to the practice. Nevertheless, it was a strain, especially walking up the flight of stairs to the top landing where we were incarcerated. Generally we were stuck out in the cold yards all day except in very bad weather. After about a week of fasting on only water and fruit juice, Ross had to stop because of severe illness. He had a stomach ulcer. Tim and I continued the fast, feeling quite good considering our circumstances.

It did not take long to realise that for a hunger strike to be successful maximum publicity was needed otherwise the officers and authorities could let us starve indefinitely. We certainly did not intend to starve to death. I wanted to get a result as quickly as possible. After a few days I pretended to look more tired than I really felt. Actually I was feeling quite energetic but I could not show that. Instead when I was in the prison yards, I laid down in the corner and covered myself with a blanket. This was soon brought to the attention of the authorities.

"So far so good," I thought.

Worrying that something might be seriously wrong with me, the authorities put me into the prison hospital for observation. It had been a week since our fast began.

The hospital, within the confines of the MRP of Long Bay Prison, had two wards with a segregated observation room in between them. I was put into the observation room where mentally disturbed and dangerous prisoners are kept. It never was clear to me if I was being kept there as punishment because the authorities thought I was dangerous, or they thought I was mentally unbalanced. Or even because they wanted to make a special effort to force feed me.

The first thing they did to me in the observation room was to place a big meat meal in front of me to try and tempt me out of fasting. I was disgusted by the smelly meat and amused by their logic. Needless to say, I was not tempted. Clearly they weren't accustomed to dealing with vegetarians. I thought jokingly that if they had placed a nice bowl of fruit salad with cream in front of me there might have been a chance.

A senior nurse came in and demanded that I eat the meal. When I told her I was on a hunger strike and would not eat she angrily muttered something and left in a huff. In the end they felt responsible for keeping me alive, so the next time a nurse came by she had fruit juice for me.

For the next few days the nurses persisted with trying to break my fast by putting meat meals in front of me. It was a disgusting experience, particularly when I had not eaten for well over a week. Eventually they put me in one of the wards with other prisoners and realised I wasn't going to eat. I was in a room with about a dozen other prisoners.

Most of the prisoners in the hospital at the time had hepatitis from heroin use. A few had other diseases and others had injuries from violence.

I never felt friendly with the nurses because they seemed to be on a constant campaign to get me to quit the fast. Once they threatened to bring the prison guards and force feed me.

Two prisoners were assigned to work in my ward assisting the nurses. I became friends with them. Arnold was doing 20 years for a rather vicious assault, while Steve was in for armed robbery. I don't recall how long Steve's sentence was but I know he had been in jail for quite some time.

Arnold became interested in my protest and in Ananda Marga not long after I arrived. As with many prisoners I met in jail, he was curious to know what Ananda Marga stood for. He'd heard many things about it but he said nothing really explained it well.

"Is it a terrorist group?" he wanted to know. "Did you really do the Hilton Bombing? Are you a religious sect and do you allow sex and drugs?"

These were the type of questions we were asked all the time in prison. My answer to the questions, except the last two, was no. Sex was permitted, preferably in moderation and in marriage. The orange robed monks, however, lead a celibate lifestyle. Recreational drugs and alcohol aren't allowed.

Big Steve

Steve was a big, solid man. He was more cautious with me to begin with. When I told him I knew Ray Denning he became friendlier. They had been quite close and had done time together in the notorious Katingal prison. Steve showed me scars on his Achilles tendon were he had slashed it in order to get out of Katingal—even if only for a brief stay in the prison hospital. It was a bad prison. Compared to Katingal, the jail hospital was a much better place to be doing time. Katingal had closed down because of its inhumane conditions. In our first years in prison the officers went on strike demanding that Katingal be reopened for very violent criminals and suspected terrorists. At this time we were the only 'suspected' terrorists in Australia! Fortunately, they weren't successful in their bid to reopen the prison.

Steve seemed to have a reasonable nature, although later I heard and saw his more violent side. His imbalanced nature was a direct result of continual bashing and mistreatment in places like Katingal, Goulburn and Grafton prisons. He had a reputation at Long Bay for sudden outbursts when his mind blanked out and he went into an uncontrollable rage.

One time Steve was in a bad mood and seeing I had only a little juice, told another prisoner who was standing near him to give his juice to me. Feeling quite embarrassed and uncomfortable about this I told Steve it didn't matter. Nevertheless Steve was looking for a fight and ignored me.

"Give the juice to the Ananda Marga guy," demanded Steve.

"No, why should I?" replied the prisoner rather nervously but also indignantly. This prisoner was also quite big but knew what could happen if Steve got angry.

"Because he's on a hunger strike and you're not," came a louder reply.

I butted in again and tried to explain to Steve that it didn't matter because I had enough. This only made him angrier because by that time he was wound up for a fight.

"It does fucking matter," replied Steve. He punched the other prisoner in the stomach.

"Come on then, are you going to give him your juice?" The prisoner reluctantly gave me his juice. When Steve left I gave it back to him feeling awful about the whole incident. To compound my feelings, I found out after that the prisoner Steve punched was later taken to hospital because the stitches had come undone from a stomach operation, undoubtedly from Steve's punch.

Once the Margiis knew I had been taken to hospital they informed the media. The fast got some media coverage, so its first objective had been achieved.

After a couple of weeks, the nurses wanted to give me antibiotics that they said would protect my weak immune system. They felt I might catch one of the many diseases around the hospital in my weakened state. They were particularly concerned about hepatitis. I refused feeling it would weaken my standing as a hunger striker and would perhaps weaken me physically.

The nurses took regular blood and urine samples and checked my pulse and sometimes my weight. I did not do much because I wanted to conserve my energy since I didn't know how long the fast would continue. I also knew that the officers and some of the nurses were watching me. If they saw that I had any energy, they might say it proved I was cheating.

The Ketosis Battle

After a few weeks, a nurse complained that I was taking up bed space. I suspected her complaint was due to some officers prompting her to find reason to have me put back in jail. The nurse also claimed that my ketosis level had not gotten any worse during my time in the hospital, therefore I should go back. The ketosis indicates protein level in the urine. A high ketosis level indicates a dangerous condition.

This worried me because of the bad effect it would have on our campaign if I was taken back to prison. The authorities would say I could not be fasting because the ketosis level was staying the same. Drastic action was called for. I had to raise my ketosis level. I did this by not drinking any fruit juice for a day. At the end of that day when the nurse did her daily check, she was horrified to see how serious the ketosis level had become. All talk of sending me back stopped and I even got a bit more fruit juice given to me.

Don't Let Paul Alister Die!

That day I received a visit. Unlike other prisoners in hospital, I was not allowed to have visitors at my bed. I was made to walk out to the visiting room.

I walked slowly to the visitor's room in dressing gown and slippers. I felt quite energetic but I didn't show it, not wanting to give the officers any excuse to say that I was not fasting. As with previous visits my Margii visitors showed pain on their faces as they saw how much I was wasting away. Today however, I looked worse than normal. I mentioned that my ketosis level was very bad and the head nurse was concerned I might get permanent damage if it didn't improve soon. But I felt I would be okay. Unknown to me, the Margiis returned home and organised a demonstration about my deteriorating condition. That evening, to my great surprise, I watched the evening television news with several other prisoners and saw Margiis protesting about my condition. They were outside State Parliament with placards and were carrying a coffin. It had a big sign that read 'DON'T LET PAUL ALISTER DIE.'

One prisoner exclaimed, "Hey, that's you they are protesting about, isn't it?"

Feeling a bit embarrassed but also moved I replied, "Yes it sure is."

Another prisoner remarked how my 'mates' had stuck by me and said, "They always seem to be doing protests for you guys."

And they were.

Thin Tim

I had been wondering how Tim and Ross were going back in the prison. Not long after the protest Tim arrived at the hospital with throat and chest pains as well as general weakness. This was November 1, 1978. When I first saw Tim I felt a mixture of joy and shock. His thin appearance was distressing to see and I understood how others must feel seeing me. Nevertheless, it was great to see him and Tim seemed happy to see me. I asked how Ross was as I'd heard he'd resumed the hunger strike early in October. Tim said he was coping all right.

We had lost considerable weight during these three weeks. Tim said he'd gone from 81 kilos to 70 kilos by the time he entered hospital. We found out later that the Corrective Services had been telling the Commonwealth police that we were secretly eating, despite prison records which showed clearly that we were only drinking three litres of fruit juice a day plus water.

Victory Then Defeat

After some more weeks fasting on juice, the medical staff became concerned with our ketosis level, which by now had become quite dangerous. There was a lot of pressure to take vitamin supplements but Tim and I refused, feeling we would lose credibility. The jail doctor asked us to make written statements saying that we had voluntarily refused to take hospital food, supplements and vitamins that were offered to us. We agreed to this, adding that we would not hold them responsible for what happened as a result of our fast.

Very soon after we made this statement, the acting Commissioner of Corrective Services, Mr Noel Day, conceded the issue of our fast. On November 16, he wrote to Amrsta Morrison of 'Campaign for the Acquittal of Alister, Dunn and Anderson' (CAADA) and the jail authorities, outlining the conditions of our visits by our spiritual teachers. CAADA was an organisation of Margiis and sympathisers who were working for our release. Acharya visits were to be allowed once a month for 30 minutes. This was a great victory for us and we looked forward to breaking our fast and getting a contact visit with an acharya.

Ross had been with us in hospital for ten days when the promise of a visit came. He decided to break his fast and return to the Remand Centre for the visit. Due to past experiences of broken promises, Tim and I refused to break our fast until *after* Ross got a contact visit. This turned out to be a wise move because the Prison Officers Union decided to block the visits.

Ross had been fasting 98 days and weighed just 42 kg when he broke his fast. Needless to say he was angry to find he was not getting the visit.

We were angry at being betrayed by the Deputy Superintendent who promised the visits and said we should break our fasts, and even angrier at the Prison Officer's Union for blocking the Commissioner's order. Tim and I decided to stop drinking fruit juice and drink water only in protest. After two days of this we decided to go back to juice because of the bad effects we were suffering. Our ketosis levels were serious again, which meant there was the possibility of permanent organ damage. We were now beginning to feel extreme weakness and hunger and spent most of our time in bed. It was November 24th and we had been fasting for 103 days when we resumed drinking juice. This stopped the ketosis.

Another Battle Begins

Tim and I settled into more weeks of weakness and malnutrition. Ross didn't go back to the fast because he had gotten too sick. We found that juice was just enough to keep us going provided we didn't walk too much. At one stage the officers and even some nurses blocked our juice supplement. Tim and I immediately wrote out a statement to the effect that if we should die from lack of juice we would hold the officers responsible. This must have given them a bit of a scare because suddenly juice started to 'appear 'or be 'found' in the store rooms. But it wasn't enough for our three litres a day and we could only buy a small amount from the canteen. On January 4th, the Prison Superintendent, Mr Campbell, gave permission for us to receive some juice from outside the jail in response to our threats. This allowed us to go back to three litres a day of juice, ending another major ketosis problem.

By now we were being taken for visits in a wheelchair. It had become too dangerous for us to continue walking as we were experiencing dizzy spells and extreme weakness.

One time while Arnold was wheeling me out for a visit he commented, "I asked [Officer] Smith why they were so dirty on giving you guys visits. He said that it would be like giving strawberries to pigs."

I felt shocked. Until then I never fully realised how much they hated us. Another prisoner commented that he wished us the best of luck with our protest but said he doubted if we would achieve our objective. He said if we did, it would be the first time prisoners had beaten the Officer's Union. That gave me more incentive not to give in. Tim by now was no longer a reluctant striker but was determined to beat the screws.

For awhile a psychiatrist was interviewing me to see if I was insane or not but stopped when he realised I was not. (I think!)

Tim used to spend his time writing poetry and studying, while I also wrote some poetry and wrote in a journal. Both of us used to read the recipe section of women's magazines. We discussed the many dishes we would have liked to have eaten. We cut out some of the recipes so we could make them when we got out of prison. I found that fantasising about the recipes helped ease my constant hunger. It gave me some kind of psychic satisfaction and I found that I could not go a day without fantasising about a food dish.

Throughout the entire fast, I continued to practice my meditation four times each day. One good side-effect of the weight loss was that I noticed that it became easier for me to sit in a lotus posture as my legs became thinner. Generally, it was difficult for me to meditate because I felt so weak, but occasionally I had experiences of deep bliss. On a few occasions I had dreams of Baba that helped restore my spiritual feeling.

Having not eaten for so many months, I got to the stage where I'd forgotten what it was like to eat. I used to wonder what it would be like to eat again. It seemed it would be too good to be true—I could never be so fortunate again. Indeed, years later, I had the same kind of thoughts about what it would be like to experience life outside of jail. It had become a sweet memory and I wondered if it would ever be a reality again. Deep inside I felt God surely must eventually give us justice and set us free, but for a long time there was not much hope in sight. I only had my faith in God.

Because I was only drinking about six cups of liquid a day, my stomach had shrunk quite a bit and I found I could only have two cups of juice at a time, otherwise I would feel bloated. Sometimes I would joke to myself, "You pig, Narada, how could you have *two* cups of juice!" Seeing my skinny body in the shower, a prisoner joked that I had to run around in the shower to get wet. I added that I had to watch the drain or I would fall down it, and that instead of counting sheep to go to sleep, I counted my ribs!

On January 12th, 1979, a Sydney judge, Justice Day, of the Industrial Commission recommended that our visits be allowed. He thought the security reasons given by the Officers' Union were genuine but thought the Commission's arrangements for monthly half hour visits should be implemented but remain 'under review'.

The Officers' Union refused to give in because in reality they saw it as 'them against us' and could not tolerate the thought of having to back down. Late in January, Justice McClelland ordered the Union to allow us visits or face deregistration. The union told the court they were afraid our acharyas would brainwash us into violence. The Judge correctly rejected their arguments in a firm manner, describing them as nonsense.

This Industrial Court Order came just in time for me. A doctor had examined me the week before and told me that if I did not break the fast in another week, I faced permanent organ damage. I was suffering from vitamin B malnutrition and I often felt disorientation and had strange sensations in my chest, numbness in the head and amnesia. For that last week, I experienced pressure building up in my head until I felt it was going to explode! It was only when I repeated my mantra that the feeling would dissipate. Each time the feeling returned, I would apply my mantra to relieve it.

In mid-December, Tim noticed that his weight had now dropped from about 81 kilos to 64 kilos and his blood pressure had dropped to 70/40. I noticed that my pulse was also at a low 36 beats per minute.

Victory is Sweet and Fulfilling

I spoke with Tim about my health and we decided I should break my fast since one way or another we would get the visits. The officers could not go against the Industrial Commission or they would face deregistration. We were also concerned that I should be in good condition for our trial that was due to start the following month.

Tim decided to continue fasting until we got the visit since his health seemed much better than mine. Perhaps my previous long fasts in Canberra affected my inability to go that much extra, or perhaps Tim just had a stronger constitution.

After 150 days of taking only fruit juice I ended my hunger strike. I was literally skin and bones. I had lost 16 kilos and now weighed just 53 kilos.

At last the long awaited moment had come to eat. On February 1st, 1979, at 4 pm I had a small tin of peaches and pears and some fresh apple pieces.

5 pm: One quarter of a cup of vitamin-enriched milk drink.

6:30 pm: Tinned fruit with a tin of reduced cream (very exciting— I love cream!)

8 pm: A cup of tinned orange juice.

9 pm: Two Weet Bix pieces, processed All-Bran, sugar, apple and hot water in milk.

And so it went. In four days I gained one and a half kilos. Whatever I ate tasted divine, especially the first few times. My sensory organs went wild with delight each time I got to eat. But after a few days food became unusually boring. I never did take any interest in the recipes I'd collected from the women's magazines. It was a spiritual lesson to me about how something we fantasise about can seem totally mesmerising, but once we achieve it, it loses its appeal.

Weight and strength rapidly returned to all of us. Tim broke his fast nearly seven days after me when we got our first visit. The fast succeeded in making us many enemies in the Prison Officer's Union. Their discrimination and harassment continued for many years. Among the prisoners the three of us and Ananda Marga gained a new respect. This was the first time the Prison Officers' Union had been beaten by anyone.

While we got our visits, the officers, still sulking over losing to some Ananda Marga crims, refused to supervise our visits. Instead, the executive officers did the job. Dada was of course very happy when he finally got to visit us in his capacity as our religious teacher. So were we, although Ross and Tim still had misgivings about the whole thing, feeling our time and energy could have been better used in preparing for our upcoming trial. I saw the fast more idealistically. It was a major battle between the positive and the negative forces. Justice, or dharma, had won in the end, as usual.

Needless to say Mum, Dad, my twin brother Mark and my two older siblings, Richard and Fern, were all very relieved to hear the fast had ended and that I could get contact visits with them. Richard and Fern were both married with families in Perth but kept in touch about our case through Mum and Dad.

Mark visited and wrote to me occasionally, telling me of the conflicts he had at work trying to get his work mates to believe we were innocent. Mum also told me of arguments she had with friends and relatives. "Where there is smoke there is fire" they would respond, which was intensely frustrating for Mum. She said Dad did not seem to be so bothered by what their friends thought. He knew we were innocent and would not stop until we were free!

11
The Trials

A spiritual seeker is verily a soldier. The pricks of thorns on the difficult path signifies one's progress. The collective welfare of the universe is the crowning glory of one's victory. — Baba

WITH THE HUNGER STRIKE VICTORY BEHIND ME, I WAS LOOKING FORWARD to another victory in court. Tim and Ross were also looking forward to our trial. At last we thought we would be able to present our side and clear our names once and for all. We had lived with the 'terrorist' tag now for about eight months, as had Ananda Marga. Eight months in jail felt like a very long time and I was eager to get out soon. The Margiis were also confident of our acquittal and eagerly sought the inevitable "not guilty" verdict. They had been visiting us at every opportunity, giving us support and inspiration. They said they also received inspiration and strength from our firm protest in jail. We were certain it was only a matter of time now.

Our lawyers were public defenders through legal aid. We had no money, and Ananda Marga also had no funds to help us. Tim's parents also paid for a top Sydney Queens Council, Marcus Einfeld. Ross's barrister was Michael Adams again and mine was Ken Shadbolt. Shadbolt and Einfeld later became judges. Marcus is a tall, solid man with a commanding presence both in and out of court. He was the first barrister to really shake Seary in the trial that followed. It was quite something to watch.

Although Einfeld was Tim's senior counsel, he only appeared in court for a few days to cross-examine Seary. During the remaining weeks, his defence was held by Michael Bowdor, the barrister Tim had in our committal hearing. Bowdor was a soft spoken man with little overt strength of personality compared to Einfeld.

Michael Adams is also quite a tall man, but much heavier than most men his size. His manner was very dramatic. In contrast, Ken was quiet and methodical, although very firm and defiant. He and Bowdor were a good balance to Adams and Einfeld.

Going to Court

The trial began in mid February 1979. One of the things I liked about going to court was that we got to wear normal clothes that were comfortable and fit properly! What I didn't like was going back to the old court routine of having to get up very early, rush through meditation, yoga postures and breakfas (if we ate at all). Then we would spend hours waiting in the cold cages before being put in meat wagons like sardines (or more precisely, smoked sardines) and being shipped off to court.

While the stuffy, claustrophobic vans were uncomfortable to say the least, one thrill we looked forward to was seeing the world outside the jail again. For some unknown reason, the air vent was covered with a large flap which prevented fresh air and light getting in and prevented us from seeing out. Still we managed to peer through the gap and see some trees or people in brightly coloured clothes. That was such a treat for me after the grey walls and clothing of prison. It also made me impatient to get out!

As the van went into the courthouse, we could hear a large steel gate clang shut behind us. When the van had stopped we heard the sound of jingling keys before the van door opened up. A group of policemen stood in a line to guide us into the doorway that led to our cells. Once we were in a cell a policeman unlocked our cuffs. We stayed there until we were called for our trial.

The cells varied in size, some not much bigger than a jail cell, others twice as big. The main difference is that the front of the cell was only bars and wire mesh. There was absolutely no privacy and no way to escape from noise or other people. Each holding cell had a toilet and a little wash basin or water fountain. Their ability to function varied considerably from cell to cell. The toilets had a waist high wall in front, which gave little privacy.

Before our trial started, we were taken away to another cell beneath the court.

"All right, you Ananda Marga boys, it's time to go," alerted the policeman who was to take us away.

"Good luck" was the usual comment prisoners made as we walked off. By then we had often had plenty of time to talk about both of our cases and Ananda Marga. "Thanks," came our reply. "Same to you."

We went down several steps and along a narrow damp tunnel. It was not very high and in some places we had to watch our heads for overhanging beams. The tunnel curved at several points before reaching our destination. "Stay here," the policeman would command. Two other officers also accompanied him. Before us was a stairway that lead up into the courtroom in which we were to appear. After Judge Nagle had entered, we were called up. A policeman led the way, another came between us and one followed behind. When we got to the top, they went to the left into the courtroom. We turned right at the top and walked into an enclosed seating area for the accused. A door was shut behind us and a policeman sat guarding the door outside the courtroom.

It was quite a contrast to come up from a dark, silent underground tunnel into the bright lights and noise of a crowded courtroom. First we saw our lawyers, then the police and the public at the back of the room, and of course the media, lots of them!

The First Days

The first time I came up into court I felt a hum of excitement in the air. I was excited, too, and felt positive and confident.

"How are you, Paul?" Ken Shadbolt asked in greeting.

"I'm fine." I assured him. I looked around the court to see if there was any Margiis I knew. I saw some and smiled at them. They smiled back, sharing my confidence.

It was a packed room, mainly because of the police and the media. Tim's parents were there, but I am not sure about Ross' parents, although they gave evidence later. My parents were not able to afford another journey across the country on top of my Dad's trip to visit me at the time of my arrest.

Sharp-shooters were on the roof and surveillance cameras scanned people coming into the building. Everyone entering had to be checked by security police with metal detectors. Our prison van was followed each day by a helicopter. After a couple of days we cynically noticed that the sharp-shooters and security check had vanished. But not before the media had painted a picture of us as dangerous terrorists guarded by security police in case of a daring breakout attempt. This was exactly the impression the security police were trying to create to prejudice our trial.

Seary Again

The first part of the trial was jury selection. We were allowed to reject several of the people on offer to us. We exercised this right fully, as did the prosecution. Eventually a panel of twelve jurors was selected, but I still didn't think these people would ever be able to understand our perspective.

The trial began with the police prosecution outlining its case against us. From the outset the jury was influenced by the police fabrications (which we called 'verbals') and Seary's lies. This included the Hilton Bombing allegation. Ross looked agitated as our so called 'confessions' were briefly mentioned. He turned to Tim and they both muttered something in a sarcastic tone.

Then the prosecution called its witnesses. The police were called first and repeated their verbals just as they had at the Committal Hearing. Although it was disgusting to hear them tell these lies again, it didn't bother me as I believed no one in their right mind could believe the police. I watched the media busily write down the police verbal whenever it became sensational. Later we would predict to each other what the headlines or news would be that night.

In the committal hearing Seary testified first, however at the trial the prosecution saved him for a dramatic ending, despite our lawyer's objections. By now the jury had heard all kinds of terrible things about our alleged violence and extremism. When Seary echoed much of what the police had said, it gave credibility to his otherwise implausible story.

When Seary came to stand in the witness box, a hush of silence spread over the normally noisy courtroom. The media had their pens to paper and their eyes glued to the witness box as they waited to pounce on every sensational allegation Seary made, especially about the Hilton bombing. When Seary finally told his story about how we had admitted to the Hilton bombing during the car ride to Cameron's house, the media seemed to treat it as if it was the first time they had heard it! The usual headlines covered the papers the next day, implicating us in the Hilton bombing. Not a single newspaper noted the discrepancies and contradictions of the case.

Our lawyers unearthed a major discrepancy while cross examining Seary. They found out that Seary made no mention of our so called Hilton bombing admission in his interview with the police the night of our arrest. It was not until his fourth interview in July, over two months after the supposed fact, and just before our Committal Hearing, that Seary spelled out the whole of his fantasy story.

We didn't hear the full details of Seary's fantastic claims until the trial. Now records of his police interviews were read out and we were amazed at the lies he had concocted to describe how we had done the bombing. He claimed I was the one who planted the bomb in a rubbish bin outside of the hotel. He said I told him that I wore a disguise to walk through the crowd in Sydney's George Street, outside the Hotel. Apparently I wore the same clothing he claimed I was wearing when I told him the story on the way to Cameron's House. At that time I had been wearing dark heavy winter clothing in preparation for some night time graffiti. I had jokingly pulled my turtle neck jumper up to my mouth and pulled my beanie down to my eye brows. Seary added in the fantasy that I also put on thick clear classes! With this ridiculous 'disguise' I was meant to have gone through a crowd in Sydney in the middle of a hot summer's day, and planted a bomb! I would have stood out like a sore thumb!

Frustratingly, I was never allowed to mention my most important defence: the fact that I had 16 witnesses who could have testified to prove I was in Adelaide, 1,500 kilometres away, leading a retreat at the time of the bombing. This could have killed any doubt about my innocence. But we were not on trial for the Hilton Bombing so my whereabouts at that time were not relevant, or so they said. I hoped someone would ask me about it—defence or prosecution—but no one did, so I could not mention my alibi.

Needless to say, our barristers made much of the discrepancies in Seary's unbelievable story. However by the time the police prosecution had finished calling witnesses, the jury seemed already to have made up their minds that we were guilty. Although they may not have been convinced we had conspired to kill Cameron, they were convinced we had done the Hilton bombing, so they felt they had to convict us, even though that's not what we were on trial for.

The jury foreman, Ross Hilton Clark, later wrote to the Attorney

General. He said:

> Much of the evidence of the Hilton Bombing that was allowed...prejudiced the jury... Some of the jurors held the opinion that we wouldn't worry so much about the evidence [of the Cameron case] (and there was a great deal of evidence) because the judge will direct us what to do in his summing up... Some of the jurors could not believe that any of the police might lie, even when totally contradicted by other police.

When interviewed on a film about our case, the foreman said if he saw some of the police allegations on TV, he'd turn over to another station— it was that implausible!

Giving Our Evidence

Finally, two weeks later, we were allowed to present our side of the story. Tim gave evidence first, then Ross and then me. I felt nervous giving evidence, but by the time my barrister had finished asking me questions, I felt relaxed and confident. Consequently when I was cross-examined by the prosecution, I was not nervous or intimidated. Indeed towards the end of his cross-examination I was enjoying being able to refute his allegations and felt disappointed when it ended. I felt God to be close by my side during the whole experience.

Our lawyers thought we all did well in the box: None of us were shaken by the cross examination. The fact that the prosecution made virtually no criticism of our actual evidence said a lot about the credibility and strength of our case.

Each of our barristers summed up with skillful eloquence. Some of the jurors seemed convinced by their arguments, particularly the foreman. Because the prosecution lawyer had his turn after our lawyers, he was able to criticise their arguments and have the last say. The judge, Justice Nagle, summed up after the prosecution. We had mixed feelings about what he said.

We were led back down underground to our cells to prepare for the verdict. The long wait began.

The Long Wait

It was afternoon when we began the wait. We discussed the case and all agreed that nothing we had said during cross examination could be used against us. We felt confident that the jury wouldn't be fooled by the fabricated police evidence or Seary's contradictory story. Our case seemed to be rationally sound. Their case was full of holes.

"Has your trial finished?" came a voice from a cell opposite ours.

"Yes, mate" said Tim.

"How's it looking?" asked the prisoner.

"Pretty good. The Crown had no real case against us."

"That's great," said the delighted prisoner, "I've been following your case a bit in the papers and it seems like a set-up by the jacks [detectives]. Best of luck."

"Thanks mate!" we replied.

Ross and I decided to do some meditation. We washed in the small sink, and sat on the bench. After a while, Tim joined us.

Hours passed, and still no verdict. A few times we were called back in because the jurors had a question to ask regarding the evidence. Each question showed disbelief about the police evidence and seemed to show acceptance of our story. We felt encouraged after each questioning. But by the time afternoon had turned to night there was still no decision.

By now the cells were empty except for us. Courts had finished at 4:00 pm and the other prisoners had been taken to jail.

A policeman came in and asked how we were going.

"Fine, thank you," said Ross, a bit surprised at the policeman's friendliness. After hearing our evidence for the first time, some policemen seemed to believe we were actually innocent.

"How do you think the trial went?" asked the policeman.

Ross replied: "It's looking good. We've been back in court a couple of times and the questions the jurors ask seem to favour us."

"I've found during the years that I've worked here," added the policeman,"that the longer it takes a jury to come to a decision, the better chance you have of acquittal."

"Yes" said Ross, "I'm feeling more confident as time goes on. You'd think if they were really going to convict us they would have decided it by now. The long delay can indicate they are having some doubts about our guilt."

I interjected: "Probably one or two of them can't believe the detectives lied."

The policeman seemed a bit uncomfortable when I said that but then remarked, "Yes, well, of course at times some police lie."

Tim responded with a sarcastic smile thinking the policeman had understated the amount of police lies.

"Well they lied in our case," reacted Ross.

"From what I know of the case," continued the policeman, "it does seem suspect. I don't know much about that 'Amanda Marga' (sic), but from talking with you three and from what I know about your case, it does seem that something has gone wrong somewhere. You certainly don't fit the image of bombers."

"Thank you," I said "I hope the jury thinks the same as you!"

The policeman left and we went back to pensive silence. I took my mind off the verdict and daydreamed about my future plans. Now I could go to India, see Baba and return to acharya training. I imagined the pleasure of being with the Margiis and visiting my parents again.

Finally the friendly policeman came in and said:

"You're wanted. I think it's a hung jury." We jumped up, collected ourselves, and followed the policeman downstairs, along the underground tunnel to the bottom of the courtroom stairs. There we anxiously waited to be summoned into the court room for the verdict.

"A hung jury," I thought. "That means they could not reach a verdict and we will have to have another trial."

There were knocks on the court floor above us as the sheriff struck his staff against the floor and announced: "All be upstanding!" We could hear the judge walking into the courtroom and taking his seat, and then we heard everyone in the court sitting down. A policeman called for us and we were lead up the stairs and into the courtroom.

It was a hung jury! Justice Nagel announced that the jury had not been able to reach a verdict and after words of thanks, discharged them. We felt very disappointed by the result. We thought one or two of the jury must have believed we were guilty, and it seemed a pity to have been so close to freedom. Later we found out that only the foreman believed we were innocent and his strong conviction of our innocence prevented a guilty verdict!

In a letter to the Attorney General, the foreman wrote:

..No impartial, logical thinking person could find Alister and Dun guilty of the second charge, (attempted murder of the arresting police officers) and would have very grave doubts about the first charge (conspiracy to murder Cameron) against all three. It is much more than a reasonable doubt.

Second Time Unlucky

After the hung jury we prepared for the second trial, which was held four months later. For this trial, in July 1979, neither Einfeld nor Shadbolt could appear for Tim and I. Tim ended up with a good lawyer and former State Attorney General, Sir Kenneth McCaw. My barrister was Sean Flood, who unfortunately didn't come until a week before the trial began. Consequently he didn't have much time to prepare for it. In fact he was still reading transcripts during the trial! It was not his fault that legal aid hired him at a late stage. Generally I was happy with the way he fought for me considering the time handicap.

Since the first trial we had received a copy of a newspaper called 'Sydney Shout.' In May, it carried a front page article reporting that an ASIO agent had claimed that "the Ananda Marga religious group...had been framed," and that, "one of the senior officers...had a personal hatred of the Ananda Marga." This gave us added optimism for an acquittal.

As with the first trial, we had a helicopter following our transport to the court, sharp shooters on the courthouse roof, surveillance cameras and metal detectors at the door. Again, after a few days these elaborate, ostentatious security measures suddenly vanished. But not before the whole show had prejudiced the media and any potential jurors.

Eric Mountier, a juror in our second trial later wrote: "The police sharp shooters on top of the courthouse the first couple of days of the trial and the general security made me feel uneasy. The effect was intimidating and created a hostile atmosphere." We heard that at least one potential juror asked to be excused from jury duty because they were afraid of getting involved with the case.

Two things in this trial differentiated it from the first trial. The prosecutor, Mr Gregory, introduced far more defamatory cross-examination material and the trial judge (nicknamed in some circles as 'Injustice' Lee) appeared to be more against us than Justice Nagle. He seemed to want us convicted.

During the prosecution's cross-examination, Tim and I were asked for the first time about the Hilton bombing, which had the effect of prejudicing the jury even further. They asked us more questions about the Ananda Marga organisation and other matters not directly related to our charges. This was solely designed to sway the jury, and it did. In his letter to the Attorney General, juror Eric Mountier wrote:

> ....I have thought a lot about the trial...and have reached the conclusion that it was not a fair hearing. Firstly, although the judge told us to disregard the accusations about the Hilton bombing, there was always the thought at the back of my mind that the three Ananda Marga men were involved in some way. This was mainly because the prosecution cross-examination centred around the Hilton accusations. Some of the jurors said they thought the three men were probably guilty of the Hilton bombing. But there was no evidence at all to support this, and the charges did not relate to the Hilton bombing anyway.
>
> Even though I was very careful to avoid newspapers and radio reports of the trial, I could not help seeing some headlines or listening to some reports which refered to the Hilton accusations. The general atmosphere created by these reports made it difficult to really detach yourself and look at the case objectively.
>
> As well as printing stories about the Hilton, the papers painted a picture of Ananda Marga as a dangerous terrorist group. Whether this is true or not I can't say, but certainly I feel that this image affected us in making a decision.
>
> Also, the prosecution barristers questioned the three men for a long time about Ananda Marga. None of us knew anything about Ananda Marga or what it did, and what we did find out sounded very strange and foreign, and was prejudicial to the charges. This certainly affected my attitude to the three men.

When I was asked about the Hilton bombing, I could only deny the charges. I couldn't present witnesses or evidence proving I was in Adelaide at the time because, as in the last case, I wasn't directly charged with the Hilton bombing. The prosecution capitalised on this complication at every turn to convince the jury of our guilt. Our lawyers often protested about prejudicial material being led into court, but with little success. The judge seemed determined to get us convicted!

Seary's evidence had expanded at each and every court appearance. It had grown since the Committal Hearing and had grown again significantly since the last trial! For example now he claimed that we we had planned to kill Cameron, his wife and three children. He had made no mention at the Committal Hearing of Cameron's family.

He made up more incriminating details which indicated his inventive mind at work again. For example Seary claimed that Tim and I synchronised our watches before Ross and I drove off with Seary to Cameron's house. However police records show that, when we were arrested and all our belongings were recorded, neither of us had watches!

The Verdict

We expected another "long wait" this time, but we didn't have quite the same confidence as we did at the last trial. We felt suspicious right away when after less than two hours we were called back to court to hear the verdict.

"How could they have studied three weeks of evidence in such a short time?" But then I thought. "Maybe they could see how blatantly innocent we were."

As we walked down the stairway and along the tunnel, I was feeling happy inside, even excited, imagining we would be free soon. As I waited at the bottom of the steps into the courtroom, I walked up and down quietly singing a spiritual tune to myself. Ross and Tim were still and pensive. Ross was convinced the worst was to come. I was feeling optimistic until suddenly a dreadful feeling swept through me that made me shudder momentarily:

"They are going to find us guilty!" I thought, with my stomach churning and cold shivers running down my spine. "Has God has been giving me all this inspiration to prepare me for the worst!?"

I quickly regained control of myself, fearing I was going to panic. Logically they had to find us innocent, so why panic? Most of my optimism and confidence returned, although a little tension remained in anticipation of a bad result. But it was now all in God's benevolent hands.

Finally the call came for us to go up the stairway and face the music, be it sweet or bitter! At the dock we watched the jurors file in. They were looking everywhere except towards us. We were once told by a crim that if the jury looks at you it means they have a "not guilty" verdict. If they don't, the verdict is guilty! This crossed my mind and I felt my tenseness increased ten-fold.

"Could it be that I'm going to be convicted for an outrageous crime that I didn't do, and then spend my youth behind bars?" I lamented to myself.

"Have you reached a verdict?" asked the Judge.

"Yes," replied the foreman of the jury. "Guilty."

We had been found guilty on all charges.

Tim later said he felt his heart sink as he heard the word "Guilty." Ross said he felt dreadful, as did the Margiis, parents and supporters in the room. It was as if our future had been painted black. The possibility loomed before us of spending years, or even the rest of our life in prison.

For a split second, I was overcome with grief, but then quickly my mind shifted to a philosophical view of the verdict. I had a sense of being unwittingly thrown into a big cosmic drama and I had no idea how it would end. I had the feeling that God had tossed me into a huge, dark and lonely pit and was watching to see how I would get out.

"You're on your own now, and the only way you can get out is if you don't lose faith in Me," was the message I heard internally.

I felt I was facing the ultimate challenge and this aroused my fighting spirit. I became determined to "get out of this dark pit" by God's grace. Since the unfairness of the conviction was something far greater than I felt I could fight alone, I knew intuitively that God was going to do something great with us in order to defeat this injustice. I did not know what or how, as everything seemed stacked against us, but I felt internally a strong reassurance that in the end Dharma (righteousness) would be victorious.

Looking at my friends in the courtroom I could feel their pain and I wanted to tell them that everything was going to be all right in the end, but I couldn't. Surrounded by police, we were not allowed to speak to anyone as we were lead away. However, my inspiration was clouded when I saw the pained faces of the Margiis as we left. The room was filled with depression. Only the police were elated, as they smiled openly, shook hands, and celebrated their victory.

Post Verdict

The van trip back was a very solemn one indeed. None of us could speak. I worried how my parents would cope with the verdict. In fact they were devastated, as were Ross and Tim's parents.

That night back at the Remand centre, a lot of prisoners asked me about the verdict. They said they were sorry to hear about it but felt it wasn't over yet. I reassured them it wasn't. One prisoner said he could not understand why I did not look unhappy. There was no real reply to give him. I was feeling quite moved in a spiritual sense but it was difficult to explain. At the most critical hour of need, God had graced me with detachment and presence of mind.

When I went to Ross and Tim's cell they were already asleep. The energy in the cell was low and I guessed that's why they had gone to bed so early. The next morning Ross did not even want to get out of bed. He said he felt dead and didn't want to live. It was a very sad time.

A lot of the prison officers were very cocky after our conviction and seemed happy with the result. One grinning officer said to Ross:

"You'll get life and deserve it."

The Sentence

The next week we appeared before Justice Lee to be sentenced. By now our spirits were up again and we were in a fighting mood. We decided we could not accept the verdict or the sentence. We had to campaign to clear our names.

When we appeared before Justice Lee we each prepared a speech to show our rejection of the verdict and sentence. We expected to get life imprisonment so we weren't too concerned with what we said.

Tim stood up and to show his conviction that this injust judgment would be eventually repealed, requested the maximum sentence. With a similar sentiment and protest, I asked for life imprisonment. Ross declared himself a political prisoner!

This shocked the Judge somewhat as he was expecting us to be intimidated by our predicament. He read out his prepared speech criticising our "arrogance" and unwillingness to express remorse for what we had done. He stressed the horror of our crime of conspiracy to murder and attempted murder of the arresting police. He declared that in order to set an example for other terrorists, he would give us 16 years without parole. This was the first time New South Wales had experienced "terrorism" and he said terrorists would not get parole.

After the sentencing we were put into holding cells. Michael Adams came down to our cells to try to console us. He looked like he needed consoling himself. Ross and I were given 16 years for the attempted murder charge, and an additional 16 years for the conspiracy charge. I calculated that Ross and I would be in prison for 32 years!

"Something really is going to have to be done. I can't believe I'm going to do 32 years for graffiti!" I said.

But then Michael Adams explained to me that the second 16 year charge ran concurrently, so in reality our sentence was only for 16 years.

"Things are looking better already!" I thought jokingly to myself. Humour was a good defence against depression and hopelessness.

12
Meditation & Service

> It is action which makes a person great. Be great by your sadhana,
> by your service and by your sacrifice.
> —Baba

WE WERE NOT GIVEN ANY CHANCE TO RETURN TO THE REMAND CENTRE TO SAY farewell to our many new friends, but were taken directly to the Central Industrial Prison which was in the same complex. The Long Bay Prison complex is composed of four jails: Metropolitan Remand Centre (MRC) where we had been, the Metropolitan Reception Prison (MRP), for long term maximum security prisoners, the Central Industrial Prison (CIP) for people like us awaiting appeal or reclassification and relocation to other prisons and the Metropolitan Training Centre (MTC) for minimum security prisoners.

At the CIP reception room we went through the usual strip search and were issued prison clothing. We were also given name tags to wear. Like at the Remand Centre, not to wear a name tag was a punishable offence.

Our conviction and sentence had received considerable publicity and two reception sweepers, who were prisoners, began to make comments about our case.

"Bad luck about the conviction," said one.

"Yes, but it isn't over yet," said Ross.

"You're going to appeal, aren't you?" said the prisoner.

"Sure," said Ross.

"The coppers don't like you, do they?" the other prisoner commented.

"No, some of them don't," I replied.

"At least you are out of the Remand. It's much better here," said the second prisoner.

"They both look pretty awful to me," Ross said.

A New 'Home'

In some ways CIP *was* better than the Remand Centre. It was a great relief to be given our own jail uniforms. At the Remand Centre we had to turn them in twice a week and then be given a clean but often ill-fitting set. Here, we had our own uniforms to look after. We were given two pairs of green trousers, two grey shirts, two singlets, two pairs of green socks, a green jacket and leather shoes. I asked for two pairs of shorts as well and two Tshirts, but was refused because they were for summer issue.

The next drama was receiving our property. The cardboard boxes that contained our belongings were opened and the contents were taken out one at a time by one of the reception sweepers while the reception officer noted it all down on a property card. What he decided we could have was put to one side and what he decided we couldn't have was packed away. I was happy because we were allowed more of our property here than on Remand. We were allowed to have a watch, a television, and a cassette player, so we made sure to capitalise on that. Later, we bought other items from the canteen with money we had earned or what friends and family gave to us. Only watches could be left for us by visitors.

We had been denied these things for such a long time that it was all too easy to give undue importance to them. This was characteristic of many things in jail. Deprivation creates a distortion of values.

After loading our belongings onto a trolley, we wheeled them to our new cells, escorted by an officer. As I walked along, I looked around with much curiosity, excitement and tension. I noticed prisoners watching me and wondered what they were thinking. Some of them didn't look too friendly.

The building itself was an improvement on the Remand Centre. At least we could see trees and there was a grassy area in the middle of the prison that we had access to. We were put into the Reception Wing to wait until a permanent cell was allocated to each of us. After about a week we were put into Four Wing and each given a cell on our own. As I unpacked my belongings I felt a little sense of home, knowing I could keep much of my own property with me and that this was to be my abode for a long time. The cell was the standard 3.6 by 4.8 metres, similar to the cell in Remand. Here, I could open or close my door at will. I cherished my privacy, even though prison officers could and did stick their heads in whenever they wished. At least they bothered me less often than in Remand.

We had to be out of our cell by 7:15 am for breakfast, which was usually porridge or cornflakes, a piece of fruit and a small carton of milk. Everybody was locked in their cell again until 8:am. We went to work if we were lucky enough to have a 'job'. Otherwise we spent the rest of the day in the yard, the gym or the library.

An attendance check, called a 'muster', was at 11:45 am. Then we picked up our lunch which we ate in our own cell. At first it was a hot meal but later it was changed to sandwiches and a piece of fruit. The meals were as bad as in Remand and we really suffered because of it. We had to leave our cell again at 1:15 pm to go to work or spend more time in the yard. Dinner muster was at 4:00 pm but was later changed to 4:45 pm. We picked up our dinner and ate it alone in our cell. I liked this part of the day best because I enjoyed the time alone when I could meditate as long as I liked. It was more peaceful by myself, away from the hustle and bustle of prison life. In Remand we were only allowed in the cell after 10:00 pm, so this was a great improvement.

After our arrival several prisoners we had met in Remand came over to speak with us. We were happy to see them, as we felt a bit alienated in this new and different environment. We exchanged handshakes and joyous smiles. They filled us in on the place, telling us both good and bad things about it, advising us on which prison officers to watch or avoid and which ones were okay.

One time as I walked along I heard some prisoners call out in a mocking voice "Ananda Marga!" It sounded like a challenge to fight me. Thoughts raced through my mind as I quickly decided whether to ignore the challenge or to look up to where I heard the voices and effectively confront the mocker. I knew once I did this there would be a strong likelihood that the taunting would continue until I reacted. I decided not to look towards them. A fight was the last thing I wanted. Taunting was a petty issue but it left me with an uneasy feeling as I wondered if I'd be confronted again. Fortunately I wasn't.

The atmosphere was less tense in the CIP than the Remand Centre, but it was still stressful. Because there were fewer restrictions, prisoners naturally felt less ill at ease. The attitude of officers was better generally and we personally didn't experience the high degree of antipathy we had previously experienced. Ross later remarked about the feeling of relief he experienced at getting out of the Remand Centre. It's amazing how relative feelings can be.

Many prison officers still considered us 'Hilton terrorists' and remembered the hunger strike for religious visits. But they didn't have the same vindictiveness as their Remand colleagues. We later learned that the officers considered going on strike if we Margiis weren't put in segregation when we first arrived at the CIP. Finally they agreed to observe us for awhile instead.

The Sit-In

Within days of our arrival we were involved in a 'sit-in'. During yard time, I noticed prisoners walking towards the central grass area. Many were sitting down. I saw a few prisoners I knew, so I went over to see what it was all about. One of the prisoners, Alex Shalarla, said that they were having a sit-in. He told me what the issue was about. I remember him saying, "Now you know what jail is really about" as we waited to see what the prison officials would do. It was a tense moment for everyone although some prisoners seemed excited at the idea of a confrontation with prison officers. I must admit I felt some excitement and curiosity as well, not knowing what to expect. I later learned from experience that these types of confrontations can easily turn very nasty.

Confrontation for some prisoners was a relief from the drudgery and boredom of prison life. This applied to prison officers as well, who sometimes seemed to go out of their way to create disputes.

Some prisoners argued with one of the leaders, trying to convince him to call off the sit-in, but the majority ignored them and the sit-in went on. Tension continued to grow as we waited to see if the Superintendent would come out and speak about the prisoners' grievances, or if he would choose to send in the riot squad instead. Eventually he spoke with the leaders and the sit-in ended.

Meditation

After my conviction I thought the only way I would survive jail was to dive deep into my meditation. I was now 25 years old and decided to meditate seven hours each day. It felt like quite a challenge to me. I meditated one hour in the morning, two and a half hours at noon, three in the evening and a half an hour before sleep.

I was inspired by the ideal of the the lotus flower. It grows in stagnant, muddy ponds, yet dirt rolls off its leaves and its beauty remains unaffected by its surroundings. In India it is the symbol of spiritual purity and the ideal of 'being in the world but not of it'. The lotus symbolised to me the ability to remain unaffected by the dirt and bondages of physical existence.

At times meditation was a real struggle, particularly in the beginning. If it was not physical difficulties then it was mental fascinations or attachments that tried, sometimes successfully, to take me away from my inner search for union with the Infinite. Over time I was able to become physically and mentally stronger and my meditation became more peaceful, pleasurable and eventually blissful. Bliss in meditation is not like ordinary pleasure or intoxication. It is extremely enjoyable and brings feelings of love and deep fulfillment. I started to feel very carefree and happy. One time I shocked a visitor by telling her I would not have minded if I did the full term of my sentence. The thought of spending the next 16 years in blissful meditation was very appealing to me—it could even counteract the awful food.

For the next few months I did little else other than meditate. I began to perceive small luminous lights in my cell, which according to Tantra, are elevated beings who have reincarnated into 'luminous bodies'. It was not long before my cell became a spiritual oasis. The contrast between my cell and the rest of the prison environment was so marked that after entering my cell, immediately peace would descend upon me. This made me reluctant to leave my spiritually vibrated cell.

Baba appeared in my meditation frequently. I saw his body so distinctly that I thought my eyes were open. If I would check by opening my eyes he would disappear. Usually he appeared with a big grin, beaming love and pleasure towards me. One time he looked sternly at me when I was daydreaming and not concentrating on my meditation. Another time he appeared and began to lean over to one side. I realised he was teasing me because I was leaning to one side in my meditation. I straightened up quickly and Baba disappeared.

The visual experience of Baba is just one way to experience Consciousness. According to Tantra, divine Consciousness is One. However, when it filters down through the layers of the mind and as it comes in contact with the more conscious ego levels of the mind, it is perceived according to the individual's mental conditioning. A Christian may see Jesus, Mary or angels. A Hindu may see gods or goddesses, while a New Age seeker may experience light, guides, sounds or some other phenomenon that is related to spirituality. God or guru can therefore guide us in a form that we can love and relate to. What I was experiencing was my guru giving me inner guidance through his visual form. This increased my faith in Baba and the Tantric path. It also helped clear away some skepticism I had felt before when I had read about such experiences. My diary reflected many of these inner experiences

Prison Diary:

28 August, 1979: Had a very sweet and surrendered meditation tonight. Now it has become so blissful, I can always count on some bliss when doing Dhyana [deep meditation] for at least ten minutes...

6 September: I have just done my meditation and each time I am amazed and inspired by the beauty of Baba's form. His skin so soft and clear, his eyes so powerful and penetrating, his smile so sweet and loving, and his face so vibrant and glowing. I often feel as though Baba is looking right into my mind. Often I see little luminous specks of light glittering around Baba's face, especially his eyes. How inspiring, how warm he is. I was in a loving mood today, just thinking of God.

7 September: Fasting today. Went to English class to try to improve my grammar and spelling. Getting clash at not being able to express myself when writing. After doing 1 & 1/2 hours meditation, 30 minutes of it in Dhyana, last evening, I felt really vibrated and inspired. I mean my whole body was vibrating, especially my head and heart.

19 October: Another blissful day with God's name [my mantra] continuously on my mind. Much love today, even towards the prison officers! The daytime bliss is better than in meditation.

22 October: This evening I probably had the most profoundly loving meditation ever! The love I felt for God in the crown of my head was almost overwhelming. [This point is called, Guru Chakra, and is important in certain practices meditation.] After about 30 minutes of this, I opened my eyes and saw there were brighter than normal specks of silvery light appearing on a photo of Baba. Next to his head was a long thin

A photo smuggled out of prison during the time I was practicing seven hours of meditation each day. At that time I would have been happy to stay in prison indefinitely because I was enjoying so much bliss.

column of light. I felt deeply spiritual and occasionally luminous objects appeared in my cell. Before this blissful meditation, I was having a terrible time trying to concentrate, which shows it was all God's grace!

23 October: Head feeling light and blissful, heart feeling sweet and loving. Feeling so much love, wanting to hug everyone. The constant repetition of mantra is what does it. It reminds me that God is in everything and everyone. Baba Nam Kevalam.

24 October. Oh what a sweet battle tonight's meditation was. Had a spinning head and felt sleepy. [Later I found out I had hypoglycemia] Eventually my mind cleared for deep meditation. What a struggle it was. You [Baba] kept on giving me just a little love to coax me on. Like a madman I fell for the bait of Your love. As I followed You deeper and deeper I was overwhelmed by a bolt of bliss, like a dagger entering into my head and exploding at my heart chakra. I was completely intoxicated by the intense love.

After this meditation I awoke the next day still feeling the blissful residue from the night before. My mantra was vibrating in my mind constantly. As I walked around jail I felt intense love in my heart centre. I wanted to embrace everyone, even the hated guards. The residual of that bliss lingered for days. I had difficulty thinking of anything else. Before I had to force myself to think of my mantra and God and not worldly thoughts. Now I had to force my mind to think of worldly thoughts and not God. Just the thought of the experience brought bliss for weeks after it happened.

Previously I had experienced various degrees of spiritual bliss but nothing as deep and complete as this. It was like what I had been reading about in the lives of great saints and mystics. Now at last I had experienced *it*, I had touched God—or He had touched me. The wonderful thing about it was that I knew it was only the beginning. Now I knew what was spiritually possible. If I continued my practice with sincerity, I could remain forever in this state—at least, theoretically. I also knew that to maintain the spiritual feeling would require great effort and spiritual grace.

Delegate Drama

One night, after several months of deep meditation, I got a strong feeling during my evening practices that it was now time for me to do some worldly service. What was the point of blissful meditation if I kept it only to myself? I had to do something for others. At that time I had no idea of what I would do but within a week of this decision I was given an opportunity. I was asked to run for the post of delegate to the 'Prisoners Problems and Needs Grievance Committee' as a representative of the prison wing where I lived.

Another happy moment

Within days of being elected my mental stress increased ten-fold. Many of the prisoners had genuine problems with no simple solution. Most prisoners didn't understand the complexity of the prison system, in fact many were illiterate, and this was a big factor in the conflicts.

I was stuck between the wrath of the prisoners and the rigidity of the prison system and the officers. I would often receive the prisoners abuse. They tended to overreact when they couldn't get what they wanted and sometimes they threatened me with violence.

Some prisoners had advised me not to take on the duty because of all the stress. Most previous delegates only remained in the position for a few weeks. I felt it was what God wanted and that my experiences in meditation must be good for more than just giving *me* pleasure. It must give me the capacity to open up more to His will and flow, thus becoming a channel for His work. I surrendered my fears and continued on.

When the intensity reached a climax, I thought my tiny brain would explode. I could not take any more hassle, abuse or pressure. I pleaded to God for help. Immediately the pressure and clash dissipated and a feeling of detachment overcame me. It was quite uncanny really—a complete change of consciousness. I could distinctly feel the change. From then on the abuse and pressure did not bother me nearly so much. This created an interesting psychological change in me.

Suddenly I was not so nearly affected by my personal pains and aversions. I had read how a person can rise above great personal hardship when they have become devoted to an ideal beyond themselves—either spiritual or social. I could understand this now. They had no personal interests to hinder them.

My experience helped me to understand what I had read about the great Indian saint, Ramakrishna. Although he was very ill with throat cancer he never bothered about it at all but continued his work as a spiritual seeker and teacher. He was in such a high spiritual state that his physical suffering did not distract him. The pain was there but the bliss of God Consciousness was much greater.

The occasional rumour that someone was out to 'get me' unsettled me a bit. Nevertheless, I carried on now that I was feeling God would look after me. It was as if God was in control instead of my small ego.

Soon after, I was elected chairman and spokesperson for the Grievance Committee. A new Prison Commissioner, Dr Vinson, had been appointed. He sincerely wanted to bring some benevolent and progressive changes to the New South Wales prison system. He had been appointed by the government after a Royal Commission into state prisons found widespread abuse and injustice.

The Grievance Committee established a good working relationship with Dr Vinson and he even gave me permission to ring him directly if I felt an issue was serious enough for him to be involved. Through Vinson's pressure, the prison Governor allowed me to hold monthly meetings with the 250 or more prisoners in our jail to discuss their grievances. This was unheard of until then and most prison officers greatly resented it. Nevertheless, much needed improvements were made, although many more still needed implementing and others were never agreed to at all.

My successes helped improve the reputation of Ananda Marga among many of the prisoners. There were always some, through jealousy or ignorance, who became hostile. Most of the prison officers felt threatened by the changes and disliked us even more.

Tim and Ross, while not being delegates, did a lot of work for prisoners generally. This earned them respect as well. Tim helped with their legal work and Ross helped with literacy. One innovation that the Grievance

Committee introduced was the creation of a job that employed an educated prisoner to help other prisoners with things they could not do well, such as fill in applications and read or write letters. Ross got that position.

Because of the time my duties took up, my meditation time was drastically reduced, particularly during the day. This disturbed me at first, but soon I began to experience Baba appearing in my meditation quite frequently, sometimes twice or three time a day. Baba seemed to be giving me inspiration to carry on with my very difficult job.

Baba Scolds

God and guru can teach in many ways, both directly and indirectly. Over time, as I practiced meditation less, the spiritual high began to fade gradually. In one special experience I learned that it was still very important to stick to proper discipline. I also felt once again that Baba was watching me closely and teaching me, even when he was physically so far away. The following experience taught me that lesson.

During the time I was a delegate I also started a movement against police verbals called 'Campaign Against Legal Malpractice' (CALM). I began by collecting information from prisoners who claimed to have been verballed, which meant I had to interview quite a few prisoners. Despite my requests, Tim and Ross said they weren't interested in helping me.

One day, I was feeling particularly despondent from the pressure of my work and the lack of support. Breaking with my usual habit of staying away from prison movies, I decided to watch a violent movie that afternoon. As a rule I would not watch movies because of the negative effect they had on my meditation and spiritual ideation. However, that day I was feeling careless and didn't want to listen to my conscience.

After watching the film I justified it by saying I would not watch such a violent film again and that there was no point dwelling on past mistakes.

Then I decided to continue the survey. I was on good terms with the first prisoner I had to interview. When I went to ask him some questions about his case, he exploded into a rage and began shouting abuse about things I had nothing to do with. The force of his anger stunned me. After about five minutes of abuse he left. I was worried that he might attack me but fortunately it did not come to that.

Feeling shaken I returned to my cell to lie down. As I was resting I had a clear realisation that this abuse had been a scolding from Baba. He was letting me know in no uncertain terms that it was not all right for me to watch violent movies. That explained the forceful abuse I had just received.

When I recovered somewhat, I gathered my courage and went to speak to another prisoner for the survey. As we were speaking, the first prisoner walked in. I was terrified he was going to abuse me again. Much to my surprise and relief, not only did he stay calm but he even supported what I was doing. He answered the survey and encouraged the other prisoner to do the same. This further convinced me that it had been Baba scolding me through the prisoner.

The Strike

After a few months of research I had collected convincing evidence of fabricated confessions and police perjury. Tim eventually pitched in at the end and wrote some good articles based on information I had collected. I arranged for one Margii outside prison, Dhruva Dimelow, to make my research known to the public. Then I organised a strike with the help of the Grievance Committee. Through the Prison Action Group and delegates in other prisons, we were able to organise a statewide strike against police verbals. The strike lasted for one day and received extensive media coverage, which highlighted this major problem.

Eventually, through our work and other campaigns outside of prison, the High Court began to voice concern about police verbals that eventually led to changes in the law.

The Hit List!

A prisoner told me a funny incident. Meals were cooked in the morning and left until 4 pm to give out to prisoners. The prisoner's job was to bring the meals to each Wing in special hotboxes. A prison officer always came with him to make sure he did his job properly.

One day he saw the prison officer taking food from the hot box. He quickly snapped at him:

"Put it back or I'll tell the Ananda Marga and they will put you on their hit list!"

The officer quickly put it back and never touched the hot box again.

For once our unjustified terrorist tag was doing some good.

The Power of Cosmic Ideation
At one jail meeting with the prisoners we were discussing the results of negotiations with the prison Governor and Officers' Union. As chairman I explained which grievances they had agreed to work on and which ones they had not. As usual some prisoners were not satisfied with what we achieved and became abusive. The meeting ended and I joined another delegate in his cell to discuss some matter.

The delegate had to go out and told me to wait until he came back. As I waited a large Maori prisoner, with arms as thick as my legs, came in and started abusing me about my role as a delegate. He was drunk on a jail brew so I tried to ignore him, knowing logic would not have any positive impression on him. He started to pull my beard. The thought of thumping him crossed my mind but his size was somewhat discouraging and there was always the problem of later retaliation. His mates might try to attack me and I would end up looking over my shoulder for an unknown enemy. I thought it was better to avoid retaliation unless absolutely necessary to defend my life.

Then he started to spit in my eyes. The situation was becoming intolerable. By God's grace the idea came to think of God. I began to repeat my mantra. A very loving feeling overcame me that I projected onto the prisoner. Suddenly he stopped abusing me and left the cell. About a minute later he returned and apologised for his behaviour. Afterwards we became good friends.

Mantra to the Rescue
There are two other similar examples where cosmic ideation saved me from a violent confrontation.

One time a normally friendly but violent prisoner stormed into my cell ready to do battle with me. He had misinterpreted what I'd said that morning and had taken offence to it. Had I gone into a defensive position a violent struggle might have ensued. Instead, I kept calm and repeated my mantra. I began to feel relaxed and calm. I kept my hands by my side to show I was not going to be hostile towards him. He immediately responded by calming down and listening to my explanation about our previous misunderstanding. We shook hands and he left.

Another incident happened when a boxer I'd been training with misunderstood a comment I made about his boxing skills. Being a proud boxer there could be nothing worse than to have his fighting skills questioned. He stormed after me and wanted a fight. Again I kept cool with my hands down and mantra up and running (quite quickly!) He calmed down and left peacefully.

Screw's Revenge

The delegates and many of the prisoners were amazed that the officers had allowed so many reforms to go ahead. We wondered when they would react. Finally, the day came when they did. It manifested in the form of a common response: an officer's strike.

For prisoners, a staff strike meant we were locked up in our cells indefinitely until prison officers came back to work. The atmosphere was especially tense as there was no exercise, no visits, solitary confinement (albeit with radio and television if you owned one) and an escort to the showers if we were lucky. During some strikes, showers were not allowed every day or even at all. A strike also meant police or senior executive officers ran the jail, which brought out even more hatred in the prisoners. They yelled abuse from their cell windows at police in the guard towers. The prisoners also yelled back and forth at each other to break the monotony of solitary confinement.

A few days into this strike, it was finally my turn for the first shower since the strike began. Up until now showers hadn't been permitted. I was escorted to the shower block with about half a dozen other prisoners. I turned on the hot and cold water to get a temperature that was comfortable. The cold water suddenly stopped running, which I meant was standing under boiling hot water. I jumped out with a yelp, as did the other prisoner in the shower block. The officers all laughed. Feeling angry I confronted one of them asking why had the cold water gone off. He played dumb and said he didn't know. Of course we all knew one of them had turned it off. They controlled the main taps.

Shanghied

The strike ended after about a week. I was disappointed when it ended. I was enjoying being alone in my cell with no one to bother me or abuse me. It was just me and God. I spent my time meditating and studying spiritual books. I felt like I was in a monastery and I enjoyed the resultant spiritual peace and bliss.

My legs were weak from lack of exercise when I first came out of my cell at the end of the strike. My vision was also strained and everything was out of focus because I was so used to only looking only a few metres away to the walls of my cell.

The delegates called a meeting of all prisoners as there was a lot of anger and talks of rioting. During the strike police had bashed some prisoners and there was general anger at being locked up unjustly for a week. A few prisoners were so angry that they wanted to burn the prison down.

We tried to calm everyone down as much as possible since we knew a riot would be just what most prison officers hoped for. They then would have an excuse to attack us and demand severe restrictions on us, including disbanding the Grievance Committee. We proposed that we go on strike as a protest against the bashing and general mistreatment.

While eating dinner that night in my cell, I heard the heavy echo of footsteps outside my door. There was a jingling of keys and the door swung open. I was sitting at my small table getting ready to take a bite out of a Ryvita biscuit covered with peanut butter and alfalfa sprouts, (grown in my cell) when I looked up to see a big burly 'screw' standing before me.

"Grab a few things, you're going!"

Quickly I put a few essentials into a pillow slip. The large officer took the pillow slip and handed it to another officer.

Being alone and surrounded by half a dozen large prison officers didn't invite rational or reasonable dialogue like, "Can I just finish my dinner?"

I never did finish that biscuit. Ross said when he saw my cell the next day he noticed a half eaten meal still on the table.

I was handcuffed and led out of the Wing amidst cries of abuse at the screws from other prisoners. I was being 'shanghaied'. This was the prison word for a punitive transfer. I asked several times where I was being taken. Finally one officer answered, "Goulburn." This was the worst jail in the state.

It would have been understandable to feel quite frightened in this situation. I was surrounded by specially trained prison officers with a reputation for violence and was being taken alone in the night to an unknown destination. But when things get difficult God is always there to smooth things out. His presence made me feel relaxed and unconcerned. Indeed, I really enjoyed the two hour trip. I was in a car and not the usual uncomfortable meat wagon, which was a big treat. In the twilight I could see 'normal' people in colourful clothes, green trees and grass, lights, houses, hills and countryside. Such a novelty!

13
Not a Merry Christmas

The sky of the external world is glittering with God's light and the sky of the inner world is also gleaming with God's effulgence.
—Baba

GOULBURN JAIL WAS THE WORST MAXIMUM SECURITY PRISON IN NEW SOUTH Wales. The officers were mostly very conservative country 'red-necks' who hated prisoners or 'scum' as they called us. Even though assaulting prisoners had been made officially illegal by the Nagle Royal Commission a few years earlier, many of these officers still favoured this form of 'discipline', and openly resented the new laws. Prisoners were still bashed in some instances, such as during strikes or when a prisoner was segregated.

When I arrived at my cell I asked for my belongings, which one officer was carrying. This request was promptly refused and I was told to "see about it in the morning." As the cell's thick steel door was slammed shut, I stared at my bare new 'home'. The room was cold and austere with the usual cot, small table and chair, a few shelves and a toilet. The entire vibration of the jail was miserable and tense.

This was the first time I'd been separated from both Tim and Ross. I found out several days later that some of the delegates, along with Tim, were shanghaied the same night. They all went together to Parramatta jail and Ross joined them a few days later. For some reason, I was the only one sent to the infamous Goulburn jail.

It was a hot November in 1981. I spent the first day and many others after, pacing up and down in a yard. The yards were all concrete with brick walls on three sides and fronted by an iron bar grid. There was one wooden bench and an open flushable toilet. When enthroned, you were in full view of all of the guards and prisoners.

As I walked up and down I noticed a group of rough looking prisoners staring at me every now and then. My experience at Long Bay in the yard flashed before me. Up to this point, I had not felt much fear or tension. I had become more confident although this did not mean I had no fear at all. Besides, I felt these prisoners were acting tough rather than being tough. Nothing happened to me so I presumed their 'heavy' looks were more bluff than intent.

The morning after my arrival I made inquiries about my belongings. No one seemed interested in helping me. The contempt here towards prisoners was very apparent. I only got my things after a persistent struggle over a few days.

I had to wait a week before I received the other items I had left in my room. The worst thing was that I had no money to buy food from the canteen. Vegetarian food did not exist here. I couldn't eat most of what was given me, so I lived mostly on the weekly ration of margarine, sugar and white bread plus some milk and boxed cereal for breakfast.

The Troublemaker

Soon after my arrival I was called before the Officer's Reception Committee. I hoped I would find out the reason for my abrupt transfer. The only answer I got was, "You're here because you are a troublemaker."

"Why?" I asked, "Did I do something wrong? Did I break some rules?"

They said I hadn't done anything legally wrong. All they knew was that my file said I was a troublemaker.

Normally prisoners are classified by a special board. During the classification process the prisoner is also interviewed and is allowed to say if they have a good reason why they shouldn't go to a particular prison (such as studies or pending court cases).

I knew I hadn't been classified yet, so why had I been transferred? And why to this place? They also could not give any satisfactory answer: "We know it's unusual, but according to your files you have been classified to come here."

I was clearly getting nowhere with the Reception Committee so I wrote to the Prison Commissioner, Dr Vinson, with whom I had been in regular contact as a delegate. Two months after my transfer I received his letter. It said, "The official reason for the transfer is easily enough stated.

The Superintendent reported that you, together with a number of other inmates, were inciting prisoners to set fire to the CIP."

Apparently, this was said to have occurred after the prison officer's strike. Of course, the other delegates and I had been trying to prevent the prisoners from burning down the jail. Once again I had been made a scapegoat on a ridiculous charge! This accusation was just a malicious act by the officers to get rid of prisoners who were bringing too many reforms into their entrenched and brutal system. Dr Vinson was unable to explain why I was classified to Goulburn without going through the normal channels.

While my experience was not pleasant, Tim's experience was much worse. He was shanghaied the same evening. He later wrote about the cruelty he experienced:

> At about 8:30 pm on Sunday evening, a day and a half after we had been let out of our cells...I was typing up my university essay for the year. There were sounds of screws moving in the Wing, but I carried on typing. Then my door opened and an executive officer said, "Right, you're going to Parramatta." He was backed up by three or four others, some wearing overalls. Surprised, I asked for a reason.
>
> "Never mind that. Are you going the easy way or the hard way?" I absorbed what was happening and put a few items in a pillow slip, picked up the typewriter and put on a jumper. The officers took and searched my things, handcuffed me and one began to drag me towards the stairs. I told him to ease up on the handcuffs, as they were cutting my wrists but he dragged me down the stairs even harder. When we got to the bottom of the stairs, I pushed him into a wall near the hot water urn and, unbalanced, he let go of the handcuffs. Other officers grabbed me from behind, pulling my hair, and dragging me to the other side of the Wing.
>
> The Wing had been fairly quiet until now, with many of the seventy people in cells silently listening and watching through the peep-holes. When the officers jumped on me there was an explosion of banging on the doors and shouting: "Leave him alone, you dogs!"

Jailhouse Drama

Rather than spend my day in the hot yard with people who had nothing better to do than fight or harass others, I found a job in the tailor shop sewing gowns for a hospital. It was a chance to earn a little extra money. In addition, I could see the countryside from the jail factory windows. It was a real treat to see greenery each day instead of the stark, bare, grey concrete walls of the prison.

It was one of the worst times I experienced in prison. I was lonely and felt oppressed by the mood of violence and cruelty. Christmas came after two months with an uninspired visit by the Salvation Army who handed us a few lollies. Life dragged on as usual with barely a break from the bleakness.

There were a few bright moments. During the time I was at Goulburn Prison I got news about the formation of a public campaign called CAADA, which stood for 'Campaign for the Acquittal of Anderson, Dunn and Alister'. It was launched by journalist and later member of parliament, Irena Dunn, with the help of Mark Dhruva. This was to become the major driving force for our vindication and was made up of Margii activists and non-Margii sympathisers. It was great to hear that we were being so well supported by people 'outside.'

Another encouraging experience was meeting jail activist, Steve Sellers. He knew a lot of the same prison activists I knew and he had a good opinion of me and the other Margiis 'inside.' He had been a delegate at his previous prison and was particularly interested in police verbals. We spent a lot of time together, which attracted some attention from the officers who saw us as two troublemakers together. We also made friends with another young prisoner who had a good heart and wanted to do something for prison reform but was a bit naive about jail politics.

Some prisoner complained to us that delegates here were lackeys for the officers and did not represent their interests. They asked if we would be their grievance delegates. Both of us were trying to get out of this jail and we didn't want to get caught up here, so we declined the offer. However, we did agree to arrange for a new election of prison delegates.

After the election it turned out that all but one of the old delegates was replaced. This caused some concern amongst the senior prison officers and the old prison delegates. The Superintendent of the prison refused to recognise the election because 'his' delegates had not run the election. Meanwhile the officers started to harass us and our naive friend was assaulted by one of the 'old' delegates. On hearing this Steve issued a threat to the ex-delegates saying we would take them all on!

Baba Speaks

Just after he issued this threat, Steve was taken to hospital due to an illness. This left me feeling very vulnerable. The officers kept on bringing false complaints and charges against me. Their aim was to have me put into segregation so they could do what they liked to me. Each time they brought a charge against me, I brought the case up to the Superintendent. By God's grace I beat every one of their charges and brought charges against them! They did not like this and started to back off a bit. Nevertheless, the tension was strong. On one side the prison officers were trying to put me in the front yards, on the other side some prisoners were out to assault me. This new drama made an already bad situation much worse.

One night while this was going on, I did my usual mediation before going to sleep. It was late and I started to feel a rush of energy through me and my head began to spin. My mind felt like it was being sucked into an abyss. I was scared. I heard loud voices in my mind that sounded like gibberish and I felt dizzy. Was I losing my mind?

Suddenly as clearly as if I'd turned on the radio, I could hear Baba talking to me above the other voices. With his characteristic accent (like what I had heard on cassettes of Baba's discourses) he said, "I don't care if (and I couldn't remember what the rest was), and I don't care if (again I couldn't remember or hear because of the loud voices), and I don't care if…"

As Baba spoke in this firm 'be strong' tone I became a bit frustrated, "Why is he lecturing me now when I'm losing my mind?" Then in final desperation and surrender I thought, "All I want is your love."

As soon as I said that, Baba stopped talking and the loud voices became silent. My head stopped spinning. Later, I realised Baba was trying to tell me not to worry about what was going on and just to be strong. If I kept faith in him, everything would be okay. And it was. About a week after this incident I was transferred to Parramatta jail where Tim and Ross were.

14
Divine Loneliness

That which makes the mind soft and strong and strenuous, so it may keep itself in a balanced state even in the condition of pain - that which perpetually creates a pleasant feeling within, is called love.

—Baba

PARRAMATTA JAIL IS AN OLD, HISTORIC BUILDING LOCATED IN AN OUTER SYDNEY suburb, that was constructed during the last century. The old steps in the first three Wings of the jail ascend gradually to accommodate shackled leg chains of convicts sent there during early settlement days. The prison is divided into two sections: an older section with an administrative block, cookhouse, chapel, visiting area, auditorium, football oval and three wings of cell blocks. The second part has three more cell wings, gym and shower block, maintenance and printing press facilities, a laundry and the infamous 'circle'—a jail within a jail for special punishment and protection of certain prisoners.

Attached to Parramatta is another walled institution called the Parramatta Linen Service, simply known as the PLS. This is where prisoners work and have their contact visits. The prison is divided by what was once the main street of Parramatta in the early days of settlement.

My first arrival there was quite an experience. As I walked through the first three Wings the atmosphere reminded me of Sydney's Kings Cross or some other sleazy place. Walking along the narrow pathway that weaves through the Wings I walked the gamut of violent looking prisoners who stood along the sides of the entrance to each Wing. They eyed us as we walked past and whispered secretly amongst themselves.

It was a totally different atmosphere from Goulburn. Although this was also a maximum security prison, the crims seemed much freer to do as they pleased. They wore whatever they wanted, they didn't have name tags and they didn't have to get gate passes to go from one area to the next. The prison officers left us alone and we only spoke to them if we needed something from them or wanted to make a telephone call.

Meeting Tim and Ross again was a joyous occasion. Jiivan (John Palmer), who had become a Margii when he was with us at Long Bay had also been shanghied because of his work as a delegate. It was also good to see the other delegates and prisoners who had been shanghaied from Long Bay.

On arrival I was taken to see the Prison Governor. He immediately threatened to have me shanghaied back to Goulburn if I caused any trouble. I assured him I had no intention of causing trouble.

I shared a cell with two other prisoners the first few days. While I had to put up with their smoking, meat eating and loud rock music, they had to adjust to my meditation and weird looking yoga postures (especially one called 'difficult tortoise posture' where I would tuck my ankles around my neck.) I thought I'd get an adverse reaction, but they quickly accepted me as one of those strange Ananda Marga people.

I was soon given my own cell and later I got a job as Wing sweeper. I settled in quite quickly, enjoying the relative freedom and relaxed atmosphere. In any jail, the atmosphere never allows you to totally relax because of the types of people in prison. While there were fewer fights at Parramatta, when they did happen they were more violent. The large amounts of heroin contributed to the increase in violence. There were far more 'crazy' crims who were likely to go off at the slightest provocation.

Murder

Within a week of my arrival two murders occurred. This concerned me especially, not because I feared for my own safety but because I might be blamed for them. I imagined them thinking, 'a prisoner arrives with a reputation as a troublemaker and a fanatical religious terrorist and one week later two prisoners are dead.'

My fears were unfounded for once and as it turned out other prisoners were arrested for the murders. One of the victims was a young prisoner who had expressed an interest in meditation. Apparently, he was murdered for resisting homosexual advances, which were not uncommon. It was such a sad waste of life.

Ross once expressed discomfort about the pressure he was feeling from one prisoner for homosexual favours. Fortunately, I knew that prisoner well and after talking with him the pressure stopped. One prisoner also tried to 'check me out' to find out if I would accommodate his desires. When I made it clear I was not inclined that way, he left me alone. Nevertheless, both incidents left me with an unpleasant feeling, particularly because I had experienced a traumatic episode of sexual abuse by a man when I was a young teenager.

We spent some years in the Parramatta maximum security jail. Generally, life was incident free but there were always exceptions. While I enjoyed 'Parra' jail I missed not being able to do more meditation or be involved with prison politics. My work as a sweeper did not allow much meditation and shanghai threats discouraged me from getting involved with another Grievance Committee. Nevertheless, God sent along some interesting experiences that showed me how much I needed Him and how much He loved me and looked after me.

Occult Forces

Prison cells host a long history of various personalities, some very strange and violent, which created an unusual atmosphere. I was especially susceptible to the vibrations around me as a result of my meditation and sensitive nature. One man was involved in the occult and gave me a distinctly eerie feeling. Whether it was because of him or because of the cell I was in, or a combination of both, I don't really know. The following experiences were strange and quite frightening.

One night a week for three weeks I experienced a strange occult attack. The first night I did meditation and lay down to sleep. After going into a half dreaming, half conscious state, I experienced a most terrifying thing. While my eyes were closed I perceived a large animal like a big cat, walking next to me. Indescribable fear swept through me as I felt its whiskers brush up against me. I felt too paralysed to move. It growled ferociously. I repeated my mantra and suddenly it was gone.

The next week I had another experience before going to sleep. This time I felt I was walking down some steps when suddenly I felt cold hands around my neck! Then I experienced being thrown down the steps. I began repeating my mantra and the experience went away. When I stopped saying my mantra, however, I felt the hands return around my neck and I was thrown down the steps again. I repeated my mantra and it stopped. Frightened, I said my mantra until I finally was able to fall asleep.

During the last occult experience I felt I was a woman and experienced being raped. I could not stop what was going on and felt very powerless and humiliated. It was similar to what had happened to me when I was thirteen, but worse. For some reason, I didn't remember to say my mantra and could not escape from the terror. This experience was so horrific I could not sleep the following nights and became exhausted.

Fortunately, during that period I had a regular visitor from Sydney, a Margii woman named Janaki. She was a herbalist and had been given permission to treat me with herbal medicines. I explained what had happened and I finally slept after she gave me some medicinal herbs.

Strange Love

Our weekend visits were the highlight of the week. Visitors were allowed to sit with us around a table and they could stay for several hours. We were allowed to take them food, although they could not bring us any. I made a special ice cream and burfi (an Indian sweet made of milk, butter and sugar.) The ice cream, which often tasted like cheese cake, was very popular. Once a crim saw me carrying an ice cream and said, "I'd kill for that!" He may not have been joking.

Many different Margiis came to visit and we would hear all the latest gossip and stories about Baba. We also met new Margiis. One new Margii was introduced to me through another woman. At first I did not take much notice of her, but then a most remarkable thing occurred with her.

The afternoon visit had ended and we started to say our goodbyes. As I said goodbye to this woman, I perceived an effulgent aura emanating from her. I thought to myself in a rather detached way that I was being shown an interesting experience of God Consciousness through her. I did not give it much thought other than that.

That evening in meditation the image of her and the radiant white aura came back very vividly. I was intrigued but a bit disturbed, as I was wanting to think about God rather than her. I thought of Baba to get my mind off her but Baba kept turning into her and then she would turn back into Baba.

The next week she came again and immediately my mantra started mentally, which normally centred me on God. This time however, the thought of her accompanied my mantra. By the end of the visit I was as high as a kite with blissful feelings. After she left my mantra continued for much of the day. This went on for the whole week until her next visit. I was beginning to feel uncomfortable and confused. I felt no physical attraction or even particular affection for her. Indeed, I hardly knew her and besides she was already in a relationship.

By this time I had decided I didn't want to become a monk but I still had no attraction to marriage or relationships. I saw them as a hindrance in coming close to God. While this is not Ananda Marga's view, I felt that it was true for me.

Nevertheless, I found being around her definitely heightened my spiritual feeling. What I felt for her was very spiritual, as if she was the Divine in a female form. Finally, I decided to tell her what was happening and suggested that she not visit me. She was inspired by what I revealed to her and wanted to continue visiting even though she made it clear she also had no special attraction for me.

After that she visited me weekly and I just enjoyed being in close proximity to her because it helped me feel close to God. I felt no passion or attachment but I wanted to serve and please her. It gave me pleasure just to see her even if she didn't speak to me. The feeling reminded me of what Margiis experienced when they were around Baba.

All good things must come to an end. Attachment and physical passion started to creep in very gradually. It got to the stage when I would start off in a detached blissful state during her visits and then begin to feel attachment and jealousy if she was not talking to me.

Interestingly, I was able to clearly notice that different chakras were affected with the different feelings I experienced. When I felt the non-attached passionless love, I experienced a sweet benevolent state in my anahata chakra region in the centre of my chest. When I felt strong attachment, jealousy and passion, I experienced crude feelings in the *manipura* chakra in the naval area and the *svadhistana* chakra in the genital region. When I experienced the latter, I would think benevolent thoughts and the sweet heart chakra feeling would come back again.

Nevertheless, the feelings increasingly degenerated into common lust and attachment. The bliss had gone and an acute and chronic depression set in. Whenever I would meditate I'd think of her, so I lost all the old peace and bliss of meditation. To not experience spiritual sweetness and bliss made life seem dry and worthless. From the time I woke to the time I slept, I felt depressed.

Prisoners asked me what was wrong because they had never seen me looking so gloomy. I was usually cheerful. But I could not explain, not even to other Margiis as I felt they would dismiss it as an ordinary worldly infatuation with a woman. I had previously experienced unrequited passion and lust for women but this was definitely not the same. She made me think of God and God made me think of her.

At one time I seriously thought of suicide but by God's grace decided against it. After three months of this chronic depression, it came to an end as suddenly as it had started. One day I woke up and decided I was sick of being depressed and was not going to be depressed any more—and I wasn't! It was all most remarkable.

Reflecting on what had happened later, I came to the conclusion that God was teaching me that marriage was not an obstacle to him. By practicing the spiritual love he had given me, I could experience him and serve him in the form of a wife. I realised that a wife could, and should, be viewed as an expression of God and served with that ideation. I imagined that I could feel great reverence and even some worship because she was a personification of God, rather than just a person fulfilling my own personal desires and needs.

The experience also taught me that the true nature of spiritual love is benevolence and altruism. It is unconditional and not dependent on how the partner responds. When I felt my mind going down to a less exalted level and losing the spiritual feeling, I remembered these qualities and the spiritual love would return very quickly. I would feel blissful again when I stopped thinking about what I wanted or what I was feeling and instead concerned myself with what my beloved wanted or needed then.

Another feature of this love was that it radiated out all around to everyone, not just to the beloved, although I felt a special fondness for her. These realisations benefited me greatly when I eventually did get married.

Divine Loneliness

After that experience life went back to normal for a while. However, a deep discontentment gradually overcame me. I was feeling a lot of love and compassion for others and this manifested in a strong desire for close friendship. In my life I had not had many, if any, really close friends but now I was feeling this need very strongly. One Margii man used to visit me and we began to feel quite close. I was thinking how nice it would be to have a friend I could relate to on a deep level, about personal and spiritual matters. Then about a week after we had formed some brotherly bond, I received the news that he had drowned in a rafting expedition. I felt deep pain and had no option but to surrender it to God and look for someone else.

I gradually became friendly with a prisoner who had been initiated into Ananda Marga meditation. We got on well together and started to deepen our friendship. He was put into segregation and I never saw him again.

"God, what are you doing to me?" I thought. Whenever I get close to anyone God seemed to take them away from me. I even had a pet cat in jail that I grew very fond of but he disappeared. The pangs of loneliness were beginning to grip me intently. I felt God's presence strongly but my desire was for worldly closeness, not that seemingly intangible spiritual companionship.

Weeks dragged on as I looked for some relief from this great burden of loneliness. Finally, I decided only God could relieve it. I tried to turn to God but He seemed to keep at a distance.

For two days I became obsessed with coming close to God. All I thought about was God. My mantra continued most of the day. I wanted tactual contact. Only that would give me satisfaction. But alas He had other plans and my pain continued unrelentingly.

I continued to pursue human friendship as well as my relationship with God. In retrospect I can see that loneliness is something that has always both bothered me and helped me. It helped me by making me feel that there was no one else but God and forced me to search deep into my meditation. But the loneliness still caused pain and sadness.

The Cat

One time at Parramatta I came across a dead kitten. It seemed like the kitten had just been born and I wondered if it was dead because of a miscarriage or if some sadistic prisoner or prison officer had killed it. It was a painful sight and I looked around for its mother. Then I saw her and she was crying. She cried more piteously as I walked towards her. I had a sense that she was reaching out to me, as I reached out to her. Without a word from me, she seemed to hear my mental call and ran to me. I could sense her distress and despair as I picked her up and stroked her. She began to purr and cry at the same time. I could strongly sense the support and comfort she was feeling. It was really very moving and my whole being melted with sympathy and empathy.

I continued to caress and stroke her for some time her until I realised it was time for my noon meditation. Such a look of pain and despair was in her eyes as I put her down. My meditation was distracted that day as I thought of the cat's pain and felt sadness that I could not have helped her somehow.

This experience reinforced in me Baba's teachings on Neo-Humanism, the concept that all forms of life experience pleasure and pain and hold their life as dear to themselves as we humans do. We must respect and care for all animals and plants as well as other humans.

This incident reminds me of a story I heard about koalas in a bush fire. Firefighters came across a mound of koalas. They were all huddled together so that only those on the outside would be killed and those on the inside would be sheltered from the deadly flames. When the firefighters arrived, the koalas ran over to them crying and clung onto their legs.

The next day I saw the cat and she seemed to be back to her normal self. Only God knows what inner trauma and scars were left from the death of her kitten. Her recovery reminded me that no matter how terrible or cruel life may seem, pain can be overcome with time and we can move on.

This realisation helped me cope with the struggles I experienced in jail, and afterwards. Just as a single event or even a single word can cause much pain, so too they can cause much happiness or relief.

Divine Dance

After one particular visit from a Margii woman who worked for women's rights, I felt depressed as I realised how women are oppressed. Realisation after realisation dawned on me about the unfair and miserable plight many women face, as well as the often gloomy plight of humanity in general.

I was locked in my cell for the night, still feeling this universal pain. I picked up a copy of *Time* magazine to distract my mind from the torment. On the front cover was a man lying dead in a pool of blood. My weary heart could take no more and I burst into tears as I felt misery all around me. Everywhere there was suffering, personally and socially. I felt totally miserable. When I regained some composure I decided to sing kiirtan (chanting a mantra aloud).

Soon I began to clearly feel God's presence. I was desperate for God's love but the intensity I longed for seemed just out of reach. Soon I began to cry and the tears that poured down my cheeks expressed my joy at the closeness of God as well as the acute pain of separation. I could sense God so closely but I wanted to merge with God completely, leaving behind my painful separate existence. I realised God was playing with me but I could not, or would not, get past his play to find Him. A sense of surrender finally surfaced out of my deep frustration. I accepted that my time for a deeper contact was not now.

Romance Fulfilled

Most of my years at Parramatta jail were physically more comfortable and relaxed than the previous years, but they were emotionally very trying. I was gripped with all sorts of personal desires, fears, emotions and longings with unusual force. Normally, I might have taken an easy option and escaped them with some worldly distraction, but there were few avenues of escape in prison.

An image kept coming into my mind, particularly in meditation and when I was falling asleep, of wearing a suit of armour in an old castle. I was in a very dark room or cell feeling very tired and weary from constant battles that I had to engage in every time I went out of that cell. I vividly saw the dents in my armour. All this represented my seemingly endless emotional and spiritual struggles. The desire for God had become intense but so too had the obstacles that arise in attaining Him.

I began to daydream about a future marriage that would express the spiritual ideals I had experienced. I decided that such a marriage would not be a hindrance to my spiritual growth and I began to keep an eye out for the 'right' woman. Fortunately I had many visitors but the search still seemed to take a long time. On a few occassions I was tempted to return interest shown to me by some of the women I met but I knew that once I got out of jail I would not want to marry them. So I resisted forming a close relationship.

Finally, I met Jenny Fitzgerald during a visit with several other Margiis. Her spiritual name was Jayanti, which means 'victorious.' She had moved down to Sydney as a lawyer and was working for the Australian Law Reform Society. One of the cases she was researching for them was our wrongful incarceration. In her spare time she worked for CAADA, our support group.

After her first visit I felt she was a strong possibility but I did not let myself jump to conclusions too soon. She visited me regularly though, and it soon became apparent there was mutual attraction. A relationship quickly followed. Much of my loneliness dissipated as a result of her regular visits and our close conversations. The romantic feelings I felt for her clouded the deeper void I felt in me from being separate from God. In time the pain of separation resurfaced to haunt me and the eternal game of hide and seek with God continued.

Past Lives

During one meditation I had a clear vision of what appeared to be a past life. I was walking across a field with another person. In the background was an old castle on the edge of a cliff overlooking the sea. It was cold and misty with a Medieval English or European feel. As we walked we communicated telepathically. I felt that I was a person involved with occult powers.

Later a clairvoyant told me I had had a life in the Middle Ages where I was developed occult powers as a sorcerer's apprentice. It was my misuse of these occult powers that resulted in my imprisonment now, in *this* lifetime. This story correlated to my early experience. Whether or not this is true I cannot say but I can relate to it nonetheless.

The Video

At one time a prisoners' club that we belonged to invited a video production engineer to come in to show us how to make videos. We got the idea to make one about our case and to smuggle it out to CAADA. To our pleasant surprise the video teacher had the same idea and quietly suggested we do a similar thing. So one day we stayed after the meeting and he made a video of us explaining how we had been framed. This footage was used in a brilliant video programme called *Frame-up* by Irena Dunn. *Frame-up* was shown throughout Australia in alternative film houses and to interested groups. It became a major tool in our campaign.

Baba's Whirlwind Tour

Meanwhile since Baba acquittal and release from prison he had been touring Europe, Taiwan, Philippines and Jamaica which was a wonderful experience for the Margiis. The government of Australia, like the USA and England, would not give him a visa. I think this was because of his stand against capitalism and Ananda Marga's link to the Hilton Bombing.

Baba had predicted that communism would soon die a natural death, because it was fundamentally an unnatural concept. However in the future capitalism would "burst like a fire cracker" and this would be preceded by a global depression.

He was also to give some talks in the late eighties on the coming poleshift. This would cause not only great calamities and destruction, but leading up to it there would be an increase in weather changes as well as an increase in the psychic speed of the human mind. Many people, he said, would not cope with these radical changes resulting in an increase in mental problems such as depression, confusion, negativity and suicide.

However, after the pole shift people's fascination for materialism will be changed to a fascination for spirituality. Baba said society will then make great advances and people would become much happier and progressive.

15
Personalities

People have one thing in common: they are all different.
—Robert Zend

OF ALL THE MAXIMUM SECURITY PRISONS WE EXPERIENCED, PARRAMATTA WAS EASILY the best. The freedom compared to the other jails was remarkable. An unwritten policy was to let prisoners do as they please within the prison as long as there was no serious breach of security. This, unofficially, allowed illegal drug use and officers allegedly peddling drugs inside the prison. Prisoners were smuggled small amounts in through their contact visits but large amounts, usually of hash or heroin, came from prison officers. While I was there an officer was convicted of drug smuggling.

Besides the long contact visits, which were the highlight of each week, clubs we were allowed to form. Since religious worship was allowed in the form of a club, we were able to organise weekly group meditations with visiting acharyas and Margiis. One memorable gathering was a special celebration at the end of the year. There were almost 20 acharyas and Margiis and it went all afternoon.

It was great. The kiirtan (chanting *Baba Nam Kevalam*) was divine, like a soothing stream on a dry summer's day. I noticed that the prison guards posted to watch over us were absentmindedly humming the tunes. (But I don't think they knew that it meant 'Love is all there is.') I even thought they looked a bit blissful at the end of it.

Another club that I was involved with was the 'Parramatta Resurgence Club,' which brought in guest speakers each week. One visitor was a Margii woman called Jaivanii (Kerry Lawrence). She was a professional masseuse and gave an inspiring talk and demonstration on massage, Shiatsu and bone manipulation. Afterwards I told her I'd like to learn more. She agreed to send me more material on the subject and said I could telephone her anytime for assistance. She often came out to visit us so I had the opportunity to confer with her then as well. From then on I began treating prisoners with massage and other techniques. Word soon got out and I could not meet the demand for my services, usually for help with sporting injuries or stress and drug-related problems.

Heads and Hearts

Ross, Tim and I got on quite well. In fact, some long term prisoners commented on how they admired the way we stuck together and rarely saw us arguing. We did differ on many things but not usually in public. What kept us together was our common spiritual ideal as well as our shared passion to clear our names.

Although we got on well, our personalities were different. Ross and Tim were similar in that they were, in my opinion, more intellectual, although Tim much more so than Ross.

Tim lived more from his head while I operated from my heart. Ross I guess lived in both, fluctuating between the two. Ross was very much affected and disturbed by the gross injustice of our case and his incarceration. Sometimes when I spoke to Ross about our predicament he would lose his temper with frustration at being in jail for something he didn't do. Tim also voiced his frustrations about being in jail, especially after the inquest. This was uncharacteristic of Tim who, by nature, was very reserved and rarely showed his feelings.

While I was not bothered much about our case, I fretted and worried much more about personal relationships, especially when I began to develop one myself. I had relatively little difficulty in accepting my plight as God's play but I couldn't surrender so easily when it came to personal matters such as relationships or the battle of keeping my mind high in a degenerate place like jail.

Being an eternal optimist, I always thought the next avenue for our release would be victorious, which kept my spirits up. Ross was much more pessimistic, while Tim was a mixture of both at different times. Of some small comfort to me was the realisation that we were not the only ones suffering from a gross miscarriage of justice. Several other prisoners we met were undergoing the same fate. It is a sad indictment of our so-called justice system.

What the Stars Said

While I was at Longbay, I developed an interest in palmistry that later expanded into astrology and graphology. As my knowledge of astrology developed, I sometime joked about our different personalities in astrological terms. Astrology explained, to some extent, why the three of us got along so well. Interestingly, all three of us had a predominance of earth and water qualities (in contrast to the other two qualities of fire and air). This gave us a tendency for persistence, practicality and emotionally sensitivity, although these qualities were expressed very differently in each of us.

My Cancerian Sun explains my emotional vulnerability regarding personal matters while my Capricorn Ascendant gives me a more serious, restrained and at time shy personality. This sometimes contradicts my emotionally impulsive side. My Taurus Moon helped me remain emotionally stable throughout the many changes of prison life and added to the stubbornness of my nature. (I was born on 15 July, 1955 at 5:17pm in Perth, for the astrologically inclined.)

Ross's Capricorn Sun and Virgo Moon explain his down-to-earth nature, his many practical skills and attention to detail along with his tendency towards worry and pessimism. His Pisces Ascendant gives a sweet and somewhat shy appearance and a heightened sensitivity.

Tim's Taurus Sun with Scorpio Ascendant and Scorpio Moon explain his very practical, intense, and private personality. All that Scorpio energy gives him great tenacity and the ability to research deeply into matters. It also gave rise to a stubborn, argumentative side that often clashed with authority, both in prison and with our lawyers. He also sometimes argued with Ross and me. We could be quite stubborn as well, but not as often as Tim.

Tim had a great intellect that was constantly absorbed in fighting for our cause. Ross and I joked at how Tim would not go anywhere without his clipboard holding pen, paper and our case documents. He would amaze our lawyers with his insight into legal matters. Most of the submissions and advice that came from us originated from Tim. We would make a few suggestions and changes and not much more. I was quite happy to let Tim carry most of the case as I knew he could do a better job than I could. He also seemed to like being in control of things which is a typical Scorpio trait! I thanked both God and Tim for not having to do it all myself.

When talking to a prisoner about our differences, Tim remarked, "Paul is more inclined to spiritual things and is more of an emotional person. He can be swamped by emotions, goes up and down and becomes moody. When depressed he becomes very withdrawn. " A typical Cancerian!

"Ross and I are more political in outlook. Ross is a more contained person generally. He is also very practical with a good systematic intellect."

Despite these big differences in our personalities, the prison guards,

Margiis at Parramatta Prison chapel:
(Left to right) Me, Babu, Ross, Tim and John Palmer.
We were more free at Parramatta and could
hold regular group meditations.

the prisoners and the media often looked on us as one entity. It was all too easy for them to see us as mindless fanatics without any personality of our own. If one did something then we had all done it. If we tried to say about some incident, "It wasn't me who did it but one of the other two," a common response was, "What's the difference?"

This de-personalisation annoyed us at times and we looked forward to the day when our independent personalities could again be appreciated by others.

Friends

Some of my other close friends were men who became Margiis in jail: John Palmer (Jiivan), Walter Maresh (Shakti), Garry Purdy (Ganesh) and Madhusudhan. I had warm and happy times with all of them. John

Margiis with visitors at the annual Parramatta Gala Day: (Top, from left): Georgina (CAADA), Tim, Me, Amrshta and Kerry (CAADA), Garry Purdy. (Seated): Ross with his future wife, Jenny, and Madhusudhan with his wife and the jail-concieved baby.

Palmer liked sparring with me. Often when we visited each other we greeted each other with punches and kicks and rolled around our cells fighting each other. At the end we would laugh and slap each other on the back as puzzled prisoners looked on wondering what to make of us. John, like the others, was in jail for violent crimes.

Garry was a very dynamic and optimistic person who despite the jail system, did his best to rehabilitate himself by attending courses and reforming his character. Madhusadan was more secretive and therefore harder to get to know. He once told me how he bribed a jailer to allow his girlfriend into his cell. They conceived their child who's age was less than his years in prison.

Walter was a serious but big-hearted person who had a sad story to tell. He had made an arrangement with his wife that if ever they were caught for their robberies they would say she was forced into it. They made this agreement to make sure that she would be able to raise their young daughter. In the end they were arrested and stuck to their agreement. As a result Walter's wife was released on a good behaviour bond.

Later, a film maker approached her about making a movie about her life of 'forced' crime, according to Walter. Apparently she turned nasty and began to say that it was all true and that Walter was violent towards her. And that he was a Nazi! A film called 'Hostage' was made about their story. It was shown on television just before Walter was due for parole. He escaped from jail to protest about what he saw as lies in the film, before giving himself up. He was deported to Germany, his country of origin. Years later he was on television again. He had come back illegally to Australia to see his daughter who was now a teenager. A television station arranged for the meeting before he gave himself up to the immigration authorities for deportation.

16
The Hilton Bombing Inquest

Struggle is the essence of life. Yours should be a pauseless struggle against corruption, hypocrisy and animality. -Baba

NEARLY FOUR AND A HALF YEARS AFTER THE HILTON HOTEL EXPLOSION, A Coroner's Inquest was finally held to investigate the deaths of the three bomb victims. The fact that it took this long to hold an inquest seemed very suspicious to us. Normally, a Coroner's Inquest into the cause of death occurs within days, or weeks at most, after the death occurred. I suspected that the inquest was held largely because of the efforts of Terry Griffiths, one of the policemen injured from the blast. He believed we were innocent and was trying to uncover the real perpetrators. CAADA had also campaigned for years to have an investigation into the bombing. We wanted to clear our names. Even though we weren't charged with the Hilton Bombing we were definitely linked to it through media and police speculation, innuendo and outright slander. The following article is an example.

> Members of a religious sect set off the Hilton Hotel bomb blast which killed three people. Sheather said yesterday the police knew who were responsible. He said he was confident those responsible would eventually be charged. 'We knew who did it from the first day after the bombing but lack of evidence to stand up in court had prevented us from making arrests,'

> Inspector Sheather said. 'We know three and possibly four individuals were involved."
> Bill Jenkins, 'Police Know The Hilton Bombers'
> *The Daily Mirror.* 14 February, 1979.

This article appeared just before the first trial. We thought cynically the well-timed police announcement was intended to prejudice the jury and I believe it did! Sheather was obviously referring to us, based on Seary's Committal evidence. He claimed to have known since the bomb went off that it was us. However, an article just before our arrest in the *Sun-Herald* of 11 June, 1978 contradicted him.

> Security Chiefs believe they know the identity of the terrorists responsible for the Sydney Hilton bomb outrage. They believe the bombers are a young man and a girl, both members of the Ananda Marga religious sect.

But then, after all the prejudicial media coverage had done its damage, Superintendent Reg Douglas, head of Security at the Hilton Hotel at the time of the explosion, admitted on Channel Seven's national current affair programme, *Willesee At Seven,* in February 1980, two years after the bombing:

> We're in the same position now as we were then. There just isn't any evidence to even question anybody...We've got no evidence to point the finger at anybody. We haven't even got any suspects.

These contradictions by the security men only served to confirm our belief, and that of many others, that we were being made scapegoats for the Hilton bombing. Evidence was growing that only security forces had anything to gain from the bombing. The bombing was probably an internal job by the security agencies themselves:

> In objective analysis, the only group seemingly to have gained by that bombing has been ASIO and the Special

Branches, who were under public pressure at the time. In the investigations taking place, has any attempt been made to determine whether or not the bombing was a bungled attempt by any section of the security forces to justify their existence—that it was intended to scare, but backfired due to the unfortunate involvement of the garbage disposal unit?

Bob Hogg, State Secretary of the Victorian Labour Party, quoted in the *The Australian*, 14th March 1978

Court Politics

When we heard about the inquest we wanted to attend in order to clear our names and, hopefully, find new evidence by discrediting Seary. CAADA made a large submission for us to attend so as "to take this most appropriate opportunity to clear ourselves once and for all of this unfounded allegation. Only then can our own case be looked at with eyes unprejudiced by the Hilton crime."

We and CAADA felt it was essential to clear ourselves of the Hilton outrage in order to get an inquiry into the Cameron conspiracy convictions. Although we had an appeal lodged with the High Court of Australia, we didn't have a lot of hope about it. Still, we had to exhaust this avenue before the Attorney General would look at holding a special inquiry into our case.

At first our application to attend the Hilton Coroner's Inquest was opposed by the police on the grounds that there was nothing to link us with the Hilton bombing. The police officer assisting the Coroner, Sgt Mason, made a public statement to this effect. The Coroner, Magistrate Norman Walsh, also stated, "I have been assured that there will not be any evidence led to implicate these people."

Some of our supporters thought after hearing Mason and Walsh's statements that we shouldn't attend the inquest because, in effect, we had been cleared of the bombing. We still felt allegations could be made against us. Moreover, it was an opportunity to get at Seary again. By now we had better ammunition to use against him in the witness box. Loaded with this we hoped to get better and new evidence that would further destroy his credibility and strengthen our chances of an inquiry.

Unfortunately, it soon became apparent that we were not the only ones who wanted our attendance at the Coroner's Hilton Inquiry. Roger Court, QC, replaced Sgt. Mason and in May made a statement to the Coroner:

"Your Worship, for the record might I say that Anderson, Alister and Dunn certainly appear in my brief, and indeed there is a possibility that a *prima facie* case might be established against one or more or them."

This sudden about face had ominous signs for us. They were going to use the inquest to try and make a case *against* us.

Court had the same evidence as Mason, which was only Seary's year-old testimonies, which we thought were so inconsistent that they lacked any credibility to be used against us. In addition, CAADA had provided volumes of documents in our favour, including statements by people who had spent time with me in Adelaide at the time of the Hilton explosion. These alibis should have in themselves destroyed Seary's allegations that I was involved in the Hilton bombing. How could I be in two places, 1500 kilometres apart, at the same time?

We do not know why Court was allowed to take over from Mason. He had been a prosecutor in the Cameron conspiracy case that lead to our conviction. Later he opposed us again during our appeal. He continually supported the case built around Seary's conspiracy story. His support of Seary's evidence was so consistent it almost seemed he was Seary's lawyer. No one could understand why Court was allowed to represent the government again at the Coroner's Inquest for the Hilton Bombing, which was supposedly a separate affair. In this role, he was meant to be impartial and simply acting as an assistant to the Coroner. Some of the media were equally puzzled and suspicious of the sudden turn around.

Let the Show Begin!

We were not only allowed to attend the inquiry, they were requesting our presence. For the next two weeks we went through the normal stress of waking early in the morning, being shipped out in the meat wagons and 'welcomed' home in the evenings with a full strip search. For a while I found it degrading and humiliating but as I got used to it, I didn't care. What little pride and modesty I had left was ripped away.

At the beginning of the inquest, Ananda Marga, CAADA and the

Prisoners Action Group staged a demonstration and street theatre called the 'Hilton Bombing Show'. People dressed as spies and clowns and acted out the ridiculous drama. They made a true circus out of a claim made by respected journalist, Evan Whitton, implying that the Coroner would have to have the police jumping through hoops to get around the inconsistencies of the inquest.

As usual there were many journalists and quite a few people from the public attending the Inquest. Michael Adams and Helen Barry represented Ross and I, while John Batten and Robyn Lansdowne appeared for Tim. The inquest began on the 17th of September, 1982 with an opening address by Roger Court inviting members of the public to come forward if they had any information related to the bombing.

Tim wrote the following to describe our first day at the Inquest:

> We were taken, handcuffed, out of the van in the basement up into a sort of concrete tomb that passed for a holding cell. Police who'd taken our biros and other items, so that we couldn't use them in the van, now handed them over to police at the cell area, so we couldn't use them in the cell. I made a brief struggle and retained my glass's case, and so won some instant resentment from the cops. Some of them hated to give in on even the smallest things and they remember such insights when making little things harder for you at the next opportunity.
>
> We paced up and down in the bare cell, a few steps long, did some push-ups, tried climbing the walls of the narrow alcove that held toilets: anything to occupy ourselves till court began. Just before 10 am we were taken through an adjoining court, through a carpeted corridor used by the magistrates, and into the packed Coroner's Court. Large cops sat on either side of each of us as we took positions behind the Bar Table and our lawyers. We were reasonably relaxed, as we were not facing any charges, but the courtroom mixture of cops, Special Branch, lawyers, journalists, and the public was tense and expectant... We had our lawyers near us and Roger Court was at the far left of the Bar table, flanked by Geoff Graham for the Police

Commissioner, a barrister for one of the Hotel employees, our lawyers and others led by Barry Hall for the Police Association and ex-cop, Terry Griffiths. A jury of six was empanelled.

(Tim Anderson, from his book, *Free Alister, Dunn and Anderson*)

Except for one or two days, I attended all of the inquest. Tim and Ross attended less because of study and disdain, respectively. As far as Ross was concerned the inquest was set up to scapegoat us for the Hilton bombing. One night Ross showed me an article sent by his parents from the prestigious *Age* newspaper in Melbourne. In effect, the article said the inquest would find a *prima facie* case against us, but we would not be charged. This would prevent any further investigation into the Hilton matter while leaving us still to take the blame. The article was written a week before the inquest began.

"The whole thing is like a Moscow show trial," lamented Ross. He couldn't believe how blatant it was that we were going to be made into the scapegoats, despite strong evidence in support of us. Ross also worried that if he went to trial for the Hilton bombing he would be convicted. He and Tim had both been in Sydney on the day of the bombing. Tim had even been inside the building delivering a protest letter from Ananda Marga to the Indian Prime Minister.

Tim did not express any particular concern, but then again he often did not express his feeling to us except when he felt very strongly about something.

The inquiry seemed more like a circus to me and I found it hard to take seriously. While I shared Ross's belief about the outcome, I wasn't concerned. My alibi was solid and there was no possibility of a police verbal at this trial. Seary's word was all there was against us. My only real concern was the worry it would cause my parents if we were committed to trial.

Going into court each day was enjoyable from the point of view that I got to see many of my friends who were sitting in the back row behind us. Occasionally we could speak to them, much to the annoyance of the court guard.

Inquest Witnesses

The only witness other than Seary that was significant was Terry Griffiths, one of the police injured in the bomb blast. He gave evidence of his experience of the horrific explosion and the wounds and injuries he received there. Griffiths, who had now left the police force due to his injuries, had done a lot of work personally to find out who had really done the bombing. His evidence painted an entirely new picture of the bombing. Griffiths' story confirmed the theory that was prevalent among many people that the NSW Special Branch had done the bombing themselves in order to justify its continued existence.

Prior to the Hilton bombing the New South Wales Government had been considering disbanding its Special Branch (the state security force), following the disbanding of the similar Special Branch in South Australia. New South Wales Special Branch was rife with accusations of illegal spying on government officials and leftist groups and there was a general sentiment that it had abused its powers by spying on innocent people rather than real terrorists.

Many people theorised that Special Branch had themselves planted the bomb in a rubbish bin on the sidewalk outside the Hilton and had intended to also discover and disarm it in order to prove that they were needed to protect the people from terrorism. The theory went that, due to a miscalculation by Special Branch, innocent garbage men had arrived at the scene to empty the bin earlier than expected and were blown up when the bomb exploded in the garbage compactor of their truck.

Griffith presented evidence for the first time in support of this theory. He claimed that the private secretary of an unnamed Australian senator told Griffith that he had spoken to an ASIO agent who had said an army bomb disposal vehicle was waiting in the city and Special Branch were observing the hotel from nearby as part of a prearranged action.

Griffith also gave evidence suggesting that even the then Prime Minister of Australia, Malcolm Fraser, may have known about the bungled attempt.

He also said that a man called William Reeve-Parker had told him that an army officer had admitted planting the bomb by switching rubbish bins 24 hours earlier. A statutory declaration by Reeve-Parker was shown to the court.

A Special Branch officer told Griffiths that his colleagues were observing the Hilton when the bomb went off and had tried to warn the police who were guarding the hotel on regular duty with a phone call. Griffiths said that he inferred the warning call had been an "attempt to save our lives," but that it also revealed security force involvement in the bombing.

A stunned courtroom, including us, listened in silence as Mr Griffiths gave this startling evidence. Even more startling was Court's reaction to this evidence. Rather than investigate his claims, as one would expect him to do, Court attacked Griffiths' evidence by bringing in Special Branch and police officers to contradict him.

Court said Reeve-Parker "was certainly not on my list" of witnesses to be called, despite Griffiths' assertion that the man could identify the person who placed the bomb. Why Court did not call Reeve-Parker is something only Court can properly answer. Court claimed to be impartial but we thought his reaction to Griffiths' evidence proved there was no genuine concern to find the Hilton bomber(s). He clearly regarded Griffiths' unexpected evidence as an annoyance. The media followed Court's lead and also barely commented on Griffiths' important testimony.

It certainly seemed that the whole inquest had indeed been set up to give credence and support to Seary's evidence that made us the scapegoats for the Hilton bombing, exactly as the Melbourne *Age* newspaper had predicted a week before the inquest began.

Enter Seary

The moment that everyone had been waiting for finally arrived when Seary stepped into the witness box. We wanted him there to extract more vital evidence to hopefully strengthen our case for an inquiry into our convictions. The public and media just wanted to see this mysterious man whom they had heard so much about, mostly in unflattering terms. However, it seemed Court (and Coroner Walsh) wanted him for the purpose of ending the inquest with a *prima facie* case against us. Court was probably eager to get to Seary to draw attention away from Griffiths comments and on to the three of us.

Court began by supporting Seary's assertion that he'd been involved in a 'military wing' of Ananda Marga (ie, the Social Service group, which I had been running at the time.) Our objections to the phrase 'military wing' were over-ruled by Walsh. Court then repeated the phrase several times. "As if to spite us," Tim sarcastically remarked.

Seary recited his old allegations that Ross and I had confessed to the Hilton bombing. It all seemed a bit 'ho-hum.' Seary had said all this several times before at the Committal Hearing and trials. No charges were ever brought against us then and we didn't see how charges could now be laid considering there was no new evidence.

Seary made his allegations more implausible this time by retreating from his own central allegation by now saying that it all "could have been bravado". In the trials Seary had given detailed accounts of an actual event, but now he said he had doubts about whether we were lying or telling the truth! Perhaps now he knew that I had witnesses to prove I was in Adelaide and wanted to distance himself from his earlier claims. Whatever the reason, it destroyed any little credibility his Hilton allegation may have ever had.

We started to feel even better about our chances when our lawyers did a brilliant cross examination. They showed that in Seary's first 'Hilton' record of interview, he had simply memorised a 1600-word passage from his own journal rather than telling directly what he claimed had happened only a few days earlier. Seary strongly denied this, saying that he wrote and spoke the same way. Our lawyer remarked that the real reason he had had to memorise his testimony was because "it was not true and learning it by heart was Seary's way of making sure of it."

Magistrate Walsh was obviously displeased when it was further revealed that Seary had been secretly paid $6,000 by the New South Wales police after we were convicted. Walsh then refused further questions on Seary's financial gains. He also would not allow medical and psychiatric records that would have shown his mental disturbance and unreliability.

Seary was a cunning witness. He recited his testimony without a flicker of guilt or uncertainly, even when he told the most outrageous lies. One of our lawyers, Tom Molomby, wrote: "Seary is an extraordinary witness...Through this whole episode, he is exposed not only as a liar but a liar of extraordinary daring and skill."

On Wednesday, October 13th, after Seary's cross-examination had been completed, Court recommended to Walsh that the inquest be terminated and the jury discharged. He said the Coroner (Walsh) should find a *prima facie* case against Ross and I and also that "the evidence possibly discloses" a conspiracy between us and Tim. While we had known that this might happen, particularly because of the media reports and the way the things were going in court, it was still a bit of a shock.

To make it worse, Walsh went totally against normal practice and reneged on an agreement with lawyers to allow submissions before ending the inquest. Rather than hearing recommendations from all the lawyers present he simply adopted Court's recommendations. This was an outrage and our lawyers were angry. Walsh knew about my Adelaide alibi yet did not allow any of this evidence to be heard though it would have directly refuted Seary's accusations. He didn't even make any reference to it. He also should have allowed submissions by our lawyers as a principle of natural justice. In effect we had been condemned by Seary's implausible allegations without the right to reply.

The public were equally shocked and disgusted by the sudden events with one calling out:

"What a farce!" and, "Bring in a lie detector!"

The gallery booed and hissed. Ross being unable to contain his anger and disbelief jumped up when Walsh said, "I terminate the inquest."

Ross said in a nervous and angry voice, "Your Worship, wait a minute. This man (pointing to Court) has in his possession evidence that can prove that Richard Seary is a liar."

Coroner Walsh ordered, "Sit down."

But Ross ignored him and continued, "Are you telling me that…"

"Please sit down," interrupted Walsh. "You're not doing yourself any good, please sit down."

Undeterred Ross continued, "We had to fight to get into this inquest. I want to speak the truth here today…"

Walsh snapped, "Look, if you don't sit down I'll have you taken out of the room. The inquest has now been terminated."

A woman in the gallery called out, "Bring in the lie detector!"

Ross continued: "I want to speak!"

Coroner Walsh: "Please sit down!"

Ross was still standing, "… something that hasn't been stated in this court before…"

Walsh cut off Ross again and ordered, "Take the prisoner out would you please, Sergeant."

The woman from the gallery yelled out again, "Bring in a lie detector!"

Walsh ordered: "Madam, you can leave the room straight away, please."

Meanwhile Ross was being dragged out of the courtroom still shouting, "I'm prepared to do a lie detector test!"

After the inquest ended Tim and I were taken back to the corridor before we joined Ross and were then taken back to our cells. As I walked through the crowded courtroom, I passed a journalist I knew. She looked very upset by what had happened, so I told her reassuringly, "Don't worry, it will be all right."

It was ironic that I was trying to cheer *her* up, I still had an underlying optimism that in the end everything would be fine, by the grace of God. I thought this accusation would cause a delay, but it would not prevent our eventual release. Delays were an unpleasant feature of our case, which I'd come to tolerate.

Ross was very upset and very angry with Court and Walsh. Although it was unlikely we'd be committed to trial, he was afraid that if we were, we would be convicted and put away for a very long time. Our parents and supporters were also upset. There never seemed to be any end to the injustice and persecution we were being put through.

The prison officers showed a lot of contempt towards us after the inquest, as if it proved what they had always suspected, that we really were terrorists.

Up to the end of the inquest many of the officers had given up on the idea of us as terrorists and started to believe we were probably innocent. That all disappeared in one swoop after the inquiry. Again we had to put up with their slander, negativity and victimization.

Lie Detector

A year later Ross took a lie detector test in March 1983. The questions were about the Hilton and Cameron conspiracy charges. Ross answered no to all these allegations. A report on the test stated:

"It is the opinion of the examiner that he was telling the truth to the above listed questions."

In mid 1983 the New South Wales Government passed a bill banning the use of lie detectors. This prevented us from using these results. Seary never agreed to a lie detector test. I'm not surprised.

Tim tried in his own way to get justice by sending a complaint against Court to the New South Wales Bar Association. He cited nine breaches of Bar rules in Court's behavior at the inquest, especially claiming that Court should never have agreed to act as Counsel assisting the Coroner when he had been the prosecutor in our previous case.

But nothing came of it except a curt reply from the Bar saying, "The Bar Council has resolved that the complaint be dismissed." No reason was given. In fact, shortly after his complaint, Roger Court was made a judge of the New South Wales District Court.

Twelve years after the inquest the New South Wales Government released to the public documents related to the Hilton bombing. These papers showed that the security forces had withheld documents that would have helped us in our case. Nothing has been done about it. Nor has a Royal Commission ever been held into the unsolved bombing, despite repeated calls from various concerned individuals, politicians and groups.

After the inquest, journalist, lawyer and supporter Tom Molomby wrote:

> It is timely to ask—though the media have not done so—what is going on? How is it that an inquest can be terminated, and enormous prejudicial publicity generated against three people on the basis of evidence which the police themselves clearly regard as worthless? It is not surprising that no answer to this has been provided, but it is profoundly disturbing that the Australian media are not interested in the question.

17
The Tide Turns

Remember that light, not darkness is veritably the truth of life.
—Baba

Towards the end of 1983, our ratings were finally reclassified from maximum to medium security. This meant we could apply to be transfered to a medium security prison. Within weeks of getting the new rating we were told we would be going to the new $52 million *high* security prison at Parklea, Sydney. Victimisation and injustice strike again!

The decision to send the worst prison officers to control the worst crims defies rationality. What should have been a place to set a new standard of enlightened and humanistic values became more of the old destructive ways in a new setting: old wine in a new bottle.

The prison officers sent there all had a reputation for overreacting to prisoners, while the prisoners initially sent there were generally regarded as uncontrollable 'heavies,, or in our case, extremists or terrorists. It is therefore not surprising that within a short time of our arrival (we were in the first batch of prisoners sent there), trouble began.

Prisoners called a strike against the ill-fitting and ridiculous looking uniforms we were made to wear. Prisoners were also upset because most of our belongings, allowed in other prisons, were not allowed at Parklea. For example, prisoners were only allowed four books each!

Tim and I were elected delegates of our respective wings but I later dropped out because of concern expressed over undue 'Ananda Marga influence in the Delegate Committee.'

We succeeded in getting some of the more ridiculous directives changed but then the prison officers went on strike against their own working conditions. This meant prisoners were locked up for the week or so that it lasted. The officers weren't satisfied, so for the first few months there was at least one strike a month. This infuriated the prisoners and some of them ended up burning part of the jail in protest at the continual restrictions.

When we were not striking or being locked up while officers were on strike we were working in the factories inside the prison. Ross and Tim worked in the print shop (as they had in Parramatta) and I worked as a secretary in the carpentry shop. We only earned about $10 a week.

The Herbal Tea Drama

One example that typified the pettiness that was rampant in the prison system and its stifling bureaucracy was the issue about herbal tea sales. The vegetarian prisoners wanted to be allowed to buy herbal tea, in the same way they had been allowed to in other prisons. This included many maximum security prisons. But no, the authorities wouldn't allow it because it looked like marijuana and it was just a fad anyway, according to the prison superintendent.

When it was pointed out that herbal tea could be bought in tea bags, they responded by saying we might open them up and put dope in them. We pointed out that the same could be done with the normal tea bags that everyone else used in prison but they didn't seem to think that was relevant. Nor were they interested in hearing that we had been drinking herbal tea for a decade and, therefore, it wasn't a fad.

After giving up on trying to reason with them, I tried my old avenue of complaint, the State Ombudsman. Several months later I had been transferred to a new prison but I finally received a document from the Ombudsman's Office. On the cover was the following:

CONFIDENTIAL DRAFT REPORT
The Department of Corrective Services
Refusal to Allow Herbal Tea
Not to be disclosed other than to your legal or other professional advisers

The document continued for five lengthy and irrelevant pages. I was amazed to see such a fuss being made over herbal tea! I had written a letter explaining that herbal tea was important since it was the only hot beverage many vegetarians drank and it also had important medicinal benefits. The Ombudsman gave weak excuses to support the refusal of herbal tea and didn't even address my points. Sometime later, I heard herbal tea was eventually introduced at Parklea. I wonder why it wasn't allowed sooner?

Massage of a Madman

The worst types were sent to Parklea. The following conversation typified the mentality of many of them, as well as the wrong perception that many people still had of Ananda Marga. I had this conversation with a prisoner as I was giving him a massage. I was friendly with a variety of prisoners and I also had an interest in getting to know some of the stranger types. This particular prisoner was well known for his violent character. He had a reputation for torture and in one case he electrocuted another prisoner's genitals in order to get information out of him! He got the information.

"You must be dirty on Seary," he remarked.

"No," I replied "not really."

"Arr, you must be, the dog."

"No, he was used by Special Branch and I don't see the point in getting upset over him."

"The Ananda Marga must be dirty on him then?" he asked.

"Some of the Margiis don't like him."

"Are you going to knock him off?"

"No, we don't do things like that."

"Why not, he's a dog and put you in jail!"

"Well, we don't believe in killing people. Despite what the police and Seary say, we are not terrorists."

Then he said in a matter of fact way, "I'll knock him off if you like."

Taken back a bit by the offer I replied, "Thanks, but as I said we don't do those kind of things."

"Well if you ever need anyone knocked off, let me know. I'll do it."

Bathurst Jail

In February 1984, our High Court Appeal was dismissed. We didn't attend. This was despite the fact that prior to the appeal, Justice Murphy of the High Court had called Seary, "the most unreliable person ever presented as the principle prosecution witness on a charge of serious crime."

Support for our cause was growing. CAADA had been working hard publicising our case, demonstrating and pressing for a Special Judicial Inquiry into our convictions. The documentary *Frame Up*, which we had contributed to, was being shown around Australia. This included a screen-

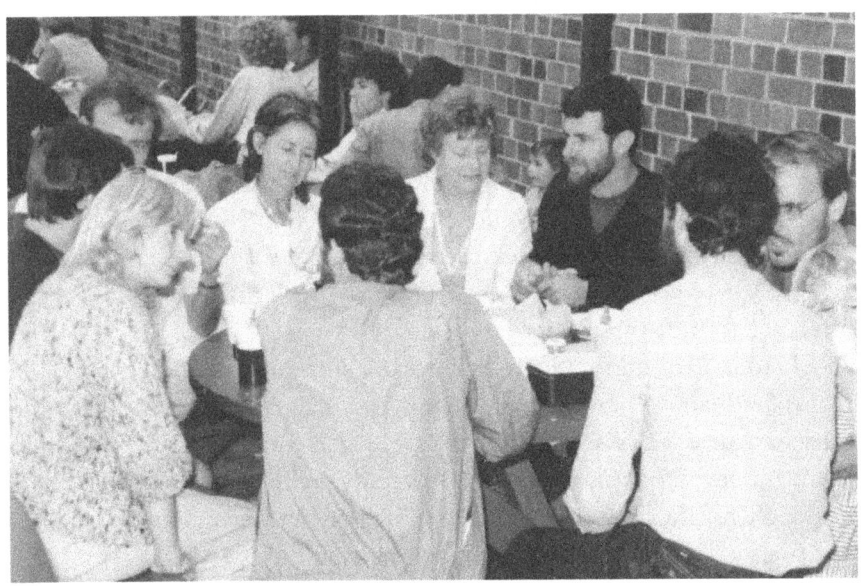

A lighter moment at Bathurst jail. A table of visitors, including Margiis and CAADA supporters. In the middle is my mum, who is visiting to inform me about her decision to begin her hunger strike.

ing for the Labor Party in Federal Parliament. We were getting increasing support from the general public. This included Civil Liberty branches throughout Australia, as well as members of State and Federal Parliament. We were hopeful but cautious.

Six months after our transfer to Parklea, Ross and I managed to get a transfer to a medium security prison at Bathurst, a country town in New South Wales. Tim decided not to come because he was seeing a tutor for his university course and so had to stay in the Sydney area. He also wanted to stay near Sydney to keep our communications with CAADA alive regarding the inquiry. Ross and I decided that if an inquiry were held we would request a transfer back to Sydney.

The ride to Bathurst, despite the usual meat wagon transport, was the most enjoyable ride I ever had going to a jail. We spent most of our time standing up and looking out of tiny cracks to see the beautiful countryside. Lush green valleys, tall soaring mountains, beautiful flowers -- it was mesmerising. I hadn't seen anything like this since being shanghaied to Goulburn, but that was at night so I couldn't appreciate the beauty as much. The only thing I didn't like about it was the realisation of how much I'd been missing such things for all these years—about six now.

As soon as I arrived at Bathurst I noticed how much less tension there was after my years in maximum security prisons. Prisoners in these medium to low security prisons usually did not have much more time to serve on their sentences. This meant they were more inclined to behave in a way that would not jeopardise their release. The officers were even civil and there was more freedom and more privileges which made a big difference to the atmosphere.

It took Ross and I a little time to adjust to prison officers calling us by our first names. Education was emphasised a great deal and I was able to run a course for prisoners on massage. I also completed a course I had begun at Long Bay through Deakin University on Religious Experience that included Christian Mysticism, Eastern Religions and Australian Aboriginal Spirituality. Ross continued his university studies.

Super Mum Takes Action

Two memorable things occurred while I was at Bathurst. The first was snow. I got to touch it for the first time in my life. There wasn't much but it was still an interesting moment for me.

Far more important was though my mother's bold action. She decided to go on a hunger strike! It was a major turning point for our court case.

In April 1984, just after I arrived at Bathurst, my mother, Eve, visited me. She told me she had decided to go on a protest fast. She would join Dada Japasiddhananda, the Australian head of Ananda Marga, on a public fast in Martin place in the heart of downtown Sydney. They both decided they had had enough of all the delays and broken promises. They wanted action now!

I was proud of mum and touched by her sacrifice and dedication to us. I was also moved by Dada's dedication. As the fast went on, I would often see them on television. Mum's involvement in the action brought the media around to our side. Australian's couldn't help but feel sympathy for an elderly woman going out on a limb for her son.

I watched with some concern because mum was in her early sixties and I worried that her health would not hold out. Usually, mum worried about me but now it was my turn to sit helpless and hope she would be okay. I thought how much she must love me to suffer like this.

All three of us felt very grateful for what they were doing.

Later Eve wrote to me:

> Overall I felt good about it, despite the cold and fatigue, mostly because after the High Court's decision I regarded the fast as a last resort and I couldn't see I had anything to lose. I could perhaps bring the sad plight of you three men a bit more into prominence.
>
> Regarding Dada, he was fantastic, a quiet tower of strength and a great sense of humour. In between talking to people and early in the mornings we would read the paper and write letters. Dada was forever writing about something and I was trying to send letters home. Sometimes Dada had to leave to make telephone calls and I would stay to hold the fort, and vice versa. Sometimes he would sit back a bit and say: "I'm going to meditate, Eve." I felt a real harmony between us and hope he felt the same. [Dada did]
>
> Regarding the Margiis, all I can say is that their love and support was overwhelming. They had a roster made up so that

everyday someone would bring in juice for me...and they all spoiled me very much and I didn't ever have a problem as they were all too supportive and kind. Going back home each night to [my twin brother] Mark's flat and the walk from the train station wearied me though.

Eve fasted on juice for two weeks while Dada continued fasting for longer. During the strike, Member of Parliament, George Peterson, made two speeches calling on the New South Wales Parliament to "correct the perversion of justice." He called Seary "a mentally disturbed fantasiser" and said Special Branch was a "threat to the life and liberty of ordinary people."

Meanwhile Peter Wilsmore, a member of the Prisoners Action Group, visited Ross and I in Bathurst on his way to Perth to begin his trek across

A turning point in public opinion about our case was when my courageous mum, Eve, went on a two-week hunger strike calling for an inquiry into our case. She was joined on the fast in downtown Sydney by Dada Japasiddhananda, the Australian head of Ananda Marga.

to Sydney for our release. He was on a 'freedom march' for our cause. He walked solo 5,000 kilometres across Australia, pulling a trolley with his necessities and signs calling for our release. I was very impressed that Peter would make such a huge sacrifice for us. We followed his trek through media reports as he went across the country.

On May 28th, CAADA staged a major demonstration, including a sit-in at the Attorney General's office. As a result of the sit-in Dada met with the State's Attorney General, Paul Landa. They reached a confidential agreement about an inquiry into our case and Dada ended the fast.

On the 16th of June 1984, Justice Staples of the Arbitration Commission called for an inquiry into our case saying it had "all the hallmarks of a classical frame-up of unpopular minority dissidents." The following day a large public meeting was held to commemorate the sixth anniversary of our arrest, organised by the Sydney University Australian Labour

A CAADA demonstration in March 1983 with a banner that read: "Dump ASIO, Not Nuclear Waste. Release Anderson, Dunn and Alister." CAADA seemed to be constantly in action.

Party Club. The speakers included John Marsden, President of the NSW Council for Civil Liberties, Glen Bachelor of the Plumbers and Gasfitters Union, Tom Molombi, senior journalist of the Australian Broadcasting Commission, Barry Cotter and George Peterson.

Finally on the 18th of June, Attorney General Paul Landa announced at a press conference that an Inquiry under section 475 of the Crimes Act would be held concerning our convictions! Needless to say, Ross and I were very pleased to hear this announcement. What was equally pleasing was that Landa and Premier Neville Wran announced that they would support our application for release on license, pending the outcome of the inquiry. We immediately made an application to the Licensing Board. The next day Landa announced that the Hilton Inquest *prima facie* case against Ross and I had been 'no-billed', that is, it had been dropped because of lack of evidence to commit us for trial.

We sent out most of our belongings as we expected to be released soon. We knew from Dada's agreement with the Attorney General that we might finally be getting out. It was very exciting. We were then informed that our application for license had been rejected because the Licensing Board felt they didn't have the power to release us. We were also told that our trial judge, Justice Lee, had informed the board that he feared for his life if we were released. We heard that the board only released on license those who had admitted their guilt and since we were contesting our convictions we had to stay in jail until the matter was finalised.

Ross was outraged when he heard of the decision. I felt confident the inquiry would put it all right. But as Ross said annoyingly and accurately, "For the last six years you have been feeling confident something favourable was going to happen soon!"

CAADA had a demonstration against the license decision that was shown on television. Ross was shocked and concerned to see his girlfriend Jenny dragged away during the demonstration. This rough reaction to a CAADA demonstration had become an all too familiar sight that disturbed us deeply. Margiis and non-Margiis, particularly from the Prisoner's Action Group, went through so much for us and for justice.

By now, we had been given a minimum security rating due to our good behaviour over time and were able to get transferred back to Long Bay Prison in Sydney. This time we went to the minimum security jail in the same complex, called Metropolitan Training Centre (MTC). We met up with Tim again who, true to form, had started preparing for the inquiry.

MTC

While the MTC had the lowest security rating, many prisoners didn't like it there because the officers treated them like children. They were very arrogant and condescending. They knew the prisoners were due to finish their sentences soon and wouldn't do anything to jeopodise their release. So they took the opportunity to treat prisoners like dirt. The following exchange with an officer exemplifies their general attitude. This dispute happened when I went for one of my twice weekly phone calls and the person I rang wasn't at home. The officer insisted that this be counted as one of my calls.

"Why do you count that as a call," I argued, "when the person I've asked you to ring is not there? I haven't made a call have I?"

"You get two calls a week," the officer said in his usual unreasonable manner.

"That's ridiculous, not even in maximum security do they count that as a call."

"I don't care what *they* do, I'm telling you what the system is here."

"But none of the other officers do it, they just hang up and say try again later. Some charge you 20 cents for the call and I don't mind doing that. Do you want me to pay for it?"

"No!" he shouted, "You're not getting more than two calls a week. If you can't arrange with your people to be ready when you want to ring them that's your problem."

"How can I arrange to call them when I'm in jail?"

"That's your problem, you've been in jail long enough. You get two calls a week and that's it. Now get out of my office!"

I saw the acting Superintendent about it but he said he wasn't going to interfere with petty phone disputes and that I had to work it out with the officer. He added that if I caused any trouble I'd find myself next door. That meant I could be shanghaied back to the maximum security prison, the CIP, which was the next building over.

18
The Judicial Inquiry

Life is the art of drawing sufficient conclusions from insufficient premises.
—Samuel Butler c. 1880

MANY PEOPLE WERE HOPEFUL ABOUT THE INQUIRY. MY MOTHER WROTE:

> Your father and I were very pleased to hear about the inquiry because we had lost all hope that you'd get out justly. At the beginning only a few friends and relatives believed in your innocence and stood by us but everyone else adopted the attitude 'where there is smoke there is fire' and some didn't even want to read material I'd gathered together to prove your innocence. It was all very hurtful but now I think everyone believes us and we get a lot of support which is good.

CAADA people were very pleased about the inquiry but like others they were also angry at the decision not to grant us a license. We three felt good about the likely outcome of a proper inquiry, especially since our lawyers told us that the judge, Justice Wood, was conservative but fair. We thought that if we had an unprejudiced judge, we would get a good result.

This time we all had good lawyers. Some worked at much less than their normal wages as we couldn't afford to pay them much more than our government allotment for public defenders. Tim got Bill Hoskins (who was Queens Counsel and public defender and went on to become a

Sydney district court judge) and retained Will Hutchins as solicitor. Ross retained Michael Adams or 'Mr Continuity' as he called him, since he had been with us since the beginning. By now Michael had left being a public defender and taken up private practice on his way to becoming a judge. My barrister was Marcus Einfeld QC, who had represented Tim at the first trial for a while. (Tim couldn't afford him for very long!) Einfeld later became a Supreme Court Judge and head of a human rights organisation. Our solicitors were Michael d'Arbon and Tom Molomby. As an Australian Broadcasting Commission legal journalist, Tom received permission to put his lawyer hat on and work for us. M. Gleason, a public defender, also joined our team.

All in all we felt good about our lawyers. Most had proven records, especially Marcus Einfeld who was highly regarded as one of the country's best criminal law barristers. The meetings and preparations we had up to commencement of the inquiry reminded me of people preparing to go to battle or a team training to play in a Grand Final. It had that sort of atmosphere and excitement. Indeed, Einfield's chambers, where we had our meetings, were referred to as the 'bunker'.

By now the public and importantly, the media, no longer perceived us as terrorists. Many people doubted Seary and the police evidence. The inquiry was a testimony to the changed perception of our case. We were also minimum security prisoners now and were taken to the inquiry in a small car rather than in a meat wagon.

Because we did not have the lowest minimum security rating, we were not entitled to go to the inquiry unescorted. Instead, officers came with us. But the good thing was we could leave at 8 am instead of 7 am like before. We also went straight to the lawyer's chamber until the inquiry started at 10 am. Prison officers waited outside the chambers. After the inquiry ended at 4 pm each day we stayed at chambers until 5 pm.

It was quite an experience for us to go from a car parked in the middle of busy Sydney, walk through a crowd and enter a lift to the luxurious chambers. It was very foreign to us. It was hard for me to not keep staring at people in the street and wonder what they would be thinking to see us handcuffed and escorted by three officers. Ross and Tim eventually expressed displeasure at the way people looked at us but I enjoyed being out regardless. I thought *they* looked strange too!

After some time we were allowed to go to the inquiry without handcuffs but prison guards remained with us. One prison officer even remarked that guarding us was a waste of taxpayers' money because everyone was expecting us to be released soon.

Our first day in court, in December 1984, was quite a spectacle. The large room was full of lawyers and media and the gallery was packed with Margiis and the public. After seven years, our case had become a major news item.

As the inquiry went on, crowds lessened somewhat although there were always a healthy presence of media and the public. We got to know some of the journalists personally. (One of them, Julia Sigworth, later helped me edit this book.)

We thought our lawyers performed brilliantly. 'Performed' is the optimum word here as it was all a great drama. Marcus with his usual charisma, commanded great respect from the judge and was always in full control when he addressed the court.

While Marcus was forceful and at times loud, he was moderate compared to Bill Hoskins who was by far the most aggressive of the barristers. His cross-examinations and submissions were cynical and mocking. Sometimes it was hard to keep a straight face and maintain proper court decorum. This is not to say Hoskins took it as a joke. His style of expressing himself often came across as funny. Then again as the inquiry dragged on month after month, some deliberate humour was injected to break the tension and monotony.

One of our witnesses was being cross-examined about his drug habit. Justice Wood warned him he didn't have to answer questions about drugs if he thought he might incriminate himself. The witness declined to answer the questions so the lawyer took up different approach to try to incriminate him. The lawyer asked if he used tobacco. Immediately Hoskins jumped up and thundered, "I object!" with such deadpan humour that the entire courtroom broke out in laughter. It was funny because tobacco is not an illegal drug. It was also a great relief to have a moments escape from the boredom and tension of the court.

While Hoskins was loud in court, out of court he was humble and polite. Humility is not something most lawyers, especially QCs, are renowned for.

Michael Adams was also quite remarkable. His voice fluctuated between soft and loud, depending on what was appropriate in the circumstances. He was not quite as dramatic at the inquiry as he was during our trials because he was not trying to persuade a jury, only the judge. At the trials he sometimes got carried away with his theatrics, thumping the table and waving his arms around as his solicitor ducked. One time he nearly knocked over one of his solicitors.

Counsel assisting the judge, Mr McGregor QC, and the prosecutor, Mr Finnane QC, were quite boring by comparison. They were both slow and plodding, examining all the details and making sure not to miss anything. The prosecution had to search hard for material against us because their case was so utterly feeble and false.

Our Case

Justice Wood stated that he was only interested in evidence that had not so far been presented. He didn't want to hear from the police or us unless there was new evidence.

Fortunately we did have some important new evidence which had been a factor in calling the inquiry in the first place. Since our first trial we had been trying to get access to transcripts of tape recordings of interviews between Seary and Detective Krawczyk while Seary was spying on Ananda Marga, as well as a few other items Special Branch had in its possession. Prosecution continually blocked our request. Finally, after our last appeal, Adams was able to persuade the NSW Solicitor-General to obtain and read these transcripts. The information in these transcripts conflicted seriously with Seary's court testimonies and put his evidence strongly into doubt. The discrepancies were so major that the Solicitor-General recommended that we be released immediately. However, the Attorney-General decided to hold an inquiry instead and allow the information from the tapes to be used in our defense.

These important tapes showed that:

- Seary had suggested at that time that a Hare Krishna group was responsible for the Hilton bombing. He had been a member of this group when he was trying to knock a heroin habit.

- This Hare Krishna allegation was not investigated at all by the

police. They ignored this and told him to spy on Ananda Marga instead.
- Seary infiltrated Ananda Marga one month later than he had stated in court.
- Seary knew how to obtain explosives illicitly. He had lied in court previously when he said he did not.
- Five days before our arrest, Seary told police about our alleged bomb attack on Cameron's house. In earlier trials Seary had said he did not know of the 'plan' until that morning.

Our lawyers demonstrated that Seary was neither a reliable nor credible witness and brought in a number of professional witnesses who had treated Seary for mental illness or drug problems. They gave clear evidence of his extreme mental imbalance. They also clearly demonstrated his long history of drug abuse, including LSD and heroin. Seary had denied his history of drug abuse during our trials.

Dr Emanuel Fischer, who had assessed Seary for psychiatric treatment, commented:

> I am of the view that Seary's reliability as a witness is very suspect to say the least. As a rule, people with this type of personality are extremely manipulative and will invent things for their own purposes. Seary is schizoid and a psychopath.

The $100,000 reward that had been offered for evidence leading to conviction of the Hilton bombers would have been sufficient motive to explain Seary's behaviour—along with probable police pressure. He had been involved with a friend's death from a drug overdose and police may have offered to 'get him off' if he would help them. He was also initially a police suspect in the Hilton bombing and didn't have a reliable alibi.

We also had new evidence for the case in two new witnesses: Wendy Hunter and Ken Jerome. Wendy had been Seary's girlfriend. Among other things she said that after our arrest Seary told her that he thought we were going out to Cameron's place to do postering or "something like that" and was surprised to see we brought explosives.

Of course, it was he who brought the explosives but the rest was correct, contradicting what Seary had told police and had repeated in court under oath. Seary always said we were going out to bomb Cameron, not to do postering as his girlfriend said he told her.

She also said that Seary had not volunteered to infiltrate Ananda Marga but that police had pressured him. Apparently Seary had told Wendy that Margiis were very nice people, in stark contrast with the picture of dangerous terrorists painted by Seary on the interview tapes.

Ken 'Dok' Jerome was also a very close friend of Seary from 1970 to 1978. Dok told of a plan by Seary to bomb an abattoir while they were both members of the Hare Krishna. The intended bomb was generally similar to that involved in the Cameron case, in that it contained sticks of gelignite with a timing device and a detonator. Later on in a police interview, Seary attributed his abattoir plan to a radical member of the sect but didn't mention that *he* was the radical member. This is remarkably similar to what Seary alleged about us; he tried to claim that *we* were the radicals.

The judge wanted Seary to attend the inquiry to give his evidence but he was overseas and had refused to attend. The inquiry ran for about three months and we were all glad to see it come to an end. We hoped to be released very soon. On the last day of the inquiry, there was a loud knock on the courtroom door. Bill Hoskins joked, "That's Seary come for the inquiry!" There was also a responding laughter from our lawyers saying, "Please don't say that—it might be true and the inquiry would have to continue!"

Frustratingly, Bill's joke came true. In early December 1984, while the judge was still deliberating the case, Seary suddenly returned to give evidence. I thought he just couldn't resist the opportunity for public attention and notoriety. Because the judge wanted to hear his evidence, Seary also requested government funding for a trip to Australia for himself, his wife and four children. He wanted accommodation, 'perhaps somewhere on the coast' and legal representation. We were disgusted with his opportunism and amazed that such a man could be the factor that would keep us even longer in prison.

Our lawyers wanted the chance to cross-examine Seary on the new evidence but nobody was looking forward to more months of an inquiry. That's exactly what happened. The inquiry was re-opened.

Seary looked as pathetic as usual and tried in vain to answer our lawyers' questions. We presumed that this time he would not be able to pull the wool over the judge's eyes as he had with most of the jurors.

The inquiry finally ended in mid February. We were relieved and excited at what we hoped would be a positive verdict. Justice Wood thanked us and the lawyers for our good conduct. We felt Wood was clearly on our side by his many looks of disbelief at Seary's evidence and the fact that he said at times he disbelieved the police. Later we learnt that Wood actually supported the police.

Media Turning Point

One very encouraging event that occurred towards the end of 1984, just before Seary came back, was by the Australian Broadcasting Commission's national current affairs television program, 'Nationwide'. It devoted the last screening of its show for the year to our case. Presented by the highly respected journalist Geraldine Douge, it showed our case in a positive and balanced way. This was a turning point in the media coverage of our case. After that program the media treated us with much more respect and credence, which had been mostly missing up until then.

A Glimpse of Freedom

The inquiry was adjourned for nearly a month at Christmas, which upset everyone as we were hoping we would be out by then. The one good gift we received for Christmas was re-classification to lowest security risk, (after months of applications), which meant we could go to the inquiry unescorted.

The first day out was a strange experience. We were allowed out at 8 am and had to be back by 6 pm. We walked past the jail gates with bus fares in hand and one dollar for a cup of tea. We caught a bus to the lawyers' chambers, then walked through town to court. Afterwards we went back to the chambers and then took a bus back to jail.

Walking out of the jail gates was a very pleasant feeling. For once an officer was not close by and it was wonderful to walk without handcuffs. We knew that while on day release, security police monitored our movements to be sure we didn't break the conditions of our release. They included no alcohol or illegal drugs (certainly not a problem for us) and no speaking to the media or attending meetings.

Two experiences impressed and surprised me during our first day of 'freedom'. The first was when I got on a bus. For a long second or two I couldn't remember what I was suppose to do, either give the driver money or sit down and wait for a ticket collector. Quickly I tried to think back six and a half years to the last time I was on a bus. I told the driver where I wanted to go and gave him the fare, which turned out to be right thing to do. It felt great to be among 'normal' people with their diversity and colour. Compared to jail the bus felt much less tense than the usual atmosphere in jail. I enjoyed the opportunity to be anonymous in public, rather than one of the central figures in a criminal trial.

The second experience involved crossing an inner Sydney street. For a moment I stood on a white line with cars racing past me on both sides. I froze. Fear swept through me as I adjusted to this forgotten experience. After a few seconds I relaxed and could cross the street, but it left a lasting memory.

We entered the inquiry through the front entrance with everyone else. Tim commented that it was fitting we go through the front entrance like free innocent people while Seary had to go through the back entrance like a criminal. The police probably feared the public would abuse Seary if he went through the front.

One time while walking to the inquiry I came across a dead man on the side of the footpath. Blood came from his head and his face was ashen. I wondered if he'd been murdered. As I stood by him trying to figure out what to do, an ambulance and the police arrived. In the paper the next day it said a man had committed suicide by jumping from a church. I mentioned this experience to the others and added, "It's safer in jail." Michael d'Arbon, one of our solicitors, quipped, "You're lucky the police didn't know who you were or they would have charged you with his death!" He was probably only half joking.

19
Freedom

When the ends are just and noble, success is inevitable.
—Baba

WE HAD HOPED JUSTICE WOODS WOULD FINISH HIS REPORT BEFORE HE WAS scheduled to leave for his country circuit. He didn't finish it however, and we had to wait months again to find out if justice would prevail. We were angry that he hadn't been allowed sufficient time to make his findings and had the added pressure of having to go on a circuit so soon after the inquiry.

Meanwhile, we were granted 'day leave' which meant we could go out of jail for a day, unescorted. We were each given two day leaves. The first time we went out Tim and I went swimming and then visited Jaivanii, my massage teacher and her friend Bronwyn. Bronwyn had just given birth to a beautiful little girl the day before. It was such a remarkable contrast after jail to see the purity of the new child and the joy surrounding the birth. I visited some Margiis for lunch and then had time to spend with my girlfriend, Jenny Fitzgerald.

The Margiis I visited typified the cross section of society that belonged to Ananda Marga. There was a scientist high school teacher, a singer, a singer/comedian, a yoga teacher, a lawyer, an alternative healer and a sound technician.

On the way back to jail I realised I felt strangely happy to be returning. While I clearly didn't like prison, after seven years it had become the only place that was familiar to me and that I could easily relate to. Some of my friends remarked later that I looked overwhelmed by them all, which was probably true, though I didn't realise it at the time. Certainly when I got back to jail I felt very disorientated. It was as if I'd been in a dream and now, back in jail, I was awake in reality.

The first day leave was just after the inquiry had ended; the second one wasn't granted until two months later. The second time I made it a point not to do so much or see so many people. I spent the whole day with Jenny. We spent the morning at Lane Cove National Park and an afternoon swimming at the beach.

We met some Margiis at the beach. While enjoying ice cream, we noticed a man in a suit taking photos of us with a little camera. He looked very suspicious. He was also conspicuous as everyone else around him was dressed for the beach. I presumed it was someone from Prison Security checking up on me.

This time when I returned to jail I felt sad and wished I could stay out. I was starting to realise what I'd been missing for so long.

Eye Operation

After the excitement of the inquiry and the freedom of day leave, jail life was even more boring. Time dragged on ever so slowly as we waited for the report. During this time I was taken to hospital to have a terageon (a growth similar to a cataract) removed from my eye. Two officers escorted me to the operating table. I was given only a local anesthetic to the eye concerned, which meant I was conscious the whole time the growth was being cut. It was quite terrifying to watch a knife coming towards my eye as they sliced a piece off. When they finished I was put into a van and taken back to jail. The officer in charge of my cleaning duty, seeing my eye all bandaged up, graciously said I didn't have to work that day.

Normally I worked at my job a few hours and spent the rest of the time learning to play tennis, attending some classes on communication and doing some astrology charts and palm readings. I also started to write down the beginnings of this book. At this point, for a variety of reasons, I wasn't practicing as much meditation as I had previously, though I always meditated four times each day.

Reflections

While waiting for our decision I had plenty of time to reflect on my time in jail. On the positive side we all felt there had been some benefits. Tim felt jail developed him personally. He had become politicised and had developed his intellect through study and writing. He had earned a Bachelor of Arts in economics and politics and an honours degree. He had completed a course in journalism and written some publications on police verbals. He also wrote a book on the legal side of our case that was later to be published.

Ross benefited in similar ways. He partly completed studies with a double major in social and political theory and history.

I had benefited educationally as well. I completed two semesters in Religious Experiences which was a major triumph for me considering my very limited educational background. I ended up with an A. I took some basic English courses and a painting course and had taken an interest in

Relaxing in the park during a break at the inquiry. Ross, me, my girlfriend Jenny, Sundari, Tim and lawyer Will Hutchins. While we got to enjoy some freedom during our days at court, our nights at prison were a cruel reminder that we were far from free.

Western classical music as well as astrology and palmistry. I had met Jenny who was to become my wife. Ross also met his future wife, who's name was also Jenny. I had learned a lot from my involvement with prison issues as a delegate and in my work against police verbals.

But the greatest benefit I received from my time in prison was spiritual. I viewed the whole long episode as a test of faith in God and Ananda Marga's ideology. Intuitively I felt everything would turn out right in the end, providing I did not waiver in faith, moral principles and spiritual discipline. It is purely God's grace that I never lost faith and at times I felt very blessed. I had grown much closer to God and had had experiences in jail that was beyond anything I had experienced before. In that regard at least, I did not regret what had happened to me. There's a quote that aptly describes my experience: "Religion is for those who fear going to hell; spirituality is for those who have already been there." It was the 'living hell' of jail that forced me deeper into my spiritual quest.

On the negative side, we all suffered physically, particularly Ross and I. Ross developed a stomach ulcer and suffered frequently from fatigue and headaches. He was too ill to attend the last parts of the inquiry. Tim often had digestive problems which he coped with by running everyday and drinking lots of water.

I suffered from weak nerves and memory, an inability to comprehend details, as well as fatigue and headaches, similar to Ross. We both developed hypoglycemia due to our poor diet in jail (too much sugar.) Around the time of waiting for the decision I developed an uncontrollable twitching in my right eye. A doctor said it was just nerves. It did disappear about a week later.

Emotionally we suffered, too. A common ailment for long-term prisoners is a tendency to overreact, often violently, to small things. We all overreacted to small problems, although not violently. The repressive jail systems world wide generates much anger in prisoners.

Before prison I had been a very jovial, happy-go-lucky person, full of vitality and inspiration. After seven years in prison, I'd become much more serious and much less animated, confident and carefree. I felt more aloof and distant. It saddens me sometimes to think how much jail oppressed my feelings. I now found it easier to be on my own than interacting with people, even when I desired to. Prison affected my ability to make close friends and later to find work as I found society generally alien and a bit frightening. It was hard for me to relate to other people. Many of these tendencies lasted for years and some still affect me today.

Our friends and supporters also suffered from our imprisonment. They often felt angry at being mistreated when trying to visit us, and powerless to help us. Others fell under the tyranny of injustice in their struggle for our freedom. My parents had a lot of trouble convincing many of their friends. Mum often would cry at night as Dad tried to comfort her, telling her that it is out of ignorance that so few believed that their son was innocent. My twin brother Mark told me on visits about the big arguments he had at work about my innocence. I think all my family had some kind of conflict with friends or colleagues over my imprisonment. It seems where justice is concerned, everyone is affected once they join the fight. Some people had dedicated years of their life to our freedom. We had a lot of admiration and thanks for these people and felt very inspired by them.

I made friends with this galah that lived in the yards at MTC minimum security prison. Prisoners had trained it to say, "I wanna get out, I wanna get out!"

More Waiting

At the beginning of May, Ross came into my cell looking very grim, "I've got some very bad news. The judge has delayed his report for another two weeks. That bloody Wood, he's done it to us again. Remember he said there had to be a stop to the submissions and that he'd give his decision in a week? Now he's taken more submissions and gone past that time...I'm furious!"

I felt some tension in our months of waiting but generally I was fairly calm, as I was able to accept that it was all in God's hands.

At the beginning of May my father, Maurice, visited me. He had spent most of the last seven years fighting for our case. In Perth he kept busy contacting the media and politicians, writing letters and doing whatever he could. He made an impressive collection of every newsclipping about our case. In fact, my freedom had become his passion.

He was also impatient waiting for our decision and had decided to come over from Perth to see me. He was having trouble sleeping at night and said that Eve's health was not so good either. I felt upset to see how all this had affected them.

Murray Farquahar

Life can have many ironies and one of them occurred during my final months in prison. Who would have predicted that the magistrate who first charged me after our arrest would end up in the cell next to me? But that is exactly what happened. Former magistrate, Murray Farquahar, had been convicted on corruption charges.

When I first saw him I went out of my way to avoid him. It wasn't out of spite but because I saw quite a few prisoners trying to ingratiate themselves with him. This disgusted me, as it did Ross and Tim. As far as I was concerned he would get no different treatment than I gave any other prisoner. As he treated me I would treat him.

Soon he was put in a cell next to mine and so it was not long before our paths met. To my surprise he was not the arrogant ex-magistrate that I expected. He had a gentle, pleasant, even unassuming manner. Perhaps because we were prisoners of some notoriety like him, or because we were better educated than others in prison, he found it easy to relate to us. I can only speculate on this, but he soon became a regular person in our lives.

One day as he was talking with me about my case, he asked why I didn't write a book about it.

"Nah," I replied skeptically, "Tim has already done that and he's a much better writer than me."

"But you and Tim are very different people, I'm sure you would write a very different story."

I thought for a while, not really wanting to admit that I would like to write but did not feel adequate.

"That's true, but I'm not very good at writing."

"That doesn't matter. If it's a good story the publishers will have their own editors who will take care of that. I have written a few books and know how they work. I'll give any help you need if you like."

Murray was really inspiring me, giving me confidence to do something I had never dreame I could do.

"Well if you don't mind helping me with grammar and English, I think I might have a go!"

"Wonderful," responded Murray as a big smile came over his face. I had access to a typewriter and later that day I began typing.

Ross and Tim went out to university twice a week and I spent most of my time typing about my experiences and waiting...

In mid-May, one day while I was busily typing, an officer came to tell me that our lawyer had left the message for us that the final report on the inquiry would be released the next day.

Excitement swept through me at the thought that our seven year struggle could be all over tomorrow! Tim was in his cell so I informed him of the news. Needless to say he was pleased, as was Ross when I told him. Everyone felt certain that the report on the inquiry would come out in our favour.

After informing them of the news I went back to my typing as I did not want to get carried away with our possible release when so many times before news had ended in bitter disappointment. God had taught me some detachment in this regard. That night I slept soundly with just a tinge of excitement.

Next morning I continued typing and had just finished the last chapter when Murray Farquahar came in and asked:

"Is there any news on the report, Paul?"

"No," I replied.

"I don't know how you can be calmly typing when the decision is coming down today," commented Murray.

"I want to keep my mind busy so I won't have too many expectations—or more disappointments."

Tim was getting ready to leave for university and Ross had already left. When Tim got to the front gate he was told he couldn't leave until further notice. We suspected that meant until the 'news' came.

I was called down to the front office at noon. My heart pounded as I waited outside the Superintendent's door. I anticipated that I had been called to be told of the decision. On entering I found that I had only been called in to sign a receipt for the Ombudsman's report regarding herbal tea at Parklea prison! The report recommended that herbal tea be allowed.

As we finally stepped out of the jail gates into freedom we were swamped by the media. It was our first time to talk directly to the press.

I passed more hours in my cell until Tim and Murray came in with big grins.

"We've kicked a goal," said a beaming Tim. "We're getting a pardon."

Murray added, "It was just on the radio, the new Attorney General, Sheaham, held a press conference and announced the pardon."

Murray went back to listen to more details on the radio. He suddenly called us in.

"Bloody not good. They have kept the convictions."

We had been pardoned, but we were not pronounced innocent. More injustice! We had mixed feelings and considered refusing to leave prison until they removed the convictions.

The Superintendent called Tim and I to the office and formally told us about the pardon.

"Now you are free men, pack your things and go."

Jokingly I thought, "Doesn't he like us? He can't seem to get rid of us quick enough."

Thoughts of protesting vanished as the excitement of release overcame me. Later we learned that the NSW Government did not have power to overturn our convictions. The pardon was the most that the government could give us, short of introducing new legislation to overturn convictions.

Excitedly Tim and I went back to our cells to pack our belongings. Murray and some other prisoners helped carry our things. We exchanged goodbyes. I felt a tinge of sadness for those who had to stay behind. We went to the reception area and collected the remainder of our belongings. Then we went to the front gate.

Tension filled the air as we waited those few minutes to be let out. Both prisoners and officers watched us, knowing we were to be released. On the other side of the large steel gate freedom beckoned us. The doors opened and out we went.

One of our Margii friends was waiting with a camera and tried to take a photo but was stopped by a prison guard, reminding us we were not totally free from jail yet.

A small group of Margiis embraced us and we joyously hugged each other. They then walked with us to a group of journalists waiting for an interview. Cries of "Jai Dharma" (victory to righteousness) rang out as we walked. It was a bit of a shock coming out of jail to land in a sea of reporters all firing questions at us. Ross came back later to prison from university and met with a similar reception from the media.

Margiis drove us back to the Ananda Marga centre where we were met by more overjoyed Margiis and more journalists. Margiis and sympathisers came to share in this happy and historic occasion. My father was there as well which was most fitting considering all those years he had struggled in Perth for our release.

Frustratingly, our joy was clouded when we got the details of the report on the inquiry that cleared police of any wrong doing. The report said there was 'doubt' as to our guilt, which would have resulted in a not guilty verdict if that had been the opinion of a jury. That was what moved the government to give us pardons. But the rest of the report gave excuses for

Dad and I just after my release. Dad dedicated seven years of his life to work for our freedom. He died soon afterwards, but Mum said those last years were some of his happiest. Despite the tragedy of the situation, Dad loved the excitement of the fight for justice. He was overjoyed at my release.

the police and spared them from criticism. We were all angry and cynical.

That night I laid my head down to try and sleep but I couldn't. My mind was literally spinning when I shut my eyes. It must have been three hours before I fell asleep. Ross said he had a similar experience.

Next day a line of media formed outside the Ananda Marga centre as they took turns interviewing us. We spent the whole day talking to the media. It was our first time to ever be able to tell our story directly. Although it was exhausting, it was a pleasure to finally have the media receptive to our case.

One interview resulted in a two page article in a major Sydney Sunday paper that earned me enough money to fly over to Perth and be with my parents. They arranged three parties for me, with the help of some Margiis. One party was with relatives and friends, one with Margiis and the last with political and media people who helped with our case. Over 50 people came to the last one. The Margiis' party was very blissful. The party with my parents and relatives was more emotional, but was enjoyable too.

Paranoia

I held more interviews in Perth and then flew back to Sydney. By now I was feeling overwhelmed and tired from so much attention and too much questioning. I decided to go for a day drive to a beach with Jenny. While we were driving, a car slowly passed us. A wave of fear and adrenaline swept through me as I relived the terror I felt when the police pulled us over at Yagoona. The image of a man pointing a gun at us became vivid. This only lasted a split second until I realised I was only imagining it. But this paranoid reaction to passing cars continued for months.

Going Different Ways

After a week the media interest in us faded, although occasionally people walked up to me to say something supportive about our case. At last the majority of the public seemed to have a good impression of Ananda Marga. Initially our case had made Ananda Marga well known throughout Australia as a terrorist organisation. Now we were seen as scapegoats for the Hilton bombing. Unfortunately, the real nature of Ananda Marga remained a mystery to most. In the meantime we wanted to put it all behind us and get on with living a normal life.

Towards the end of our imprisonment Tim had decided to leave Ananda Marga. While he appreciated certain aspects of it and its philosophy, there were other aspects he could not accept and live with. Basically, he was a socio-political person while Ananda Marga was on a socio-spiritual path. Ross stayed a Margii for a few more years before moving into Zen meditation. He expressed aversion to the controversy and discrimination he had experienced as a Margii.

Baba's Good News

In India, Baba had been out of prison for some time. He had been released with a total acquittal of all charges not long after our imprisonment. Each day Baba asked for reports of Ananda Marga activity around the world. He especially liked to hear 'good news'. On the day of our release acharyas were telling Baba some good news from Ananda Marga around the world: 300 hundred people benefited from food distribution in Bangladesh, a primary school opened in Nairobi and so on, but Baba was dissatisfied.

"That's not the news I'm wanting to hear," Baba said stubbornly.

No matter what people reported that day, Baba was not happy.

Finally there was a phone call from Sydney telling of our release. Baba was immediately informed.

"That's the news I've been wanting to hear," replied Baba with a very happy, satisfied look.

I didn't hear this story until many months after it happened but I when I did I was very touched. It confirmed what I felt inside; that Baba as my guru was personally concerned with my well being at every moment.

A New Ananda Marga

One of the things that I noticed after coming out of jail was how Ananda Marga had changed. It was much bigger and more complex. While Baba was in jail the Indian security police offered him release and a comfortable life if he promised to give up trying to establish PROUT, the social-economic system he propounded. Baba rebuked the offer saying, "Let the PROUT movement die, when I come out I will establish 16 similar organisations."

Certainly there were many more departments in Ananda Marga than when I went into jail. This made me feel like a newcomer—I often couldn't understanding what Margiis were referring to when they mentioned these new departments.

Since Baba's acquittal, Ananda Marga had grown rapidly and was established in almost every country of the world. Australia was an exception to Ananda Marga's growth but elsewhere its reputation became more respectable. Ananda Marga's service work earned national and international praise and awards. Baba was also awarded international prizes in the area of culture, in recognition of, among other things, the 5,000 songs he had composed. I understand he declined most of the awards. Baba was a very private person and did not like much public recognition.

Compensation

Soon after our release, we applied for compensation for our years of wrongful imprisonment. We expected to receive between $300,000 and $500,000 each based on comparable cases. Finally, the Government awarded us each $100,000 "to help rehabilitate us back into society." They would not call it 'compensation' as that would have implied that we were wrongly convicted and that would reflect badly on the police. Police tried to stop any payment being made to us at all. It seems injustice followed this case from beginning to end.

Hilton Bombing 2

The case dragged on far beyond our release. Five years later, in 1990, Tim was arrested again and charged with the Hilton bombing. An ex-Margii, Evan Pederick (Om Prakash), had given himself up to police claiming that Tim had brainwashed him into planting a bomb at the Hilton Hotel.

Pederick was sent to trial and convicted with life imprisonment. Tim was imprisoned while awaiting trial for several months but was able to beat the charges. Pederick had weak and conflicting evidence that suggested he probably didn't do it but might have been pressured into admitting it to avoid some other charges. Another theory was he was brainwashed into thinking this by the new Christian sect he now belonged to. He could just be a bit mad, which is quite possible. It's not unheard of for people to admit to crimes they didn't commit. They do this to get recognition, or in an attempt to remove feelings of guilt from some other crime they have committed, or both.

Tim's arrest aroused much passion in the community and a large, influential movement was formed, mainly of non-Margiis, to secure his release. To their credit they were successful. Seary popped up and tried to influence the trial, as well as ASIO who dragged in an old Margii. He claimed the then Secretary of Ananda Marga in Australia was the mastermind behind the Hilton bombing. Nothing has come of these wild allegations and it seems the government is still reluctant to look at the most probable Hilton bomber: ASIO, in complicity with Special Branch. To this day, the Hilton bombing remains an unsolved crime.

20
Meeting Baba

> God alone is the Guru. He alone directs the unit beings to the path of emancipation through the media of different bodies.
> -Baba

THE FIRST THING I DID ONCE I GOT OUT OF JAIL, AFTER ALL THE MEDIA HYSTERIA, was to apply for a passport so I could visit Baba. This took several months because I was still on ASIO's list of known terrorists. Finally, their bureaucracy got around to noticing that I'd been given a full pardon and therefore ASIO had no valid reason to withhold my passport.

As soon as it was issued I was on a plane for India. I was so eager to go I did not even bother to find out where Baba lived. Such a detail seemed insignificant when I was finally to meet my guru.

During the plane journey I had plenty of time to imagine what it would be like to meet Baba. I had heard so much about him from other people and in meditation I had had many experiences with him.

I once asked a Margii why more people didn't know about Baba, given his occult powers and amazing capacities. She told me that a Dada had told Baba that some university professors were very eager to hear about his occult powers. Baba got upset and said, "What foolish thing is this? Do you want to surround me with millions of people who only want a show of occult powers? Do you want them to block me from fulfiling my real purpose on earth by taking up my limited time with people like these?" Baba's real purpose was individual and collective advancement.

Another time Baba described occult powers as mundane rather than spiritual. They are not an indication of spiritual success and can be a hindrance.

Baba didn't seem to be impressed by rich people who tried to buy his favour. There were stories of Baba throwing them out of his house with their money. Baba would say something to the effect that he was only interested in those who were interested in God, not money, power or prestige.

Arrival at Last!

At Calcutta airport I felt a mixture of excitement and trepidation. Stories of security police watching out for anyone who might be a Margii and having them deported were fresh in my mind. Consequently, I had prepared myself to look like a non-Margii. I had shaved my beard, cut my hair short, wore leather shoes and displayed a pack of cigarettes ostentatiously in my shirt pocket.

While waiting in line to be processed through customs I noticed a man looking at me. He wasn't in uniform but I felt sure he must have been a plainclothes detective. I felt nervous.

"I've been spotted," I thought. "This calls for drastic action!"

I pulled out a cigarette, lit up and attempted to smoke it. I thought that if I did not inhale fully the man would be able to tell that I was faking. So saying my mantra internally I inhaled fully, praying to Baba that I would not start coughing, which I normally would do since I hadn't smoked in over 13 years. To my relief and delight, I experienced no reaction. I inhaled and exhaled with ease as if I was a regular smoker. As soon as I began to smoke the man seemed to lose interest in me and walked away. I went through customs and immigration like a breeze. It was as if Baba had thrown open the door for me to enter his abode.

Once I had stepped out into the warm September afternoon sun, a feeling of excitement and grace overcame me. So too did a crowd of hustlers, trying to get me to go to their taxi. After some arguing over fares, I got into a taxi and was off to Lake Gardens, a Calcutta suburb where I was told Baba lived.

As I got closer to Lake Gardens the taxi driver wanted to know exactly where I wanted to go. I said, "to Baba's house, Ananda Marga," but it drew a blank response. I told the driver to ask another group of taxi drivers sitting nearby. They immediately came alive when he asked for Baba's house. I knew then I was on a roll and would soon be enjoying Baba's presence. Better late than never, I thought, even if it is 13 years late.

Down narrow stone streets we went, weaving in and out of the multitude of people walking, riding bicycles and scooters. Suddenly I noticed a Didi (a female acharya) and stopped the taxi to ask directions. She pointed down a street. We turned down it and my heart went into my throat as I saw a crowd of orange-robed people outside a gate. It was Baba's house for sure. It was several stories high and inside the walled enclosure was a garden packed with green plants, almost like a botanical garden.

Excited, I quickly paid the taxi fare and jumped out. I had arrived just in time for Sunday afternoon meditation with Baba called 'darshan' (to view the guru). I quickly found where to have a wash and then dumped my belongings in the garage. Nervously I moved to the entrance of the darshan room. Over a sea of shoes I walked into the small hall. It was packed. I never thought that so many people could get into one room. How was I to find a place?

Some serious concern gripped me at the thought that I'd miss out due to lack of sitting space. I felt more determined to find room. I had not come this far to be stopped by lack of seating space.

Pushing my way in past people standing at the door, I maneuvered through the sea of people sitting on the floor and found a small space against a wall. With knees up against my chest I began what was to be a familiar experience: waiting for Baba in a crowded, cramped room with aching knees and backside.

Then I was called to the front by an acharya who knew me from when I had been in India in 1975. I was soon in front of the room listening to this Dada talking in Bengali about me and the Hilton case. I was then asked to say something. I spoke a bit about the struggle we had for so long but also how God graced me with many wonderful spiritual experiences. Then I was told to sit down, only now I was in the front. Thank you.

After what seemed like hours, voices and excitement swept through the room with a sound of "Baba's here!" and "Baba's back! (he'd been out for his daily walk). Excitedly, and with some nervousness, I waited for that long-awaited experience to finally meet my guru.

"What will Baba be like?" "Will I experience anything?" These and other thoughts went through my racing mind. I thought of the wondrous stories I had heard from people about being in Baba's presence and I wondered if anything would happen to me.

Baba's Presence

Suddenly, there was some noise, a door at the front was flung open and in came Baba, followed by a mass of acharyas. I perceived something special about Baba immediately, something divine and super-human. The air in the room seemed to be electrified. With my subtle vision I could see a different vibration around Baba—like an electric storm.

In the midst of this tremendous energy, Baba had amazing dignity and control. Senior acharyas, who could be gurus in their own right, seemed like little puppy dogs around him, eager to please. Some Margiis cried out, "Baba," while others just looked up in awe and wonder. I was also transfixed for the whole hour and a half while Baba sat and talked in Bengali. I could not take my eyes off him. I was totally charmed and captivated by him. I had never experienced this with a person before.

Baba spoke in Bengali since the majority of people there were Bengali-speaking (other times Baba spoke in English, Hindi or other languages). Nevertheless, it was easy to feel the atmosphere he was creating. He sometimes joked and I found myself laughing with everyone else. Not because I understood what he was saying but partly because he looked so funny laughing and partly because the atmosphere was so infectious. Baba created such a sweet family feeling. He would often joke individually with someone like they were a close relative or friend. Everyone was enjoying themselves, especially Baba. But I felt no bliss, love, or strong pull of devotion for him. It was more enchantment and fascination than anything else.

Finally, it came time for Baba to leave. A crowd of acharyas scrambled behind him. As he walked passed me, only a foot or two away, it felt like a powerhouse of energy passed by me. It was something I'd never experienced before.

Suddenly, Baba was gone. It was over. I closed my eyes and meditated. Bliss and love overcame me. Tears ran down my cheeks. It was as though my nervous system could not take all the energy Baba was giving out and I could only take it all in now that he had gone. Every cell in my body was tingling with ecstasy and joy. It was an incredible feeling. I sat transfixed for a half an hour before the reality of my situation set in again.

Later, I was told that during the darshan Baba had been talking about some of his own experiences in jail. It made me feel he was welcoming me and wanted to let me know that he also knew what it was like to be in jail.

I stayed at the Ananda Marga headquarters in Tiljala, an outer suburb of Calcutta and every morning I joined many others in the ritual of taking a rickshaw to Baba's house. We spent the afternoon and evening waiting to get a glimpse of Baba leaving or entering his house. Baba was driven to a park where he went for a walk. What we saw was him getting into and out of the car when going or returning from his walk in the park. This was called 'field walk'.

Margiis from all around the world gathered around Baba's car to catch a glimpse of him. Men waited on one side of his car and women on the other. I always tried to stand near the back window where Baba sat, hoping to get a look or comment from him. Often I would catch his eye, though he rarely spoke. Every time he got in and out of his car I felt him give me a one or two second stare, while greeting everyone with palms folded at the heart in the Sanskrit greeting of 'Namaskar'.

Doubts Shattered

While I was in prison I had developed a bit of a complex because it seemed like Baba wasn't really concerned about what we were going through. To my knowledge, Baba never inquired about how we were doing in jail. Years after our release, however, Acharya Abhidevananda, who was working in Australia at the time, told me that when he visited Baba in jail, Baba gave him a garland and said, "Take this garland and give it to those boys who are taking on sufferings knowingly." Dada understood that the garland was meant for us.

I didn't hear about this story until later, so while I was in jail I wondered if the reason why Baba hadn't asked about us was that according to his standards what we were going through was no big deal. After all Baba had suffered from the effects of a near lethal dose of poison administered to him by the prison doctor and had fasted on a hunger strike for five and a half years out of the six and a half years he was in prison. My own trials seemed minor in comparison to this. So when I arrived to see Baba this little doubt was in the back of my mind:

"Does Baba think much of me? Does he want to see me as much as I want to see him? Does Baba appreciate my little sacrifices since being a Margii, some of which were big sacrifices for me?"

While I knew intellectually that the answer to these questions was "yes," I still had my doubts. I guess I just wanted to hear it from him personally, although I didn't really expect anything.

"Who am I that Baba should be bothered about telling me how much he appreciates what I do for him?" I thought when my self confidence was low. Then I would remind myself, "Baba loves me no matter what and he knows and appreciates everything I do for him. But more importantly, do I appreciate all that he is constantly doing for me?"

Two experiences occurred with Baba that exploded these doubts. The first happened when I was near Baba as he left for his field walk. As usual Baba first scanned everyone with one of his long Namaskar greetings, giving me a momentary pause before ending and getting into the car.

I was now looking at Baba through the car window where he sat in the back. Normally he would look straight ahead as the car drove away. This time however, Baba turned his head to look at me and then motioned with his hand for me to sit next to him in the car. My lack of confidence did not allow me to understand the obvious; he was beckoning me to come and sit with him. Instead I became confused and couldn't understand why he was waving his hand up and down at me.

I was too frightened to get in the car with him unless there was no doubt whatsoever it was what Baba wanted. I felt I would die of shame if I got into the car and learned he did not want me there.

After a few long seconds of beckoning me, Baba stopped. I did Namaskar to Baba and he smiled saying some nice things to me before the car left. I felt quite blissful from Baba's smile and his kind words directed especially at me. But I felt frustrated that I hadn't understood what Baba had wanted from me.

Baba's car drove away. An Australian friend who had been standing next to me turned to look at me: "You dummy! Baba was telling you to get in with him, why didn't you get in?"

My heart hit the floor as I realised I had just missed a chance to ride next to Baba, an opportunity that Baba hardly ever offered. I replied that I did not understand what he was doing but that only made me feel even more foolish.

On his returned Baba stepped out of the car and did Namaskar to everyone. He then looked at me and did some unusual hand movement in my direction. I did not understand what it meant and just responded with, "Namaskar, Baba." He replied, "Namaskar," with that look of love and divinity which I'd grown to cherish so much, and left.

A man said to me that Baba was asking how I was. Apparently that particular gesture Baba had used was a kind of common Bengali sign language that everyone understood. Again a feeling of pain and frustration hit me as I realised I'd missed out on an opportunity to have a close experience with him. I resolved not to let it happen again.

The next day when Baba returned from his field walk, he offered his usual Namaskar to everyone, but then stopped in front of me. Baba did another hand movement to me which I didn't understand. Not knowing how to respond I returned it with, "Namaskar, Baba." Baba gave a loving smile and left. Again I was told afterwards that Baba was inquiring about my health. I became particularly frustrated, even annoyed with him. Why was he doing these things to me when, as an all knowing guru, he knew I did not understand what he was communicating?

Later, Baba's assistant, Dada Keshavananda, told me that when Baba returned to his room from the field walk, he asked, "Why doesn't Narada speak to me?"

Hearing Baba ask about me, was such a thrill. One time I brought a simple gift for Baba. His assistant said that when he offered it to Baba, he asked, "Is Narada Muni here?" sounding both surprised I would come this far to see him, as well as sounding very happy that I was there.

Then I understood. I had been thinking Baba would not want to speak to me. Now Baba was playing a joke on me and making it look as if I didn't want to speak to *him!* It was Baba's way of showing how foolish I was to ever think or feel that I was insignificant in his eyes.

The second incident was during a beautiful evening outside Baba's house. It seemed to me to be a special night. The garden lights shone on Baba, giving an added radiance to his already illuminated presence. Just before getting into his car, Baba stopped and said in English, "I would like to invite you all to attend a festival of light. This light is both within and without and I would like to invite you to attend it permanently."

Everyone was struck with surprise and ecstasy at Baba's unexpected mysticism, especially in English. Suddenly, I found myself spontaneously responding with, "Thank you, Baba." I just felt so much appreciation for what he said and the love I felt coming from him. Baba stopped, tilted his head forward as if to listen more closely. Then he looked straight at me with intensity, love and appreciation said, "And I thank you."

I felt such a strong wave of love with these magic words. Immediately, I knew that he was thanking me for what I'd been through in jail. As Baba got into his car his words kept ringing in my mind. Everyone else seemed oblivious to our interaction. Baba made it seem so personal and intimate. As the car drove off I was left melting in love and spiritual ecstasy.

The Garland

In all, I was in Calcutta for three weeks. What a blissful time it was! Baba seemed so loving, gracious and blissful. In his own way he did shower a lot of attention on me, despite my ignorance and reticence.

All good things come to an end (as do all bad things) and soon it was time to go home. Well, home is not quite the best word to use because I felt so at home around Baba.

When it came time to go I bought a garland of flowers at the marketplace to offer to Baba as a traditional gift from a devotee to a guru. Because so many Margiis wanted to offer garlands to Baba he didn't always accept them, or sometimes they were just given to his assistant. I wondered if he would accept mine.

I heard the sound of Baba's car returning from the field walk and excitement overcame me. I was also afraid Baba wouldn't let me garland him directly—the opportunity to touch Baba physically was very special. Baba got out and started to do Namaskar to everyone. I frantically pushed my way through the crowd to get in a position to be near Baba.

Baba finished his Namaskar and slowly turned to me. With those incredibly penetrating and loving eyes Baba slowly looked up at me (he was only 162 cm and I am 170 cm.) Looking at the garland he said sweetly, "Is that for me?"

My heart went a hundred miles an hour, my mind even faster and I froze, again afraid of responding in the wrong way and upsetting him.

"Yes Baba," I finally said. I started to hold the garland a little, but hesitated. Then I felt someone from behind pushing my arm to put the garland around Baba's neck. I resisted but Baba bent his head down to me. My dull thick brain finally realised that dear Baba did indeed want me to garland him. Nervously, I placed the beautiful flowers gently around his neck.

Baba said, "So you are going now, when will you come again?"

The Dadas had been telling me I should come back in December for the special New Year's gathering, so I said, "For the New Year's celebration, Baba."

Such a sweet joyous smile bloomed from his face as he said, "I think that is a grand idea."

Slowly, Baba turned and walked away. The bliss was overpowering. I felt like the happiest person in the world. I felt honoured to have finally met such an unusual personality. Baba was so humble, unassuming and loving, yet so powerful and commanding. It's difficult to comprehend and even more difficult to explain.

21
Dreams Fulfilled

*Mysticism is a never-ending endeavor
to find the link between the finite and the infinite.
--Baba*

I WAS ONLY IN SYDNEY A SHORT TIME BEFORE I HAD A STRONG DESIRE TO GO BACK to see Baba again. I had told Baba I would return in December and Jenny had also agreed to go with me so we could be married in India. Twice a year in India, in May and December, there was a major spiritual gathering called Dharma Maha Cakra, or DMC. Baba gave darshan and important discourses. Tens of thousands of Margiis came from all over the world. Baba gave a special blessing to couples who were married there and we looked forward to that special opportunity.

By late December Jenny and I were on a plane to India. All my dreams were coming true at once. It was astonishing how quickly my life had changed. From the degenerating atmosphere of prison, I had been released to find both worldly and spiritual pleasure. I was romantically in love with Jenny and perhaps equally spiritually attracted to Baba. Life was very sweet.

Arriving at the global office in Calcutta we set out to make arrangements for our marriage. We requested a Dada and Didi to perform the marriage, and also requested permission to receive Baba's blessing. Baba would only bless those who had a 'revolutionary marriage' which meant that the couple had in some way crossed traditional barriers. They could be from from different countries or cultures, different religions or castes, or different economic background. This adds a challenging dimension to the relationship and helps break down the unnatural boundaries that separate people. We managed to be considered 'revolutionary' because of our differing class and religious backgrounds.

Baba's Blessing

Our marriage was conducted in a huge tent with about 10,000 Margiis watching. It was quite an experience. We followed the Ananda Marga system of marriage, which is simple but very meaningful. We took vows to each other promising to care for each other's physical, mental and spiritual well-being. Then the whole audience also took an oath to support our marriage.

Feeling quite high from the bliss of the wedding we waited for the time we could get Baba's blessing. It happened the first night of the DMC gathering. We were one of about a dozen couples hoping to get his blessing. We waited anxiously in a line to the side of the stage were Baba sat before about 30,000 Margiis. The atmosphere was already electrified by Baba's presence. After hearing some devotional songs Baba signalled for the marriage blessings to begin. One by one the couples were called by name to come in front of Baba. Next thing I knew I could hear our names being called out over the PA system. It was time to receive Baba's blessing.

Baba was sitting on a dias and we knelt before him and offered him a garland. He accepted the garland and said, "Be like Shiva and Parvati and serve the universe with maximum zeal." Shiva, an enlightened master, was said to have invented the marriage system some 7,000 years ago and Parvati was his wife and spiritual partner.

I felt such a strong vibration when I was near Baba. It became quite difficult to concentrate or to think coherently, as my mind was so high and vibrated. We both staggered away after receiving the blessing and went to sit amongst the sea of Margiis, watching Baba and enjoying everything.

Baba gave a discourse on some spiritual topic but I did not absorb much as my mind was somewhere else. Jenny was 'blissed out' as well.

Baba's Mudra

It was special during DMC to enjoy two darshans each day with Baba when he would talk, joke and just sit where we could watch him. Baba gave several longer discourses, as was his habit. They were about deep spiritual topics as well as important social issues. Another specially delightful feature of DMC was the performance of Baba's own songs called Prabhat Samgiit. He had written by that time hundreds of spiritual songs. (he wrote over 5,000 in all) The songs were made up of tunes and melodies from cultures all over the world. The lyric was usually spiritual in nature, although sometimes social or cultural. Most were written in Bengali, although Baba wrote a few in English and other languages. Many of Baba's songs seemed to capture exactly my own spiritual feelings:

> You came in my heart and filled it with hope,
> In the house of hopelessness
> That which was covered with darkness
> Was mixed with effulgence...(Song no. 960)

The highlight of the DMC gathering was always Baba's *mudra*. A mudra is a special vibrationally-charged hand position. At the end of DMC, Baba held a special mudra for several seconds. I had heard many times about the incredible vibration everyone felt at this time. It was meant to be a great spiritual blessing to experience Baba's mudra.

On the night of the mudra I felt great anticipation. Since my first days as a Margii, I had been dreaming of this opportunity. Baba completed his evening discourse and chanted a special blessing in Hindu, English and Bengali:

> Let everyone be happy
> Let everyone be free from pain,
> Let everybody see the bright side of things
> Let nobody have to suffer under pressure of circumstances.

The entire tent of tens of thousands of people was absolutely silent as Baba formed his hands into the special mudra position. Then it was as if a wave of consciousness washed over everyone, or a bolt of spiritual electricity passed through the crowd. Margiis cried out, or began laughing, crying or even singing. Some fell over in a spiritual trance. I felt a very subtle feeling like electricity pass through me and I felt that my consciousness had undergone a change on a very deep level. Jenny wept next to me. She told me later she had had a wonderful feeling during the mudra and she was crying tears of bliss.

After that first DMC I was hooked on the desire to experience more and more of Baba's presence. It was so easy to experience spiritual bliss around Baba. This felt like a wonderful reward after my intense spiritual struggles in jail.

Back to Reality

After three blissful weeks in India, Jenny and I returned to Australia to begin our new life together. While life was generally very enjoyable and exciting, the years that followed presented a few adjustments and challenges for me.

As a result of the stress of my seven years in jail and the poor diet that had caused hypoglycemia, I suffered from chronic fatigue. Any kind of physical work exhausted me completely after just a couple of hours. After prison, since I couldn't do physical work and I didn't have any intellectual skills I could rely on for a job, I went on a government sickness pension until I regained my health. Fortunately, soon after our marriage we moved out of Sydney to help found a small Ananda Marga cooperative community in rural Queensland, where I still live today. In this pristine mountain environment we were able grow much of our own food, drink pure rainwater and breathe smog free air. This contributed considerably to my ability to regain good health.

Employment was difficult. This was partly because I had no skills. I had gone to jail at the age of 22 and came out at 29. I also had to explain what I had been doing in the past decade. Writing on a job application that I had been 'a cleaner for government institutions' avoided any mention of prison but also didn't do much to impress prospective employers.

I also found it difficult to adjust to sharing my life with another person in partnership and negotiating the complexities of living in a community. After seven years of living mostly on my own, it took some time and effort to re-learn some basic social and cooperation skills.

One of the most difficult social challenges for me was empathising with other people's problems. After what I had been through many of the difficulties my friends complained to me about seemed petty by comparison. I spoke with my doctor about it and she said this was a common complaint of returning soldiers. After experiencing the intensity of war few small things seem really important. I had to work hard to learn to appreciate people's struggles in their own context.

I also found that I had developed some anger in jail that was hard to control. If I was threatened in any way I would instinctively want to fight back. I had to control my instincts by reminding myself I was not in jail where a small threat could easily be followed by a full attack. This took considerable effort and meditation to manage constructively. After we had our two sons, I still had to work with my anger and tendency to react. Once when my eldest son was playing with me when he was only a few years old and accidentally kicked me in the eye. I almost punched him from pure reflex. These kinds of incidents happened from time to time.

I gradually adjusted to my new life and environment over the years. Several trips to India to see Baba made the adjustment easier. After each trip I felt that a major load had been lifted off my shoulders.

The compensation money was soon spent on land and our new house. Money continued to come in from our case, however, as a result of several successful defamation law suits against newspapers and a television station. Even some time after our release and pardon, the media continued to report that the three of us had been convicted of the Hilton bombing, when of course we had never even been charged with it. Each time the media made such a claim, we sued for defamation.

This money helped finance our trips to India and support my family for a few years. It felt like cosmic justice to me. After all, we had been wrongly convicted in the first place because jurors believed we were responsible for the Hilton bombing, largely because of the media's portrayal of us as the bombers. It seemed fair that now some of them were having to pay, literally, for their mistakes.

Personal Contact

For the next five years I was fortunate to be able to visit Baba at least once a year. During that time I had some very memorable experiences with Baba. The most profound was having a personal interview with him.

Baba had a system of meeting with each Margii personally at least once. This meeting was called 'personal contact'. Baba would only allow this meeting if the Margii had shown commitment to their social service duties. Fortunately for me I had been doing some service and I was permitted to have personal contact.

I asked many Margiis what Baba said and did during these meetings. I noticed he had a set of questions with little variation. I decided on some answers that would prolong my stay with him. Since the meeting usually lasted only about ten minutes, I was keen to drag it out as long as I could. I also had many questions I wanted to ask him. I dreamed about asking him about my past lives, my future, and what to do for a certain illness. Despite my plans, I was also aware that Baba must be aware of my desire to prolong the meeting and in the end he would arrange it as he liked.

After some days of waiting, I was finally called to wait outside Baba's door as I would be the next person to see him. Thoughts poured into my mind as I waited in anticipation. I wondered if Baba might scold me, as he had others. He had a way of finding out 'secret sins' that people thought they had done in private and then telling them about it. Would Baba embarrass me by telling me in detail of my past impure thoughts?

As I waited just outside Baba's room, I remembered my many experiences with my 'internal' Baba, such as the time he spoke to me so clearly at Goulburn jail, or when he appeared so vividly in my meditations at Long Bay jail. I felt excited that now I was going to be meeting Baba in private. Suddenly, my reminiscing was interrupted and I was told it was my turn to go in and meet Baba.

As soon as I entered his room a deep peace and calm overcame me. I felt more content and happy than I had ever felt before. Baba was sitting on his cot, smiling ever so blissfully and lovingly towards me. Baba told me to sit before him. Then he looked at me silently with just a little hint of a smile. It felt like he was looking into my mind, scanning it for who knows what? I was transfixed.

Baba then told me I had been a bad boy in the past and asked if I wanted to receive punishment (as a way of rectifying the past mistakes). I agreed. Baba pulled out a stick and made the motion of striking me but very slowly and gently so that it was only a gentle tap on my ribs. Baba asked if I would take an oath, which I agreed to do. I promised to do my meditation regularly, follow moral principles, and to serve humanity selflessly. Baba said that I'd done some great work in the past but that I would do great service in the future. Baba put his hand on my head and said a special blessing before telling me to go.

I left reluctantly. While I was with Baba I had forgotten all my plans for prolonging my stay. In the end my time with him was actually shorter than the others he saw that day. But I felt totally satisfied and contented.

Reporting

Another opportunity to be in Baba's presence was to attend a 'reporting' session. In order to supervise the work of quite a vast organisation, Baba held meetings with different groups of acharyas and Margiis who were doing work in different sections of Ananda Marga. I was a District Secretary at the time, so I attended a meeting with other District Secretaries from all around the world. These reporting sessions were always a mixture of excitement and tension. There was excitement because no one knew what Baba might do. While he might focus on the work itself, he also often gave talks on spiritual topics, sometimes giving a demonstration of a spiritual principle or even putting someone into *samadhi* (a spiritually intoxicated state). Sometimes he showed his humour or his vast knowledge.

On the other hand, there was tension because sometimes Baba would display anger if he knew the reports given were exaggerated or false, or if he felt the work wasn't up to standard(our work was rarely up to Baba's standard).

Reporting was fascinating though I was never called personally to give a report. In one session a man was giving a report on the service work he had done when Baba became agitated. Baba did not seem to believe the man. Baba asked more detailed questions until finally the man admitted he had been exaggerating.

Sometimes Baba would listen for awhile to a report about a particular area of the world. Then he would surprise everyone by telling details about the district that the person living there did not even know. Baba commented on mineral resources, population, dominant religions and languages, cultures, political systems, industries and crops and gave practical solutions to problems in the region. It was all very inspiring.

Being in complete control of himself, Baba could switch suddenly from one extreme emotion, like anger, to another, like great sweetness and affection. Often I saw him do this after scolding someone. To achieve the desired effect (usually to get one to confess his or her misbehaviour) Baba would become incredibly loving. Baba said that if he only showed love we would not learn right from wrong, but if he only scolded we wouldn't want to be near him and would not learn anything either. He had to balance the two, like a loving parent with his children.

Animal Attraction

While I certainly was aware of my own attraction for Baba and could see the effect Baba had on many people, I was surprised to note that Baba also appeared to attract animals to him.

Once I had the opportunity to go with Baba and some other Margiis for a field walk at about 10 pm. Baba was so busy that he stretched out his day by keeping a rather unusual schedule and sleeping only a couple of hours each night. Evening field walk, which Baba did before his dinner, was often very late. It was a very still night and as we walked through a Calcutta park, I noticed that the birds in the tree that Baba was walking under, would suddenly wake up and start singing. It was clearly noticeable in the quiet of the night. As soon as Baba moved away from the tree the birds suddenly stopped singing, even while we Margiis were still walking under the same tree.

On another occasion, I was sitting by the side of Baba's chair during a discourse. I happened to look out of the nearby window and saw a remarkable sight. Below us was a pond in Baba's garden filled with goldfish. As I looked down all the goldfish were gathered at the surface looking up towards Baba. When Baba finished his talk and left the room the goldfish disappeared from the surface of the pond! Since then I have passed by that pond many times but I have never seen the goldfish behave in that way again. In fact, I have seen very few goldfish in the pond at all as the water is deep and darkly coloured.

Hilton Bomber Alert!

During one of my visits to India, the General Secretary of Ananda Marga called me to his office and said I had to leave West Bengal, the state that Calcutta is in. Apparently a newspaper had published an article saying that one of the Ananda Marga Hilton bombers was in Calcutta. That of course referred to me. Even though that was clearly untrue, I knew that given Indian police and politics, I was at risk of deportation at best and imprisonment at worse, if I was found.

Jenny and I decided to go to Bettiah, a town near the Himalayas. While we were there the local Dada arranged for us to give talks on meditation to some interested community groups. Jenny spoke at a girls' college with about 600 attending. I spoke at a factory and to a group of lawyers. After the talk one of the lawyers commented on the irony of the situation. Here they were, Indians, coming to listen to me, a Westerner, speak on the Indian practice of meditation. Usually, it was the other way around. I also noted the humour in the situation but commented that meditation is a spiritual practice that anyone can do, and with time and effort anyone can become an expert. Spiritual practice isn't confined to any one culture or country.

When we returned to Calcutta we kept a low profile until we left India.

22
Saying Good-bye

There were tears in my eyes the day you left
"When will you come again?" I asked
"We will meet in love whenever you call."
—Baba, Prabhat Samgiit

THE LAST TIME I SAW BABA WAS IN DECEMBER, 1989, AT HIS HOUSE IN CALCUTTA. Baba had cancelled the New Year's DMC gathering because of ill health. I suspected that as a self-realised guru he often took on the bad karma of his devotees, which caused his illness. Baba has also never fully recovered his health since his poisoning attempt and extended fast in jail. Baba had had various ailments during the years, such as diabetes, but nothing had ever seemed to slow him down. This time it was clearly more serious and the acharyas who worked closely with him seemed to be more worried. I only saw Baba a few times as he was pushed around his garden in a wheelchair, checking the plants and commenting about them. It was beautiful to see him in the garden surrounded by the many plants that devotees had brought from around the world. This trip was one of my most special times in India.

Normally, when I was visiting Baba I meditated eight or sometimes ten hours a day. This time, for a few days, I began meditating 16 hours a day. I was feeling very introverted, detached and blissful. The internal world I was experiencing was becoming stronger for me than the external 'reality'. I perceived everything as a divine and blissful play of God Consciousness. Other times I would have been very upset at seeing so little of Baba but now I realised what Baba had repeatedly told us: the real 'Baba' was inside us and not in his physical form. I was enjoying Baba's presence so strongly internally that I didn't feel the need to see him physically as before.

After three weeks, it was time to leave and return to Australia to be with my wife and children. While I loved them dearly, there was no denying my love for Baba. Like so many others, I felt deep sorrow each time I had to leave. Besides not knowing when I would see Baba again, I also knew that back in Australia I would not have the time or inclination to spend as many hours in blissful meditation.

With a heavy heart, I prepared to leave for Calcutta airport at noon. Early in the morning I sat for my last meditation in India. I had been meditating for a few hours when I saw Baba very vividly in my mind. He was standing at the end of a long hallway. He was surrounded by darkness except for a white aura that radiated out from him. I also sensed a heavy sadness, but it was not my sadness but his. Baba's hands were folded in Namaskar and I understood that he felt very sad that I was leaving.

This experience touched me deeply. Here I was, feeling sorry for myself at leaving Baba, yet it never occurred to me that he was feeling (much more) sorrow because I was leaving him. It was not until the following October when I was at Baba's cremation that I realised Baba was giving his last goodbye to me during his time in a physical form.

Baba's Departure

News of Baba's death shocked everyone. Twice in Baba's lifetime he had announced that he was leaving his body but after repeated pleas from his followers, he remained. This time he told no one. He died suddenly of a heart failure, catching everyone unprepared.

On reflection some people who were close to Baba realised that he had said things that were hints that he would be leaving us soon. For example, shortly before his death, he called a group of acharyas into his room for a reporting session. His assistants thought he was too sick to meet with people but Baba arranged it despite them. He asked the gathered acharyas if he could depend on them to carry out his work and asked everyone present to take a vow of service. They repeated in front of Baba:

> All my energy, all my mind, all my thoughts and all my deeds are to be goaded unto the path of collective elevation of human society without neglecting other living and inanimate entities, from this moment until the last moment of my living on this earth.

Then they came individually up to Baba and he blessed them and said to each one, "Remember me."

I heard about Baba's death when a friend called me with the news. I was very upset and shocked by the news. While I had developed a very close internal relationship with Baba, there was still no denying my attachment to his sweet and special physical presence.

I had been planning to go to India several times that year but something always came up which caused me to cancel. I had a ticket ready to go, and like many Margiis, I decided to go to India to take part in Baba's cremation ceremony.

I arrived at a huge gathering of Margiis from India and around the world. It was like a huge family gathering as many of the people were familiar to me. Everyone was gloomy, distraught, and trying to adjust to life without Baba.

Before the cremation we were allowed to look at Baba's body. It was displayed, surrounded by flowers, in a special room. While I was waiting to go in, I stood near a man who wasn't a Margii but lived in the village near the Ananda Marga headquarters. He looked very upset. He said for years he had heard about Baba but he had never come to see him. Now it was too late for him to get to know this great personality.

I approached Baba's body with curiosity and sadness. While looking at it, I heard a very clear voice speaking to me. "I am not this body, if you want to know me do more and more spiritual meditation (*sadhana*)." My previous grief vanished and I went outside to meditate.

Watching Baba's body burning during the cremation did not bother me after that. I no longer related to it as Baba, who I realised was my own inner spirit or consciousness. Now that this medium to God Consciousness was gone, I had to rely more on my inner Baba or soul (*atman*), and the extensive ideology and spiritual organisation that Baba had left behind.

At the cremation ceremony one acharya shared a story. He said years before, Baba sent the acharya's mind into the future and then asked him to explain to everyone present in the room what he could see. The Dada described to the room of people the vision he saw: he was at the global headquarters and everyone was crying and very distraught. When Dada returned to normal consciousness he asked Baba what this vision meant. Baba said in time he would understand. Dada forgot about the experience until he came to the cremation and realised he was now witnessing what Baba had shown him in the vision years before.

I still am amazed that I had the privilege of meeting Baba. While I did not personally experience any of the more incredible feats attributed to him, I certainly experienced enough to convince me of his divinity. It was Baba's unconditional love that impressed me most. Baba told us there were two factors that demonstrated externally a person's level of spiritual progress: their positivity and the radius of their love. We should love unconditionally, not only all humans but also plants, animals, even inanimate objects, as manifestations of God. Baba was the embodiment of positivity and love.

Epilogue:
The Diamond and the Rose

Whatever you do, the Supreme Consciousness sees everything...
no part of your being is closed or shut.
He is the innermost part of your being.

—Baba

As I write this it has been over seven years since Baba's death. He continues to come into my dreams and indirectly into my daily life to instruct and inspire me. Once I had a clear dream about Baba and he reminded me of a specific spiritual practice. The next day I had a very serious accident when my motorcycle collided with a car. I was thrown over the car and onto the road. Fortunately I didn't hit anything when I came off my bike, but when I landed on the road I was in extreme pain and lay on the ground in agony. I thought I might have broken my back. Then I remembered what Baba told me in the dream and I proceeded to do the meditation he had taught me. Within seconds a man appeared with a mobile phone and called for an ambulance. Meanwhile, my pain receded considerably. Hours later I was discharged with nothing broken and my body healed extremely quickly.

Another time I had to cross a raging river during a flood. I lost my balance and was swept off my feet and carried off into the current. I was heading towards rocks and certain death. I began to say my mantra mentally as I became transfixed on the oncoming rocks and concrete causeway the river was rushing over. Suddenly I heard Baba's voice telling me to look up. I looked up and saw an overhanging branch. I grabbed it and pulled myself to safety.

On a couple of occasions I went through extreme emotional suffering that lasted for some months due to relationship difficulties. In both cases,

Baba appeared in a dream and smiled at me blissfully. The next day, the emotional pain vanished.

Life Goes On

Ananda Marga remains a large global social service and meditation organisation. Baba had created a complex network of departments and boards to run Ananda Marga and had organised it in such a way that his direct leadership wasn't necessary. Baba had no successor but according to the system he'd created, a new president was elected from among the senior acharyas.

Acharya Shraddhananda Avadhuta was unanimously elected as president. I met him while he toured Australia and visited our Ananda Marga community in Queensland. He is a wise, humble and spiritual person and everyone felt happy that he had been chosen. The President acts as advisor to the organisation and oversees the General Secretary and the various departments that run the day-to-day operations.

My family in 1996. Sons Krishna Ryan and Ajit Nicholas and my wife Kamala, at our home on a beautiful Ananda Marga Community in rural Queensland.

My life is now quite happy. I have remarried and have begun a new career in counseling and welfare work. I have worked with prisoners and now work with street kids in a youth refuge. Like my wife, Kamala, I am also a professional astrologer and do some graphic design work. I also love surfing and Australian football.

I am also active with Ananda Marga as district secretary for the Sunshine Coast of Queensland and am a member of the management committee of the Ananda Marga River School, an independent primary school.

Hilton Bombing Fall-out Continues

The Hilton bombing case is still discussed from time to time in Parliament. Calls for a Royal Commission have not brought any result although the New South Wales Government has opened all documents on the case to the public.

In early 1997, the Premier of New South Wales, Bob Carr, announced that Special Branch will finally be closed down. The national news reports that followed often referred to our case as part of the controversy that surrounds Special Branch in that state. It seems the Hilton bombing debacle almost succeeded in doing what Special Branch had hoped: at least it extended the life of Special Branch for an extra 15 years.

In late November of 1997 Evan Pederick was released from prison having served eight and a half years for the Hilton bombing. He still claimed responsibility for the crime, but does not seem eager to give out any useful details.

Personally I am not convinced he is responsible, given that evidence he presented in court does not match the known facts. However, if he did commit the crime, it may have been on behalf of ASIO and/or Special Branch. Ananda Marga clearly had nothing to gain from the bombing and such an act goes against our beliefs. The Indian Prime Minister, who supposedly would have been the target of the bomb, had been recently elected and had indicated he would bring about Baba's release, so for Ananda Marga to attempt to kill him makes absolutely no sense. (In fact, Baba *was* acquitted following a re-trial that occurred after Desai lifted martial law.) Baba himself said his release would not be attained through violent means but through the proper legal procedure.

Nevertheless some sections of the media continue to portray

Ananda Marga as a violent organisation. We still see the use of subtle half-truths such as a recent article in a major newspaper that mentioned Baba's imprisonment, but didn't mention his acquittal on all charges and the subsequent condemnation of his persecution by several respected international legal organisations. Or a recent article in *Newsweek* that listed Ananda Marga as one of the top world terrorist organisations, but didn't even bother to check its sources to discover that the office location they listed was over ten years out of date (and of course, most importantly, that Margiis had been acquitted of all the charges anyway!) It is a sobering lesson for me each time I read these slurs in the newspapers and magazines that I depend on for my information about the world.

The Cracked Diamond

Truth can be stranger than fiction. My life has certainly been a testimony to that. Both my spiritual life and involvement with the Hilton bombing case have been extraordinary events and remind me that some things baffle our understanding and continually remind us how little our rational mind can possibly understand. I also feel that there is an invisible hand that guides our life with compassion, no matter what it may seem like at the time.

There is a story about a king who had a favourite large diamond. One day he dropped it and the diamond cracked. The king offered half his kingdom to the person who could restore his diamond to its past perfection. However, the person who tried and failed would lose their head.

Talented jewelers from many lands came forward but no one dared to repair the diamond for fear of losing their life. Besides, how could anyone repair a cracked diamond? Finally, a jeweler came forward and said she would do the job. With great care and artistry she made the crack into a stem supporting a tiny rose engraved into the diamond. When she showed it to the king he agreed that now the diamond was more beautiful than ever.

This story illustrates how we can make seemingly disastrous incidents into something wonderful. Crises can be stepping stones to empowerment and deeper happiness and wisdom. Certainly that has been my experience.

Epilogue: Third Edition, 2016

Twenty years later, as Kamala and I complete the edits for the third edition, there have been some big changes though many things remain the same. We have two more sons, Manikya and Tapash, who are now teenagers. We continue to live on the Ananda Marga community and the Ananda Marga River School here is a beautiful example of Neohumanist Education which touches the lives of many students and families. I still love surfing and Australian football.

Over a decade ago I completed the intensive training to become a "Family Acharya." I am one of only a few family people who have the training to individually teach Ananda Marga meditation.

I film and produce videos for my business, Alister Multimedia, and we continue to work to support many aspects of Ananda Marga.

Meditation remains a central focus of my life and I am grateful for all the lessons and blessings this spiritual life has brought me.

My family in 2016
From top left: Krishna, myself, Kamala, Tapash, Ajit and Manikya

Appendix 1
Moral Practices of Ananda Marga

Yama & Niyama
These principles are considered the base of Ananda Marga spiritual practices.
Ahimsa: Not to intentionally cause pain through thought, word or action.
Satya: The right use of words with the spirit of welfare; benevolent truthfulness.
Asteya: Non-stealing or depriving others of their due through action or thoughts.
Aparigraha: Moderation in all worldly things.
Brahmacarya: Perceiving God in everything.
Shaoca: Physical and environmental cleanliness and mental purity.
Santosa: Contentment.
Tapah: Selfless service. To undergo harships in order to help others.
Svadhyaya: Spiritual study and understanding its underlining meaning.
Iishvara Pranidhana: Faith and surrender to God Consciousness regardless of circumstances.

15 Points for Character Building
These points are important in personal life and in social integration.
1. Forgiveness
2. Magnanimity of mind
3. Restraint of behaviour and temper
4. Sacrificing nature
5. All round self-restraint
6. Sweet and smiling nature
7. Moral courage
8. Setting an example by individual conduct before asking anyone else to do the same.
9. Keeping aloof from criticising others, condemning others, mudslinging and all forms of groupism.
10. Adherence to Yama and Niyama(above).
11. Due to carelessness, if a mistake has been make, to admit it immediately and ask for rectification.
12. Even while dealing with persons of inimical nature, one must keep oneself aloof from hatred, anger and vanity.
13. Keeping aloof from talkativeness.
14. Following the structural code of discipline.
15. Having a sense of responsibility.

Appendix 2

Major Departments & Sections of Ananda Marga

(I am including this list to give a glimpse at the wide scope of Ananda Marga activities. There is scope here for people to serve in a variety of ways.)

1. ERAWS (Education, Relief and Welfare). The main service section of Ananda Marga, including schools, relief work and welfare institutions.

2. WWD (Women's Welfare Department). Managed and staffed by women for women's needs in the ERAWS activities.

3. AMURT/AMURTEL (Ananda Marga Universal Relief Team). AMURTEL is the women's section of AMURT. AMURT/EL provides emergency or permanent relief to the public at the time of natural and human-made disasters. AMURT is affiliated with the Red Cross and is registered as a non-governmental organisation with the United Nations.

4. DHARMA PRACAR. The propagation of Ananda Marga's spiritual ideology, especially through teaching meditation and yoga.

5. SEVADAL. Provides relief and material assistance to economically disadvantaged people.

6. MEDICAL. Establishes hospitals, clinics and medical programmes.

7. RAWA (Renaissance Artists and Writers Association). For the development of fine arts in the spirit of service and spirituality.

8. RENAISSANCE UNIVERSAL. A part of RAWA, it promotes universal and progressive ideas and concepts among scientists and other intellectuals.

9. PCAP (Prevention of Cruelty to Animals and Plants). A practical expression of Neohumanism. It promotes vegetarianism and other life-supporting projects.

10. TRIBAL AND BACKWARD PEOPLE'S WELFARE DEPARTMENT

11. PUBLICATIONS

12. LAND

13. CONSTRUCTION (of buildings)

14. FARM

15. COMMERCE

16. INDUSTRY

17. EMS (EKA MANAV SAMAJ - ONE HUMAN SOCIETY). To create popular movements in society which promotes cooperation and justice for all people. It works against racism and other divisive sentiments.

18. NEO-HUMANISM. It promotes love for all of creation, including plants, animals and even inanimate objects.

19. MASTER UNITS. Establishes model socio-economic-spiritual communities based on Prout, Neo-humanism and Baba's concepts of agriculture and farming.

20. GURUKUL. Guides all the educational projects of Ananda Marga

21. SOCIAL SECURITY. Establishes cooperative industries and commercial companies.

22. SOCIETY BUILDING. Encourages 'revolutionary marriages' (interracial, inter-cultural or inter-religious marriages) and assists those wanting to lead a sannyansi (monastic) life by becoming acharyas.

23. PUBLIC RELATIONS

24. LEGAL

25. FINANCE

26. OFFICE ESTABLISHMENT

27. INSPECTION

Appendix 3

PROUT:
The Progressive Utilisation Theory

Sarkar will probably stand out as one of the truly great in this century, so much deeper and more imaginative than most...
He is an intellectual giant of our times.

—John Galtung, *winner of the alternative Nobel Prize, founder of the International Peace Research Institute and author of 71 books.*

P. R. Sarkar and his followers...do not stop with the theoretical comprehension of the human being. They are preoccupied with the viability of a practical and effective way for authentic human development.

—Leonardo Boff, *Brazilian founder of Liberation Theology and prominent author*

(Much of the opposition against Ananda Marga and Baba is fueled by fear of the socio-economic side of the philosophy explained here.)

Prout stands for the Progressive Utilisation theory. Baba first started talking about Prout when devotees asked him about long-term social service: how could they do service that was more than just a 'band-aid' for social ills? Baba clearly stated that an essential part of true service is creating a just human society. Prout is an alternative to the theories of communism and capitalism that have dominated human thinking in recent centuries.

Over time Baba's accumulated writings about Prout were gathered into a 20-volume set called *Prout in a Nutshell*. While it is hard to condense such an extensive theory into a short appendix, here are a few of the important points:

- "Progressive" refers to a new definition of progress. It is not about bigger and better technology, but ultimately the progress that occurs as individuals develop spiritually. For this to happen, society's technological growth must continue in such a way that dangerous side-effects do not outweigh potential benefits. This requires wisdom and long-sightedness in planning.
- Communism is based on production (people are 'workers') and capitalism is based on consumption (people are 'consumers'.) Utilisation is the bridge between the two. 'Maximum utilisation and rational distribution' is a key phrase in Prout's ecological economics. Utilisation refers to all of the earth's resources: physical, mental and spiritual.
- The underlying theory of Prout is 'cosmic inheritance'. As all beings are the offspring of the Cosmic Consciousness, all have a right to share creation. Thus Prout stands for universalism and Neo-Humanism. All beings, not just humans, must be cared for.
- Practically, Prout advocates cooperatives and local planning supported by a democratic world government. Prout believes it necessary to establish self-reliant economic zones, similar to bio-regions, based on common cultural and economic factors. Prout supports the strengthening of local cultures through support of diverse local languages and culture and the development of flourishing local self-reliant economies. Baba said we should have 'regional application and universal outlook'.
- A basic human right is the guarantee of the basic necessities of life: food, clothing, medical care, housing and education, and other needs that may arise. To assure this there should be 100% employment in local areas as well as an assurance that goods are affordable for all people. Local people are those who have merged their socio-economic identity with that of the area, rather than those who are taking money out of the region.
- Basic goods should be produced locally, from locally available raw materials whenever possible. This avoids the common Third World trap of exporting raw materials and importing expensive finished products.
- Prout's balanced economic system has three parts: small businesses, co-operatives (which is the largest sector) and key industries run by local government. The two main types of cooperatives are producers' and consumers' cooperatives, while areas such as banking and medical cooperatives remain attached to these.

- There should be not only a minimum wage, but also a maximum wage that is tied to the minimum. (they both steadily increase over time) This would eliminate extremes in poverty and wealth, creating a society that is affluent not just by an average (GNP) but in the real living standard of all the members.

(For further information and research, please note that Baba used his social name, Prabhat Rainjan Sarkar in authoring his social works, while he used his spiritual name, Shrii Shrii Anandamurti, with his spiritually- riented works.)

Glossary

Acharya : Spiritual teacher, "one who teachers by example"

Ananda Marga: "Path of Bliss (*Ananda*)." A path dedicated to liberation of self & service to all.

Ananda Nagar: "City of Bliss. " The Ananda Marga global headquarters and spiritual community in India.

ASIO: Secret Service, "Australia Special Intelligence Organisation.

Avadhuta: Senior monk

Baba: "dearest beloved one, affectionate name given to Guru. Also Cosmic Consciousness as all pervading divine love.

Barrister: The lawyer who argues in court for your case

CAADA: Campaign for the Acquittal of Anderson, Dunn & Alister. A group of Margii and non-Margii activists.

Chakra: Spiritual energy centre in the body.

CIP: Central Industrial Prison at Long Bay Prison. Maximum security prison.

Dada: Respected spiritual brother, monk acharya

Detective Krawsczyk: The Special Branch detective who Seary reported to while spying on Ananda Marga.

Didi: Respected spiritual sister, nun acharya.

Dharma: Spiritual path, one's innate nature.

"dog": Prisoner who gives information about other prisoners to the authorities.

God: Infinite, formless, blissful, loving Cosmic Consciousness. Our inner most Self.

Initiation: The process where an acharya first gives personalised meditation instructions.

Jabananda: Aboriginal friend from jail

Karma: "Action" or the reactions to previous actions

Glossary

Katingal: Special high security jail next to Long Bay Prison.

Kiirtan: Chanting the *Baba Nam Kevalam* mantra which means divine love is everywhere and is the essence of everything.

LFT: "Local Full Time" volunteer of Ananda Marga

Mantra: "A sound that liberates." Special word or phrase for meditation

MTC: Metropolitan Training Centre. Medium to low security prison at Long Bay.

MRC: Metropolitan Remand Centre at Long Bay Prison. Maximum security.

MRP: Metropolitan Reception Prison at Long Bay Prison complex. Maximum security.

Namaskar: "I greet the divinity within you with all the warmth of my mind and heart." Spiritual greeting to see the inner spiritual nature of the person rather than their outward appearance.

Narada: Paul Alister's spiritual or Ananda Marga name, meaning "one who inspires devotion in others."

Ombudsman: An authority who can investigate complaints against government institutions.

Paul O'Callaghan: Paul Alister's birth name.

Police verbals: Admissions of guilt fabricated by the police.

Queens Counsel: Senior barrister also know as "silk" or "QC"

Ray Denning: Prison activist who joined Ananda Marga while in prison.

Sadhana: Spiritual practices or meditation.

Richard Seary: The Special Branch spy who infiltrated Ananda Marga.

"screw": Prison officer.

Solicitor: The lawyer who does most of the research and paper work for the case.

www.ingramcontent.com/pod-product-compliance
Lightning Source LLC
Chambersburg PA
CBHW052130010526
44113CB00034B/1307